Succeeding in College

Succeeding in College

STUDY SKILLS AND STRATEGIES

Jean A. Reynolds

Polk Community College

ALLYN and BACON
Boston   London   Toronto   Sydney   Tokyo   Singapore

Vice President, Humanities: Joseph Opiela
Senior Production Administrator: Marjorie Payne
Developmental Editor: Carol Alper
Manufacturing Buyer: Aloka Rathnam
Marketing Manager: Lisa Kimball
Editorial-Production Service: Electronic Publishing Services Inc.
Cover Administrator: Linda Knowles

Library of Congress Cataloging-in-Publication Data
Reynolds, Jean A.
    Succeeding in college : study skills and strategies / by Jean A.
    Reynolds
       p.   cm.
    Includes index.
    ISBN 0-205-16041-7
    1. Study skills. 2. College student orientation—United States.
    3. Academic achievement—United States. I. Title.
LB2395.R48 1996
378. 1'7'02812—dc20   95-43522
                                        CIP

Printed in the United States of America

10 9 8 7 6 5 4 3 2 1 00 99 98 97 96

For permission to use copyrighted materials, grateful acknowledgment is made to the copyright
holders on page 379, which is hereby made part of this copyright page.

*To Charlie
with love and thanks*

CONTENTS

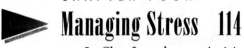

CHAPTER SIX

Taking Tests   179

CHAPTER SEVEN

Active Reading   209

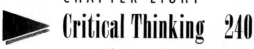

CHAPTER ELEVEN

 # Studying Mathematics   325

CHAPTER TWELVE

 # Introduction to Research   351

PREFACE

◆ TO THE STUDENT ◆

Your college years will have a powerful effect on the rest of your life. Your college achievements will help shape your career, and the interests you develop and the friends you make are likely to stay with you for many years. *Succeeding in College: Study Skills and Strategies* is designed to help you enjoy and benefit from your college experiences.

Three strategies can increase the usefulness of this book. First, acquaint yourself with its pages. Read the Table of Contents, browse through the chapters, and scan readings that look interesting. Many selections are designed to stand alone. Three-quarters of the way through this book you may find an idea that will help you with an issue you're facing right now.

Second, mark up this book. Worksheets, freewriting activities, and journal pages are designed with spaces for your ideas and experiences. But you can underline, circle, star, and mark up the margins on any pages—and you should. (Some instructors even give extra credit to students with well-marked books!) Adding your own ideas and experiences to a book makes it your own; you're also increasing its usefulness to you later, when you reread it.

And rereading is what the third suggestion is all about. Plan to keep this book to refer to again and again. Although it's primarily intended as a guide to college success, its ideas can help you in any endeavor. (You'll be reading success stories about athletes, performers, professional men and women, and leaders in many fields.) Remind yourself often that college isn't preparation for life: it *is* life.

Enjoy your college experience, and may your future exceed your most cherished dreams.

◆ TO THE INSTRUCTOR ◆

You're one of the special people who help college students achieve their dreams. No book can substitute for the role you play in your students' lives as a model, guide, and resource. What *Succeeding in College: Study Skills and Strategies* can do is offer information and activities that help you structure, deliver, and reinforce the knowledge you want to share with your students. The scope of this book goes beyond traditional study techniques. It encourages students to become thoughtful, mature learners who take responsibility for their own success.

Three central principles helped shape this book: First, active learners have the best chance of succeeding in college. Every chapter in this book emphasizes critical thinking (also covered in its own chapter) and connections between reading, writing, and learning. Every chapter has freewriting suggestions and a reading selection that includes writing activities for preparation and reinforcement. Chapter Seven suggests ways to mark up a book or article; Chapter Eight offers nine more ways to use a pencil as a learning tool. Other aids to active learning include collaborative activities, student-made memory aids, checklists, review exercises, and other strategies for college success.

Research suggests that the unique demands of mathematics and science courses present special challenges to students. This book features separate chapters and motivational content for both mathematics and science: study tips, activities, problem-solving techniques, critical-thinking skills, and insights into science and mathematics. In addition, separate chapters cover research and language skills.

Second, both students and instructors have limits on their time and energy. In addition to an extensive section on time management, this book includes many time-saving features. Each chapter begins with a preview and ends with review exercises (Using What You Have Learned) and a progress check (Evaluating Your Progress). Every chapter has an In-Class Introductory Activity that serves as both an icebreaker and a warm-up. Because the activity is printed in the student text, instructors need less preparation time.

Numerous activities, both individual and collaborative, facilitate planning. In addition, an Instructor's Manual offers practical suggestions for structuring the course, presenting content, designing supplemental activities, and evaluating students' performances.

Most importantly, both students and instructors thrive in a stimulating environment. Although you and your students are the primary creators of the learning atmosphere, this book can make an important contribution as well.

Lively multicultural readings, examples, and anecdotes describe skills, ideas, events, and people that students may meet again in other courses. A Sherlock Holmes story by Arthur Conan Doyle helps students see the value of math; educator Richard Rodriguez explains the importance of mastering a "public language"; author Stephen Hawking discusses public perceptions of scientists. Although some names may be familiar to your students (Walt Disney, Oprah Winfrey, Joe Montana), others may not (David Fairchild, Florence Griffith Joyner, Marsha Sinetar, William James).

All share a common trait: they have knowledge and experience to share with your students—as do you. The semester ahead offers you a rare opportunity to help students change their lives. I hope you will find this book both practical and inspiring in that extraordinary endeavor.

◆ ACKNOWLEDGMENTS ◆

I am grateful to many people who helped with this book. Audrey Roth of Miami-Dade Community College first suggested that I write about study techniques. Carol Alper and Joseph Opiela, my editors from Allyn & Bacon, offered boundless suggestions and encouragement. I appreciate the expert help I received from Marjorie Payne, Senior Production Administrator.

Friends from Polk Community College helped in many ways. Hugh Anderson, Director of the Arts, Letters, and Social Sciences Division, has long provided support and encouragement for my writing and teaching; he assisted me in obtaining a sabbatical to write this book. Staff members in the Learning Resources Division enthusiastically helped with research and word processing. Joan Monahan offered ideas, spotted errors, and shared supplemental material. Georgia Newman, who coordinates student-success courses and faculty workshops, first encouraged me to become involved in this area. I learned a great deal about collaborative activities from Sandra Hightower.

Thank you to the following reviewers of the manuscript for their many fine suggestions: Phil Barrineau, Pembroke State University; Thomas J. Buchholz, University of Wisconsin-Stevens Point; G. Jan Colijn, Stockton State College; Rory Donnelly, NE Illinois University; Tahita Fulkerson, Tarrant County Jr. College, N.W. Campus; Carmen S. Garland, Murray State University; Roger H. George, Bellevue Community College; Cynthia Hill, Rock Valley College; Terry Jones, California State University, Hayward; Raymond S. Ledford, Western Carolina University; Kathryn E. Moore, St. Louis Community College at Meramec; Jayne Nightingale, Rhode Island College; Judith Olson-Fallon, Case Western Reserve; Bruce Peterson, Sonoma State University; Susan Steger-Farmer, William Rainey Harper College; Jane Sullivan, Rowan College of New Jersey; and Gloria Tribble, Youngstown State University.

My lessons with Gene Kallenborn and Debbie Bethel, teachers at the Dance Connection, sparked many insights into the learning process.

My husband, Charles Reynolds, made suggestions, helped with research, unraveled problems, and encouraged me throughout the writing process. This book is dedicated to him.

CHAPTER 1

Getting Started

You see things and you say, "Why?" But I dream things that never were, and I say "Why not?"

GEORGE BERNARD SHAW

PREVIEW

1. To succeed in college, you need new study techniques in addition to the ones you used in high school.

2. In college you will be challenged by new ways of thinking and learning.

3. Writing a Personal Mission Statement can strengthen your motivation and help you stay focused on your college goals.

4. Stress-management skills can help you deal with the ups and downs of college life.

IN-CLASS INTRODUCTORY ACTIVITY: SUCCEEDING IN COLLEGE

How do you feel about this statement?

I'm confident that I'll succeed in college.

Strongly disagree	Neutral	Strongly agree
1	5	10

Mark the point on the line that best represents your position. Then complete the activities below.

1. *Finish these statements in your own words:*

    I'm looking forward to college life because _____

    _____

    Sometimes I'm uncertain about college life because _____

    _____

2. *What assets do you have now that will help you succeed in college? (Examples might include encouragement from family or friends, financial aid, good math skills, or a strong desire to succeed.)*

COLLABORATIVE ACTIVITY

Meet for five minutes with a small group of other students to discuss and compare your answers to questions 1 and 2. Then use the space below to jot down any helpful ideas you may have heard or contributed during the discussion. For example, someone may have suggested a helpful approach to a challenge you're facing right now. Or you may have helped other group members discover assets they didn't know they had.

GROUP DISCUSSION NOTES:

How Will You Meet the Challenges of College?

Every time you begin a new college term, you confront new challenges. If you've just enrolled in college, you're entering a particularly critical period. Research shows that by the end of the first six weeks, many first-year students have formed a lasting impression—positive or negative—of college life. If you enjoy your introduction to college life, you'll feel at home and enjoy your learning experiences. If college is not to your liking, you may get very little benefit from your studies.

This chapter offers a variety of ways to meet the challenges of college. While you're reading, look for ideas that match your lifestyle and special needs. "Getting Started," the first part of this chapter, will help you equip yourself for success this semester. The second part of this chapter, "Setting Goals," offers help in meeting another challenge—keeping your motivation high.

◆ GETTING STARTED ◆

Many students find it hard in the beginning to keep up with the fast pace of college. Assignments may be longer than you're used to, and college professors offer fewer reminders and step-by-step instructions than high-school teachers do. Lectures often cover great quantities of information very rapidly: College usually compresses a whole year of high-school work into one semester. Study techniques that worked well for you in high school may not be effective in college. Fortunately, careful planning can help you avoid chaos at the beginning of a new semester.

Equip Yourself

Shop ahead of time to avoid hectic last-minute trips to the store. Here's a suggested list of college supplies:

- a durable looseleaf binder with your name, address, and telephone number inside.
- an abundant supply of straight-edged looseleaf paper for notetaking and classwork. Bound spiral notebooks are less flexible to work with because pages can't be transferred easily; also many professors will not accept homework torn from a spiral notebook.
- notebook separators marked with tabs for each subject.
- a three-hole plastic zippered case to hold pens, pencils, erasers, colored markers, paper clips, a pocket calendar, a small stapler and staples, and quarters for photocopies and last-minute phone calls.
- a photocopy of the college calendar, three-hole-punched and inserted into the binder.
- a photocopy of the campus map, also hole-punched and inserted into the binder.
- a photocopy of the scheduled hours for campus services you expect to use, such as the cafeteria, records office, library, learning center, and computer lab.
- a photocopy of your own class schedule.

Your Binder. A well-equipped looseleaf binder can serve as a college survival kit. With its help, you'll never have to search frantically for assignments, handouts or materials. Some students hole-punch all the papers they're given—handouts, returned tests, and homework—and securely insert them into the binder. (It's wise to invest in a three-hole punch, or to locate one on campus that's available for student use. The learning lab is a good possibility.)

Your Dictionary. An item almost as important as your notebook is a current dictionary. Paperbacks are fine; just make sure yours is no more than five years old—essential because English, like other languages, changes as time passes. Buy a hand-held, electronic spellchecker, such as a Franklin Speller, if you can afford one; it's a great help when you're writing college papers. But there is no substitute for the extensive information you'll find in a good dictionary.

Keep your dictionary handy for learning the new words you meet in college; browse through it during free moments. Civil-rights leader Malcolm X studied his dictionary extensively while imprisoned. In addition to improving his communication skills, it broadened his knowledge of "people and places and events from history." The dictionary, he noted, "is like a miniature encyclopedia."

A Word-Processing System. The third piece of equipment you'll need is a word-processing system—essential because many college papers and reports must be typed. If you can't afford a typewriter or computer, look for a typing room or computer lab on campus.

If you can't touch-type, sign up for a keyboarding course. Start learning word processing right away, if possible, because changes and corrections are simple, and the finished product looks professional; it's not wise to struggle with a typewriter when computers are available. Don't be discouraged if your typing is poor; you'll get better with practice, and computer skills are superb timesavers.

EXERCISE 1: EQUIP YOURSELF

A checklist of suggested college supplies and skills appears below. Put a check in front of every item you've already obtained or planned for; circle others that you plan to obtain this week; cross out any that you don't think you'll need.

EQUIPMENT LIST

_____ *durable looseleaf binder with identification*

_____ *notebook section for assignments*

_____ *three-hole punch*

_____ *three-hole plastic zippered case*

_____ *writing supplies*

_____ *stapler and staples*

_____ *paper clips*

_____ *pocket calendar*

_____ *larger planning calendar*

_____ *photocopy of the college calendar*

_____ *photocopy of the campus map*

_____ *photocopy of the scheduled hours for campus services you expect to use*

_____ *photocopy of your class schedule*

_____ *up-to-date dictionary for your own use*

_____ *hand-held electronic spellchecker*

_____ *typewriter*

_____ *electronic word-processing system*

_____ *up-to-date college catalog*

Cultivate Friendships

Think of other students as both friends and resources. The relationships that develop during college can last a lifetime. Friends are a valuable resource when you're lonely or discouraged; reach out to others on your first day of college with a smile and a friendly greeting, and continue the practice daily. College activities are great places to make friends: Study college publications, posters, and bulletin boards to learn where you can meet other students.

Besides providing opportunities for fun and emotional support, friends can be valuable learning resources. As you get to know one another, exchange phone numbers with the other students in each course so that you can keep up with assignments in case of an emergency absence. Start looking for study partners in all your courses, and think about forming a study group for each course.

Collaborative study offers many advantages. Group members are usually more disciplined, motivated, and efficient than do-it-yourselfers. You're likely to understand new information and ideas better when you've talked them over with friends. Study groups

Make Friends with Calendars

You've probably seen advertisements for elaborate card and computer systems that promise to organize your life. Maybe you thought you would manage your time better if you could afford one of those systems. But even an ordinary calendar can accomplish miracles for you— if you know how to put it to work. Or, more accurately, if you know how to put *them* to work, because most students need two calendars—a small one to carry, and a larger one, used for planning, in a convenient spot at home. Neither calendar has to be elaborate. Your pocket-sized calendar should have a durable cover and extra pages for telephone numbers. The bigger calendar at home should have both large writing spaces for more detailed planning and a storage pouch. If you can't find a pouched calendar, staple a manila envelope to the back of an ordinary one.

As soon as you obtain your calendars, mark down college events, along with family celebrations and other important dates. Don't be tempted to invest in a third calendar; you'll have trouble transferring entries among all three, and information will get lost.

The pocket-sized calendar can be carried with you for on-the-spot planning: assignments, social events, appointments, meetings, and other deadlines. Use a small paper clip to keep the calendar open to the current month. A large paper clip inside the back cover can hold

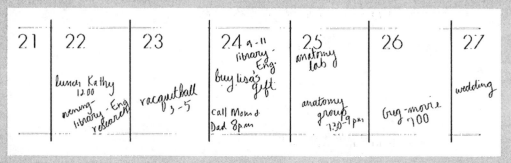

Figure 1.1 Notes From a Student's Pocket Calendar

can help you articulate your ideas more effectively—a skill vital in both college and the working world.

Inform Yourself about College

Browse through your college catalog, study your student handbook, and read college newspapers and magazines. For example, it's helpful to know that "adjunct professors" often teach part-time and may not have office hours for meeting with students. If you expect to need extra help with a course, it's probably wise to sign up for a course with a full-time professor who has office hours on campus. On the other hand, many adjuncts have valuable professional experience as lawyers, scientists, physicians, artists, business executives, and writers.

Information about financial aid can also be valuable while you're in college. Don't be discouraged if you weren't a superior student in high school: You may still qualify for

a notepad for jotting down reminders about car maintenance, home upkeep, and other responsibilities. Use the notepad also for important bits of information, but don't accumulate too many scraps of paper; you should transfer the information to a filing system at home.

Choose the spot for your large planning calendar with care—near the telephone, if you have one. Accessibility is important: You should be able to make calendar notes easily, without stretching or moving furniture. Use this larger calendar for detailed planning, and check it once a day.

Two simple steps can make you an expert planner. First, enter information into your small calendar during the day. Second, transfer the information to your large calendar daily along with reminders, where needed. As you enter research assignments, for example, set mini-goals for yourself: a library deadline, a date for completing your first draft, and so on. When you mark the date of a friend's wedding, write "Buy gift for Nancy and Dan!" two weeks before the event. The large spaces on your planning calendar will allow you to make detailed notes about coming events and assignments.

Use the pouch to prevent bills and letters from getting lost before you can attend to them. Another advantage of the pouch: If you get behind in your paperwork, you'll be forced to deal with everything when you change the calendar at the end of the month. With a little effort—and a quick calendar check at the beginning of each day—you too will be an organized person.

grant money or a student loan. Talk to a financial aid officer at your institution to learn what funds are available.

Some of your most useful information can be found on the course information sheets and other handouts distributed by your professors. Time management is easier when you know how your grade will be calculated and what assignments will be given. Suppose that 10% of your final grade comes from daily quizzes, while a research paper is worth 40%, and major tests make up the other 50%. Those numbers indicate that even a string of A's on daily quizzes won't earn you a passing grade: You'll need to invest large amounts of time preparing your research project and studying for major tests.

Establish a Routine

You can lower stress significantly by following a consistent routine for work, study, recreation, rest, and relationships. Consistency helps you move easily from one task to another. It also makes studying easier. If you sit in the library for an hour at the same time each morning, you'll soon develop the habit of focusing your attention on your studies at that time. Stress levels will be more manageable if you feel that your major roles and responsibilities are well balanced; your friends and family will appreciate your routine because they'll be assured of spending time with you regularly.

If sticking to a program is difficult for you, consider pairing up with another student for mutual encouragement and accountability. (Chapter Two offers many more suggestions about effective time management.)

Forming a Study Group

Participating in a study group can enrich your college experience and help you succeed in college. You'll make new friends, improve your speaking and listening skills, increase your knowledge, and develop the ability to interact and solve problems in a group.

Your study group can function as informally—or formally—as you wish. Most groups have found, however, that the following guidelines help them achieve maximum efficiency and effectiveness:

1. Find other students with similar goals.

Arrive for class a few minutes early—or stay a few minutes afterward—and ask who else is interested. Arrange a time and place to get together to set up your first meeting. Exchange names and telephone numbers with everyone who plans to join the group.

2. Choose meeting times and locations carefully.

The time and place should be convenient for all members and suitable for group work. Avoid places where you're likely to be distracted or interrupted, where noise levels are high, or where you might disturb others.

Joining a study group can give you valuable leadership experience.

3. Have a detailed plan for each meeting.

Each group member should have a detailed list of the topics to be covered and activities to be completed. Ideally, a new meeting plan should be drawn up at the end of the previous meeting so that group members can prepare thoroughly ahead of time.

4. Exchange roles frequently.

Rotate responsibilities among group members so that everyone has opportunities to serve such roles as group leader, presenter, and notetaker. If you're working together on a library project, give each member a turn as researcher, bibliographer, and recorder.

5. Make each member accountable to the whole group.

Divide topics evenly so that each member has a subject to cover at each meeting. This kind of accountability has three important advantages. First, when members know that others are depending on them, they're more likely to attend group meetings. Second, new experiences help group members develop skill and confidence in new roles. Third, these experiences are excellent preparation for professional life. Because modern workplaces are emphasizing cooperation, college students need to develop the ability to learn, work, and teach productively in a group.

6. End each meeting with an evaluation.

Choose one member (on a rotating basis) to chair this part of the meeting. Discuss what worked well, what didn't, and what you'd like to do differently next time. The chair is responsible for seeing that everyone has equal opportunities to speak, no one is unfairly attacked or criticized, and the discussion proceeds in a positive way. (All these skills are useful for professional and civic life.) It is up to the whole group to decide what changes to make—and how to implement them—in future sessions.

◆ SETTING GOALS ◆

If you don't know where you're going, you'll probably end up somewhere else.
LAWRENCE J. PETER

When you come to a fork in the road, take it.
YOGI BERRA

Sometime in the future you plan to graduate. When your courses are over, you'll probably look back to evaluate your college life: Did you fulfill your expectations, goals, and dreams? If all goes well, the answer to that question will be *yes*. You'll have experienced personal and intellectual growth, developed friendships worth keeping, and enjoyed a high level of academic success.

Don't let shyness prevent you from getting answers to your questions about college.

But the hectic pace of classes, campus activities, and other responsibilities can cause students to overlook the rewards of college. Once you lose touch with the reasons you came to college, minor frustrations and disappointments can seem bigger and more serious than they really are.

Your Personal Mission Statement

A *Personal Mission Statement* is a short written piece in which you state your college goals and priorities. Some students find it helpful to think of the statement as a letter to themselves about their reasons for attending college. This can help you stay focused and keep your motivation high through the normal ups and downs of college life. Many organizations (businesses, hospitals, educational institutions, churches) create mission statements to explain their goals and policies. Your college or university almost certainly has its own mission statement, which you can find in the catalog you received at registration.

Mission statements have also become popular with professionals in such fields as hospitality, law, business, education, and medicine. You can benefit from their example. Because you're the person who writes this mission statement, it is unique to you—a personal declaration of your purpose in attending college. The activities on the following pages will help you plan and write a statement about your goals for college.

Many high achievers say that success always requires sacrifices and uncomfortable choices. The person who tries to do everything often turns into the person who accomplishes nothing. Allowing others to make your choices may mean that you never get what you want. When your Personal Mission Statement is complete, you'll have an individualized guide to refer to when conflicts arise and decisions have to be made.

Opera star Roberta Peters says,

> It's only human nature to want to be liked and to go along with the dictates of your crowd. It's always a lot easier to join them, to do what they do, to think their way. But if there is something you want and have to do, there comes a time when you must go it alone. Right now, there are probably people you know who are devoting themselves to something they want and believe in. Chances are they're not winning any popularity contests. But honestly, don't you envy them? And don't you respect them for their courage to be individuals?

Here are examples of Personal Mission Statements written by college students. Notice how different they are—and how well they define each student's reasons for attending college.

From a recent high-school graduate majoring in music:

I'm attending college to prepare for a career as an orchestra conductor. I expect to meet some resistance because opportunities for women conductors are limited. Academic work is important to me because high school grades will increase my chances of attending graduate school and earning scholarship money. I'm committed to spending two hours of preparation for every hour in class.

Expanding my musical knowledge is another priority. As time permits, I will attend every rehearsal and performance I can. I'll listen to recorded music and read musical biographies, histories and criticism.

An orchestra conductor must have good relationships with musicians and all the other people who support an orchestra. I intend to take several psychology courses, and I will make the most of any opportunity to work with other people. I plan to participate in study groups and take an active role in planning musical activities on campus.

Figure 1.2 Personal Mission Statements

From a married veteran who has two young sons:

I originally planned on a military career. Government cutbacks caused me to leave the Air Force. I'm studying business management and hope to work for a company that offers many opportunities for advancement. My first goal is to do well academically. My second goal is to finish college quickly. Although my veterans' benefits are a big financial help, I want to graduate, start working and do more for my wife and children. My third goal is to be part of my children's lives while they are growing up. Since school will keep me very busy, I will limit my outside activities and instead invest my spare time with my family.

From a student on a basketball scholarship:

I'm the first person in my family to attend college. I live on campus, far away from my home and friends. My basketball scholarship will help me make something of myself. After graduation maybe I can help my two sisters and my parents too.

First I plan to build a support group. Several of the basketball players agreed that we're going to be boosters for one another. I'm going to try to make friends with people in all my classes. I miss my old friends, and I know things will never be the same for us again. None of them are trying to build a new life.

Second I want to play good basketball. I want to keep my scholarship and play for a pro team after graduation. I will work hard both at team practices and on my own to develop my skills.

Third is academic work. The coach keeps telling us that basketball isn't life. Because so few athletes make it, we need to learn other ways to earn a living. I'm working with the staff in the Career Office to decide on a college major.

Figure 1.2 Continued

What Are the Benefits?

The following comments are from four students who have benefited from writing Personal Mission Statements:

- This is my first time away from home. I love my new freedom, and it's hard to say "no" to some of the fun on campus. I read my Personal Mission Statement every day, and it helps me make sensible decisions about my social life. I don't have to go to every party I'm invited to, and it feels good to be moving towards my goal of becoming a teacher.

- I felt overwhelmed by all the activities on campus when I started college. I wanted to make friends but didn't know what clubs to join. My Personal Mission Statement helped me sort out my priorities. I decided on the Speechmakers Association because I'll need public speaking in my law career.

- I help out in my parents' bicycle shop to help cover my college expenses. At first I hated working there because it takes up so much of my time. After I wrote my Personal Mission Statement, I saw that the bicycle shop is helping me make my dream of being a nurse come true. Now I have a much better attitude—and my grades are better too.

- I signed up for five courses this semester and got a part-time job as a computer aide in the college learning center. Perfect, I thought. I was getting working experience in my field—computers—that would look good on a job application later. But after three weeks I failed two tests and realized I wasn't keeping up with my assignments. Rereading my Personal Mission Statement helped me get my priorities straight. The Financial Aid office helped me get a loan, and I quit working. They promised to help me find temporary work during college breaks and summer vacations so that I can stay in college.

In the following pages, you'll explore your reasons for attending college—the first step in writing your mission statement.

Why College?

Here's how a well-known educator—Bill Cosby—made the decision to earn a college degree, according to biographer Bill Adler:

> His four-year stint [in the Navy] taught him something very important. "I met a lot of guys," he recalled later, "who didn't have as much 'upstairs' as I knew I did, yet here they were struggling away for an education. I finally realized I was committing a sin—a *mental* sin."

And so he studied on his own while in the Navy and passed an examination that gave him the equivalent of a high-school diploma. When he was out of uniform, Cosby was able to get an athletic scholarship to Temple University, working part-time as an entertainer.

Cosby became so successful as a comic that he had to choose between show business and college. Show business won, but not for long. Cosby's mother was an important factor in his decision to return: when he'd dropped out of Temple University, the shock and disappointment led to an illness that put her into bed for seven weeks. Another factor was his dream of helping children learn both values and basic skills through television. Cosby

In his doctoral program, Bill Cosby focused his attention on television as an educational medium.

returned to college part-time, taking six years to earn a bachelor's degree. Later he attended graduate school to earn a master's degree and doctorate in education. In his television career, he used both his academic studies and show-business experience to educate millions of viewers.

EXERCISE 2: YOUR REASONS FOR ATTENDING COLLEGE

What motivates you to attend college? Write answers to these questions:

1. *What factors influenced Bill Cosby to enroll in college?*

2. *What factors influenced you to enroll in college?*

3. *What are your lifetime goals?*

4. *How will college help you achieve them?*

When you're finished, meet with a small group of other students to discuss your answers. What motivations do you have in common? Which reasons for attending college are unique to you?

Don't be surprised if you're a little unsure about the long-term benefits of college, especially if this is your first semester. It can take time to feel the full impact of your new learning experiences. The six statements below offer you an overview of what you can expect from your college experience. In the following pages you'll explore each statement in depth.

Reasons for Attending College

1. College offers you new approaches to learning.
2. College is an entry point into the life you dream of living.
3. College puts you in control.
4. College sharpens your thinking skills.
5. College prepares you for citizenship.
6. College enlarges your world.

1. **College offers you new approaches to learning.** Expect college to expose you to new kinds of learning experiences, some of which may not appeal to you at first. If you feel frustrated or confused about an assignment, remember that college demands more than memorization: you're developing the outlook and intellectual skills of an educated person. (Chapter Eight, "Critical Thinking," explores these skills in depth.)

Some of your new experiences will increase in meaning as time passes. One student nurse felt frustrated because she was forbidden to use her new skills during her first hospital visit. Instead of taking temperatures and reading charts, she was instructed to sit down and make conversation with a hospital patient for half an hour. She went to the hospital feeling hurt–why didn't her instructors trust her with basic nursing procedures? But the wisdom of that assignment became apparent later, when she realized that she had needed training to relate to patients as people rather than simply as medical cases.

Many professors are happy to explain why their assignments and subjects are important, but you may also have to discover their purpose on your own. A student majoring in ballet was infuriated because he had to take a course in kinesiology—a branch of physiology focusing on muscles and movement. The course was taught by a physician who knew nothing about ballet. At first the young dancer could not imagine how memorizing the names of muscle groups would help his ballet training. Finally a ballet instructor showed him how to make his own connections between dance movements and physiology. Seeing these connections was harder than simply memorizing the information in the text—but it also turned kinesiology into his favorite course.

Sometimes a subject's importance doesn't become apparent until later. Dr. Joyce Brothers, who has had a long career as a television psychologist, recalls a mistake she made about math. She says, "It hadn't occurred to me to study math as preparation for psychology." But her program required advanced mathematics. "I got busy teaching myself trigonometry and calculus. I was frantic. I bought review books, and then I got a tutor. That psychology course was really three courses for me: one in theories of behavior, one in trigonometry, and one in calculus." Make a commitment to trust the learning process as it develops in your college courses.

READING THOUGHTFULLY: AN UNUSUAL LEARNING EXPERIENCE

The following essay, by biologist Samuel H. Scudder (1837–1911), describes an unusual learning experience from his Harvard education, when he studied under Jean Louis R. Agassiz (1807–1873), a world-famous naturalist. Before you read the essay, complete the following activity.

BEFORE YOU READ

Answer the following questions:
1. If you enrolled at a university to major in biology, what learning experiences would you expect to find most valuable?

2. How do you deal with learning experiences that frustrate you?

---

from **In the Laboratory**
by Samuel Scudder

I entered the laboratory of Professor Agassiz, and told him I had enrolled my name in the Scientific School as a student of natural history.

"When do you wish to begin?" he asked.

"Now," I replied.

This seemed to please him, and with an energetic "Very well!" he reached from a shelf a huge jar of specimens in yellow alcohol. "Take this fish," he said, "and look at it; by and by I will ask what you have seen."

With that he left me. In ten minutes I had seen all that could be seen in that fish, and started in search of the Professor—who had, however, left. Slowly I drew forth that hideous fish, and with a feeling of desperation again looked at it. I might not use a magnifying glass; instruments of all kinds were interdicted. My two hands, my two eyes, and the fish: it seemed a most limited field. I pushed my finger down its throat to feel how sharp the teeth were. I began to count the scales in the different rows, until I was convinced that was nonsense. At last a happy thought struck me—I would draw the fish; and now with surprise I began to discover new features in the creature. Just then the Professor returned.

"That is right," said he; "a pencil is one of the best of eyes." With these encouraging words, he added: "Well, what is it like?"

When I had finished, he waited as if expecting more, and then, with an air of disappointment: "You have not looked very carefully; why," he continued more earnestly, "you haven't even seen one of the most conspicuous features of the animal, which is as plainly before your eyes as the fish itself; look again, look again!" and he left me to my misery.

I was piqued; I was mortified. Still more of that wretched fish! But now I set myself to my task with a will, and discovered one new thing after another, until I saw how just the Professor's criticism had been. The afternoon passed quickly; and when, towards its close, the Professor inquired: "Do you see it yet?"

"No," I replied, "I am certain I do not, but I see how little I saw before."

"That is next best," said he earnestly, "but I won't hear you now; put away your fish and go home; perhaps you will be ready with a better answer in the morning. I will examine you before you look at the fish."

This was disconcerting. Not only must I think of my fish all night, studying, without the object before me, what this unknown but most visible feature might be; but also, without reviewing my discoveries, I must give an exact account of them the next day.

The cordial greeting from the Professor the next morning was reassuring; here was a man who seemed to be quite as anxious as I that I should see for myself what he saw.

"Do you perhaps mean," I asked, "that the fish has symmetrical sides with paired organs?"

His thoroughly pleased "Of course! of course!" repaid the wakeful hours of the previous night. I ventured to ask what I should do next. "Oh, look at your fish!" he said. And so for three long days he placed that fish before my eyes, forbidding me to look at anything else, or to use any artificial aid. This was the best lesson I ever had.

Agassiz's training in the method of observing facts and their orderly arrangement was ever accompanied by the urgent exhortation not to be content with them. "Facts are stupid things," he would say, "until brought into connection with some general law."

After You Read

1. List any new words you encountered in this essay. What strategy will you use to learn them?

2. Reread the essay, writing down any questions that you wondered about. What strategies could you use to answer them?

3. What do you think is the main point of Scudder's story about Agassiz?

4. At first Scudder was puzzled by his professor's insistence that he keep looking at the fish. List the steps he took to deal with his confusion.

5. What is your opinion of Agassiz's teaching method? How would you feel if you were his student?

6. Have you ever felt confused or frustrated about a learning experience? How did you handle the experience? What did you learn from it?

---

2. **College is an entry point into the life you dream of living.** One large component of "the life you dream of living" is your career choice. Your college has many resources to prepare you for the future: career counseling, professional contacts in the community, and professional programs to teach you the skills you will need.

In addition, college can prepare you for the changes—some of them rapid and dramatic—that happen in every professional field. Most professionals are constantly adapting to new ideas, procedures, information, and technology. "Learning how to learn" is an important component of your education. Your ability to absorb new information, think about it critically, and apply it can play a significant role in your professional success.

While you are in college, recharge your motivation occasionally by looking beyond the immediate goals of earning good grades, graduating, and establishing yourself in a career. Search for ways to build your confidence, develop your uniqueness, and meet your deepest needs for love, joy, and a meaningful life.

3. **College puts you in control.** Who was "in control" when you were in high school? The answers are obvious: parents, school board, principal, faculty, and staff. Chances are that high school didn't give you many experiences of autonomy—of being in charge of your own life.

Colleges have authority figures too, of course: the president or chancellor, deans, professors, coaches, and others. What's different now—or what *should* be different—is you and your attitude. Feeling that they—rather than you—control your life can weaken your motivation to succeed in college.

Many successful students find it helpful to think of college personnel as resources rather than authority figures. Professors can do more for you than just assign homework and calculate grades: They are specialists in the knowledge you need for success. In this new mindset, librarians are information managers; deans, presidents, and chancellors are problem solvers. Now's the time to put yourself in control and to think of the others in your life as resources, not bosses.

What is Critical Thinking?

Thinking is the hardest work there is, which is the probable reason why so few engage in it.

HENRY FORD

Critical thinking can also be called "active thinking." When you evaluate, explore, or generate ideas, you are thinking critically. Critical thinkers practice the following mental activities:

1. Becoming aware of their assumptions.
2. Exposing faulty reasoning.
3. Looking for relationships among facts, ideas, and events.
4. Sorting and classifying ideas.
5. Uncovering possibilities overlooked in traditional thinking.

4. **College sharpens your thinking skills.** You're likely to hear the term "critical thinking" often in college. In the past, college courses emphasized transferring ideas from the textbook and professor into the student's mind. Critical thinking adds additional steps: evaluating, expanding, applying, and challenging ideas. A central task is to think about the act of thinking itself—an undertaking both fascinating and demanding.

Because critical thinking is essential to the educational process, it appears in each chapter of this text and in greater depth in Chapter Eight. You'll probably find that some (or all) of these thinking skills are already familiar to you, although some of the terminology may be new.

a. Critical thinkers look for the assumptions that shape our beliefs and experiences, often without our awareness. Samuel Scudder, you remember, assumed that ten minutes was long enough to examine his fish. Not all assumptions are negative: Roberta Peters assumed she could become an opera star. Critical thinking skills help you get in touch with your assumptions and decide which are useful to you.

b. Critical thinkers try to expose the faulty reasoning that leads to poor decisions in academic, personal, professional, and community life. For example, an industry leader may try to convince you that people who promote environmental concerns are anti-business. This kind of either/or thinking distorts the truth: Many businesses have actually *increased* their profits through recycling and other ecological practices.

c. Critical thinkers look for relationships among facts, ideas, and events. Whether they're learning about historical events or scientific phenomena, they're curious about both causes and effects. They often draw comparisons and contrasts between their own experiences and the theories they're learning. When they study psychology, for example, they might try to apply their new ideas to family life or the people they knew in high school.

d. Critical thinkers sort and classify ideas. They try to establish priorities while they're reading and listening: What's the most important idea in this journal article? What points did the professor emphasize in today's lecture? They often place information into categories—for example, the positive and negative results of automation.

e. Critical thinkers try to uncover possibilities overlooked in traditional thinking. One day Monty Hall of TV's *Let's Make a Deal* program offered $100 to a woman if she could take a nail out of her purse. After looking blank for a moment, she put her hand into her purse, pulled it out, and triumphantly pointed to her thumbnail! Hall was so impressed that he doubled the $100 he'd promised.

You might think there's little connection between that kind of cleverness and the serious thinking required in college. But the ability to think creatively—to see what others miss—is a valuable professional tool. A librarian used her creativity one summer to cut the cost of transporting the library's book collection to a new building. Just before the move, she announced that the library was trying a new vacation policy: Books could be borrowed for the whole summer rather than the usual two weeks. Then she persuaded the local newspaper to feature the new policy in a front-page story. Library patrons rushed to the library to borrow books, which they would return to the new building at the end of the summer—saving the cost of transporting them to the new building.

Critical thinking can help you discover unexpected solutions to a wide range of problems—everything from gathering information for a history paper to financing your senior year in college. You'll bring a fresh outlook to your classroom experiences, whether you're studying a Renaissance painting or the human circulatory system.

Finally, critical thinking can help you resolve personal issues. Sometimes a new approach can improve a relationship or solve a long-standing problem. One student complained that her marriage was deteriorating because her husband always wanted to go fishing on Saturday mornings, and she resented spending her free time that way. After many arguments, they solved the problem by purchasing a 35-millimeter camera and a telephoto lens so that she could take wildlife photos from the boat. Suddenly the fishing trips became fun, and their marriage was much richer as a result.

The good news is that you can develop your own thinking skills with motivation and practice—and that developing these skills is an exhilarating process, as you'll see in Chapter Eight.

5. **College prepares you for citizenship.** When you enrolled in college, you were probably thinking primarily about your own goals: a fulfilling career, financial security, intellectual growth, a better life for you and your family. But your academic achievements can have a powerful impact on your community, state and nation as well.

First, college will develop your writing and speaking skills so that you can communicate effectively with the media, community leaders, and other concerned citizens. Because college sharpens your thinking skills, you'll be able to question the shining promises of political candidates who want you to vote for them. You'll have a deeper understanding of current controversies, and a broader view of the consequences of local, national, and worldwide policies and events. Responsible citizens appreciate the importance of viewing issues from many angles. Criminal-justice procedures that make sense to police officers can seem threatening to citizens; a proposed law that community members like may seem arbitrary and pointless to government officials. College experiences in the arts, the social and physical sciences, and other areas will enable you to understand and evaluate multiple viewpoints about many kinds of issues.

6. **College enlarges your world.** Chances are you came to college because you wanted more out of life than you were experiencing in the past. If your pre-college life seemed confined and predictable, you're probably looking forward to the stimulating atmosphere of college. For many students, the hunger for new ideas, challenges, and possibilities is a major reason for attending college.

Be aware, though, that the larger world of college sometimes triggers negative feelings. The diversity you'll experience in college—exposure to people, viewpoints, lifestyles, and values different from yours—can be threatening or bewildering. Frustrated students sometimes ask, "How will I ever use the information I'm learning?" They forget that college involves much more than just career preparation: it's a place to broaden your outlook and discover a larger world.

To get in touch with your own hunger for expanded awareness, take a look at your daydreams and recreational habits. Have you ever yearned to travel to an exotic place? Do you enjoy movies or books about people whose lives are very different from yours? Have you ever had the nagging sense that there must be more to life than what you're now experiencing? College life can be an avenue into the new life you're seeking.

EXERCISE 3: WHY COLLEGE? YOUR RANKINGS

PART I

Here are the six reasons for attending college discussed earlier. Rank them in the order of their importance to you. Number 1 will be your strongest reason, 2 will come next, and so on:

_____   *College offers me new approaches to learning.*

_____   *College is an entry point into the life I dream of living.*

_____   *College puts me in control.*

_____   *College sharpens my thinking skills.*

_____   *College prepares me for citizenship.*

_____   *College enlarges my world.*

PART II

Meet with two or three other students to compare your rankings. What motivators do you have in common? Which are unique to you?

PART III

Circle your top three reasons for attending college. What college experiences have you had already that reinforce these three motivators? What experiences are you looking forward to in the future?

PART IV

List three (or more) choices you may have to make while you're in college. For example, you may have to make decisions about working part-time, getting involved in student government, handling family responsibilities, or participating in a sport.

PART V

Reread your answers to the previous question. Which choices will be most beneficial to you? Which choices will be hardest for you to make? Are any sacrifices involved?

GETTING IN TOUCH THROUGH FREEWRITING

Throughout this book you'll be offered opportunities to "freewrite"—to write your thoughts and feelings spontaneously.

"Freewriting" is more personal and less formal than academic writing. Don't think about spelling, grammar, punctuation, or neatness. Don't try to organize or develop your ideas. Freewriting is strictly an exploratory activity. You're not trying to exhibit your writing skill, and you won't be earning a grade.

Research shows that freewriting is an excellent way to explore ideas, feelings, and problems. Practiced regularly, it can also help you develop your ability to express yourself in words. Don't try to block or correct your thoughts. As you complete the freewriting activities in this book, you'll see how they help you get in touch with the issues in your college life right now.

FREEWRITING ACTIVITY

Write about your college and career goals. Don't worry about spelling, punctuation, or organization: Concentrate on describing the college experiences you hope to have and the career you want.

Writing Your Personal Mission Statement

Reread the freewriting you wrote on the previous page; then answer the questions below. Use additional sheets of paper if necessary.

1. *Write your first major purpose in attending college here:*

2. *Write your second major purpose in attending college here:*

3. *If you have other important reasons for attending college, list them here:*

4. *List three (or more) choices you may have to make while you're in college. For example, you may have to make decisions about working part-time, getting involved in student government, handling family responsibilities, or participating in a sport.*

5. *Reread what you wrote about the previous question. Which choice will be most beneficial to you? Which choice will be hardest for you to make? Are any sacrifices involved?*

6. *Now write an informal letter to yourself about your college and career goals. Don't worry about spelling, punctuation, or organization; concentrate on describing the college experiences you hope to have and the career you want.*

When you've finished your letter, you're ready to rewrite it as a Personal Mission Statement. Many students find the following outline helpful, but feel free to organize and express your ideas any way you choose. (You may want to read the Personal Mission Statements on pages 11 and 12 before you write your own.)

Personal Mission Statement

My first purpose in attending college is _____

_____.

In connection with this purpose I plan to _____

_____.

My second purpose in attending college is _____

_____.

In connection with this purpose I plan to _____

_____.

My third purpose in attending college is _____

_____.

In connection with this purpose I plan to _____

_____.

When your Personal Mission Statement is completed, display or store it in a convenient place where you can refer to it often. Review it at least once a week, and reread it whenever you need to clarify your goals or boost your motivation. Feel free to revise it if your lifestyle changes or you adopt new goals.

Setting Your Own Goals

After you've completed your Personal Mission Statement, you'll need to translate it into workable day-to-day goals. Since you can't carry out your whole college mission in one or two days, you have to plan small, specific steps to make your dreams come true. Workable goals have four characteristics: They're positive, realistic, measurable, and controllable.

1. Positive

Whenever possible, state what you're *going* to do, rather than what you're *not* going to do:

> I won't watch TV tonight. NEGATIVE
>
> I'll read my English assignment and go for a walk tonight. WORKABLE GOAL
>
> I'll stop daydreaming in class. NEGATIVE
>
> I'll take a thorough set of notes in each class. WORKABLE GOAL
>
> I'll stop shouting when the kids interrupt my study time. NEGATIVE
>
> I'll use a low, pleasant voice when I remind the kids about my study time. WORK-ABLE GOAL

Positively stated goals boost your self-esteem: You can watch yourself practicing new, desirable behaviors. Negative goals, however, constantly remind you of the behavior you're trying to eliminate—shouting, excessive TV watching, daydreaming.

2. Realistic

Prepare for success by selecting achievable goals. Don't plan to study for three hours after work if your job always leaves you drained and exhausted. Break the study period into smaller sessions, and choose times when you feel fresh. If you're *always* overextended, start planning some major lifestyle changes. An impossible goal won't get you anywhere.

Give yourself permission to modify, postpone, or cancel goals that aren't workable. One student planned to start a jogging program in June, traditionally a month of heavy rains in her state. Not surprisingly, she failed to follow through: An indoor activity—an aerobics class, for example—would have been a better choice. Another signed up for a full load of courses right before her father-in-law moved in to recover from surgery. Home-nursing responsibilities prevented her from completing assignments, and the semester was a disappointment. She could have delayed enrollment, signed up for a lighter schedule, or asked for help with the nursing care.

3. Measurable

Most people are accustomed to setting broad goals for themselves: "I'm going to study harder," "I want to get back in shape," "I've got to get organized." Broadly stated goals can be inspiring and motivating, but they also need to be restated in measurable terms, for two reasons: First, measurable goals are more realistic. It's almost impossible to tell when you've completed a broad goal like "I'm going to study harder." No matter how many hours you spend at your desk, you may still guiltily think that you could have done more. Second, a measurable goal gives you permission to celebrate. If you plan to revise an essay this afternoon, you can congratulate yourself when the revision is completed. The satisfaction you feel after completing your goals can boost your energy and fortify your motivation to succeed in college.

4. Controllable

You've probably heard many students say, "My goal is to join the Honor Society," or "I'm hoping for straight A's." Although these sound like workable goals, they're not. Professors, not students, determine the final grade in a course; membership in an honor society may be decided by a panel that votes on a number of characteristics in addition to grades.

Whenever possible, try to select goals that put you in charge of the outcome. You can't guarantee yourself an A on a test, but you can monitor your study time and assignments. Learn to reward yourself for completing a study plan rather than earning a particular grade. The same practical strategy can be applied to almost all your goals. For example, you can't control your body's metabolism, so you can't promise yourself a particular weight loss or increase in muscle size. But you can design an eating plan or exercise program and reward yourself for carrying it out.

Evaluating and Restating Goals. Here are four general goals from the Personal Mission Statements you read earlier:

As time permits, I will attend every rehearsal and performance I can. (music major)

My first goal is to do well academically. (Air Force veteran)

My third goal is to be part of my children's lives while they are growing up. (Air Force veteran)

I'm going to try to make friends with people in all my classes. (basketball player)

After writing their Personal Mission Statements, all four students set workable daily goals for themselves, like these:

I'll attend the Wind Ensemble rehearsal at ten tomorrow morning. (music major)

This semester I'm going to complete every assignment on time. (Air Force veteran)

I'm going to play miniature golf with my sons on Saturday morning. (Air Force veteran)

I'll introduce myself to two people in each of my classes today. (basketball player)

EXERCISE 4: DAY-TO-DAY GOALS

Day-to-day goals should be positive, realistic, measurable, and controllable. Put a ✔ in front of each goal that meets these criteria; put an X in front of each goal that does not:

_____ *I'm going to stop putting off my assignments.*

_____ *I will be selected for the varsity cheerleading squad.*

_____ *I will work all the practice problems in Chapter 2 of my algebra book tonight.*

_____ *I will eat only two servings of fried foods today.*

_____ *I will improve my relationship with my family.*

_____ *I will take my parents to the college open house this weekend.*

_____ *I will invite my parents to a college hockey game.*

_____ *I will memorize the vocabulary words on the handout I received in my reading class this morning.*

_____ *I will stop being shy around students I don't know.*

_____ *On all my math tests this semester, I will check my answers before I hand in my test.*

Now rewrite all the goals you marked with an X in Exercise 4 to make them meet the goal-setting criteria: positive, realistic, measurable, and controllable.

Choosing Goals for Yourself. On page 29, Exercise 5, you'll be writing three or more goals for yourself. Before you set these goals, spend a few minutes thinking about the quality of your life right now. What changes would be beneficial to you? In his book *The Seven Habits of Highly Effective People*, Stephen R. Covey poses two helpful questions (adapted here for college):

Question 1: What one thing could you do (you aren't doing now) that if you did on a regular basis, would make a tremendous positive difference in your personal life?

Question 2: What one thing in your college life would bring similar results?

Spend a few minutes freewriting about these questions. What changes would you make? Why? What results would you expect? Do you plan to make these changes? Why or why not?

EXERCISE 5: SELECTING YOUR GOALS

Using your Personal Mission Statement and your freewriting you just did (pages 28 and 29) as a guide, write three or more day-to-day goals for yourself this semester. Make sure each one meets the goal-setting criteria: positive, realistic, measurable, and controllable. Then meet with three or four other students to share and evaluate your goals.

Goal 1

Goal 2

Goal 3

If you have additional goals, write them here:

Resources

Most goals require resources. If you're writing a research paper, you need access to a library and help in finding the information you need. If you're learning how to drive a car with a standard transmission, you need an instructor and a car for practicing. If the resources you need aren't available, you need to find alternatives or postpone your goal. When humanitarian Albert Schweitzer was confined as a prisoner of war in World War I, no musical instruments were available for practice. Instead of postponing his goals for developing his musical talent, he "practiced" every day on a table, pretending that the surface was a keyboard and the boxes underneath were pedals.

What resources—or alternatives—are available to help you achieve your goals? Write them here:

Goal 1

Goal 2

Goal 3

Other goals:

Obstacles

If your goals are worthwhile and challenging, you can expect to encounter obstacles on the way to achieving them. Friends and family members may compete for your attention; shortages of time and money may block your path; you may have to overcome your own doubts, inertia, or fear. And other difficulties—both expected and unexpected—may interfere with your plans. In addition to the resources you explored on the previous page, courage, self-discipline, and persistence help create success.

Courage. Opera star Roberta Peters recalls many days in her voice training when she almost lost her courage. Sometimes, after a disappointing lesson, she would wander alone in New York City, wondering whether the struggle was really worth it. She remembers thinking, "Maybe those well-meaning friends and relatives were right—maybe I *had* set my goal too high." Even worse, her dreams were a financial drain on her family: Both parents were working to pay for her lessons.

When she was sixteen, she was faced with a difficult choice that she had to make alone:

> I had a chance to star on Broadway. It seemed like a golden opportunity, and it would have meant an end to my family's financial struggle. But every road has its detours, and I realized this was one. The strain of singing nightly in a Broadway show can wreak havoc with a coloratura voice. But more important, this was not my goal—I wanted the world of opera, not the bright lights of Broadway. So with some regret, I turned down that offer, and in doing so learned the marvelous quality of patience. Many times later I wondered if I had done the right thing.

And she had: Four years later she made her debut at the Metropolitan Opera.

Most goals don't require that degree of courage. But you may be faced with disheartening periods when you're not sure you'll ever reach the finish line. You can gain courage by focusing on your goal—as Peters did when she reminded herself that her goal was opera, not Broadway.

Self-Discipline. Doing something you don't enjoy, and postponing or giving up something you want, are forms of self-discipline. Roberta Peters learned self-discipline during her voice training; you can develop the same quality in your everyday life through daily training.

Psychologist William James (1842–1910) recommended this approach:

> Keep alive in yourself the faculty of making efforts by means of little useless exercises every day; that is to say, be systematically heroic every day in little unnecessary things; do something every other day for the sole and simple reason that it is difficult and you would prefer not to do it, so that when the cruel hour of danger strikes, you will not be unnerved or unprepared.

Persistence. More than almost any other factor, your willingness to persist determines whether you achieve your goals. President Calvin Coolidge once said,

> Nothing in the world can take the place of persistence. Talent will not: nothing is more common than unsuccessful men with talent. Genius will not: unrewarded genius is almost a proverb. . . . Persistence and determination alone are omnipotent.

Chances are you know extremely talented people who haven't achieved their goals—and less-gifted people who achieved extraordinary success despite immense obstacles. (You'll read some surprising success stories in this book.)

Often people give up on a goal not because they can't do it, but because they're *afraid* they can't do it. Thomas Edison observed, "Many of life's failures are people who did not realize how close they were to success when they gave up." Successful people anticipate obstacles and devise plans for overcoming them.

GETTING IN TOUCH THROUGH FREEWRITING

In the spaces below, freewrite about any obstacles you expect to encounter as you pursue your goals—and the resources, including self-discipline, persistence, and courage, that you will draw upon:

Goal 1

Goal 2

Goal 3

Other goals

GOAL WORKSHEET

Write a goal that is important to you right now. Use the spaces below to make a plan to complete your goal.

1. *Evaluate your goal. Is it important enough for you to tackle right now? Are there any major obstacles that might interfere with your success? If necessary, choose another goal.*

2. *When you're satisfied with the goal you have chosen, break it down into a series of steps.*

3. *Look at the steps again. Can they be broken down into micro-steps—small tasks that can be accomplished in five minutes?*

4. *Choose a micro-step for your first task. Make sure it is non-threatening and confidence building.*

5. *Take that first step. How did it feel? How successful were you?*

6. *Plan subsequent steps, anticipating any special challenges you may face. Devise micro-steps to help you meet those challenges successfully.*

7. *As you approach your goal, plan a celebration—a special meal, favorite activity, or a gift for yourself. One student bought herself a new pair of dance shoes when she advanced to the next stage in her dance training; another student spent an evening eating popcorn with friends and watching a favorite video he had rented. Be creative, and have fun.*

JOURNAL ACTIVITY: GOALS AND CHOICES

Every chapter in this book includes a journal activity: You apply an idea or skill for seven days and write about the results. Writing in a journal is much like freewriting: You don't have to worry about the rules of formal writing (such as punctuation and spelling), because your goal is exploration and discovery.

Every chapter features a different journal topic. But feel free to use a notebook to continue with a journal topic that seems particularly interesting or meaningful. Many students say that recording their feelings this way is a powerful stress reliever; often they add that they learn a great deal from rereading their journal entries after time has passed.

This week's journal is about goals and choices. In the spaces below, briefly describe a goal you worked on that day. Then mention a choice—either positive or negative—you made in connection with the goal. Finally, record any thoughts or reactions you want to mention.

Here's a sample journal entry from the basketball player whose Personal Mission Statement you read earlier:

DAY 1

Goal: To visit the learning center every day

Choice: Decided to cut short a conversation with Don to make sure I had time to work with Lisa, the English tutor

Comment: Lisa had some good suggestions about my paper

Record your journal entries in the spaces below:

DAY 1

Goal:

Choice:

Comment:

DAY 2

Goal:

Choice:

Comment:

DAY 3

Goal:

Choice:

Comment:

DAY 4

Goal:

Choice:

Comment:

DAY 5

Goal:

Choice:

Comment:

DAY 6

Goal:

Choice:

Comment:

DAY 7

Goal:

Choice:

Comment:

 USING WHAT YOU HAVE LEARNED

1. Make a list of practical information you've acquired about college life. Share your answers with another student.
2. What obstacles in the past have interfered with your motivation to learn? How might you overcome similar obstacles in college?
3. How much of your potential do you think you've used in past learning experiences? What kinds of potential do you think you have that haven't been developed yet?
4. Think of a situation from the past that gave you the feeling that you were in control. Then think of a situation in which you did not feel in control. What made the

two experiences different for you? What factors contributed to those feelings? What did those experiences teach you? Do the experiences look any different now?

5. Meet with two or three other students to compare and discuss your Personal Mission Statements. What similarities do you notice? How are the statements different? What did you learn about one another from sharing your statements?

6. Which do you think will be more important to your success in college: courage or self-discipline? Why?

7. Meet with two or three other students to compare and discuss your answers to the previous question. Have each group member share an incident from college life when courage or self-discipline (or both) were necessary.

EVALUATING YOUR PROGRESS

This checklist appears at the end of each chapter. Don't feel you have to improve in every area at once; instead, use the checklists to track your progress and set new goals for yourself:

1. As I look back on the past seven days, I've seen an improvement in these areas:

    _____ organizing my life

    _____ protecting my health

    _____ planning my time

    _____ concentrating

    _____ taking notes

    _____ active learning

    _____ reading critically

    _____ writing effectively

    _____ thinking critically

    _____ communicating with important people in my life

    _____ enjoying my free time

    _____ allowing myself to be imperfect

2. In the coming week, I plan to invest five minutes a day working towards this goal:

CHAPTER 2

Managing Your Time

I must govern the clock, not be governed by it.
GOLDA MEIR

Just when you think tomorrow will never come, it's yesterday.
EARL WILSON

PREVIEW

1. Develop your Personal Mission Statement into a written plan so it can help you manage your time better.

2. Attend to your priorities before you do anything else.

3. Break a task into small steps and work persistently towards your goal.

4. Learn to make use of the spare moments that most people waste.

IN-CLASS INTRODUCTORY ACTIVITY: MANAGE YOUR TIME

How do you feel about this statement about time management?

Spur-of-the-moment living suits me more than detailed planning.

Strongly disagree	Neutral	Strongly agree
1	5	10

1. *Mark the point on the line that best represents your position.*
2. *Recall a recent experience that illustrates your preference for either detailed planning or spur-of-the-moment living.*

3. *List one advantage and one disadvantage of your preferred style of time management.*

 COLLABORATIVE ACTIVITY

Meet with a small group of other students to compare your answers. Use the space below to take notes on other students' approaches to managing their time.

GROUP DISCUSSION NOTES:

◆ TWO STYLES OF TIME MANAGEMENT ◆

Psychologist Carl Jung discovered that most people organize their lives in one of two ways. One group, composed of individuals who might be called *closure types*, sticks with a task until it's finished ("closure" means "completion"). Many closure types say they feel heavily burdened by unfinished tasks. As one student put it, "I seem to have a cement block on my back until the job is done." The other group, made up of people who might be called *open-ended types*, prefers more flexibility. Members of this group switch easily from one project to another, and deadlines do not weigh as heavily on them.

Jung believed that a preference for one style or the other is inborn; he also noted that neither is good or bad. They are simply different. *Closure types* tend to be highly organized and efficient, but they may lack flexibility. For example, they may have trouble scheduling recreation, exercise, and family life when an important deadline is near. Their perfectionism can create stress, since they often pride themselves on following a plan perfectly.

On the other hand, *open-ended types* may have trouble following a set plan. They often feel stifled by lists and schedules, even when an important task is looming. Open-ended types often struggle with procrastination—putting off jobs until their stress levels become intolerable.

Both groups may have trouble overcoming their differences when they work together as a team, committee, or family. Closure types tend to push for swift completion of a job, while open-ended types want more spontaneity and freedom.

Effective time management begins with *self-knowledge* and *self-management*. Be aware of your own preferred style and its advantages and disadvantages as you work through this chapter. As you learn more about time management, adapt the suggestions you're reading to your own style of time management. If you're a closure type, you may prefer a tighter schedule than your open-ended friends can live with. But whatever your style, you can benefit from the time-management techniques taught in this chapter.

Now is also the time to become more aware of other people's time-management styles. Whether you're studying, socializing, working, or relaxing with your family, you must often consider the preferences of other people. Specific suggestions for working with others appear on pages 69 and 70.

Most of all, remember that *effectiveness* is different from *efficiency*—and much more important. If you're efficient at a task that's not worth doing, you're wasting your time. But hours spent struggling with an important goal—even if you're inefficient—may reap tremendous rewards. So don't try to transform yourself into a perpetual-motion machine. Your goal is to reap the greatest satisfaction from the twenty-four hours allotted to you each day.

The rest of this chapter will introduce you to a variety of time-management skills. You will learn how to lower your stress level and enjoy life more by managing your time effectively. In addition, you'll learn how to work with others whose approach to time management is different from yours.

 ## GETTING IN TOUCH THROUGH FREEWRITING

Do you think you're an open-ended type or a closure type—or a combination of the two? In the space below, freewrite about your time-management style. Mention incidents, feelings and conflicts. Remember, you're writing to get in touch with your own preferences. Don't worry about spelling, punctuation, or organization. Just keep your pen moving, and keep the ideas flowing.

College tasks are less overwhelming when you take advantage of your time-management style.

EXERCISE 1: GET ACQUAINTED WITH YOUR TIME PREFERENCES

Answer the questions below.

1. *Do you tend to be a closure type or an open-ended type? Give examples from your own experience to support your answer.*

2. *Do you know anyone who seems to be the opposite time-management type from you? What differences have you noticed in that person's style of time management?*

3. *Is it more important to you to be "effective" or "efficient"? Why?*

◆ DETERMINE YOUR PRIORITIES: A $25,000 IDEA ◆

They always say that time changes things, but you actually have to change them yourself.

ANDY WARHOL

Whether you prefer closure or open-ended living, your first time-management task is to focus on your priorities. Rereading the Personal Mission Statement you wrote on page 25 can help you keep in touch with whatever is most important to you.

College life can be overwhelming, and you may be facing other challenges as well: a full-time or part-time job, family responsibilities, community work, friends or relatives in crisis. In addition, our culture pressures us to be popular, attractive, well-informed, and wealthy. Whatever your lifestyle, you may find yourself battling feelings of inadequacy from time to time. Those feelings, while normal, don't have to control your life. It's up to you to decide for yourself what goals and values are important to you, and to postpone or ignore others.

Once you give yourself permission not to *do* everything and *be* everything, you can make practical decisions about the most important things you want to do with your time. Ivy Lee, a famous business consultant, devised a simple but effective system for time management. The secret, Lee insisted, was listing the top three priorities for each day. Charles Schwab, head of Bethlehem Steel, had hired Lee to make Bethlehem Steel more productive. But Schwab was skeptical when he heard Lee's advice—in fact he refused at first to pay Lee's consultant fee. How could such a simple trick work the miracles his company needed? In response, Lee made a generous offer. "Use my suggestion for a month," he said, "and then pay me what you think it's worth." But before the end of the month, Schwab was a believer: He sent Lee a check for $25,000.

This chapter will offer you many suggestions about managing your time. Some will appeal to you right away; others may not be as practical. Lee's one-two-three system, however, is always a winner—and you can start applying it right now.

Write down the three most important tasks you need to accomplish today. (If you haven't reread your Personal Mission Statement lately, this would be a good time to do so.) Examples might be: reviewing your notes for an important test, checking out a library book for a paper you're writing, or memorizing a list of sociology terms. (Notice, incidentally, that determining priorities this way is a critical-thinking skill.)

When your list is finished, make sure you complete all three items *today*. Soon you'll be seeing dramatic results from the $25,000 idea.

TODAY'S PRIORITIES

1.

2.

3.

Important or Urgent?

When you're selecting priorities, it's normal to think first of urgent tasks: studying for tomorrow's test, typing the final draft of a research paper, paying an overdue phone bill. But beware! If you're always focusing on emergencies and urgencies, you may be overlooking other tasks that seem less pressing but offer significant benefits to you, such as:

planning for future events and challenges

preparing for upcoming assignments

strengthening relationships

developing new interests

Your time-management style can be a factor here as well. Sometimes closure types are so intent upon completing a particular task that they lose sight of other priorities. And open-ended types, who tend to dislike detailed planning, may postpone dealing with long-term goals.

EXERCISE 2: URGENT VERSUS LONG-TERM TASKS

Label each of the following tasks "U" (urgent) or "L" (long-term beneficial):

_____ *Memorizing the symbols on the periodic table for tomorrow's chemistry test.*

_____ *Stopping by your chemistry professor's office to ask for help in solving one of the homework problems due in two days.*

_____ *Attending an elementary-school concert in which your sister is performing.*

_____ *Buying a gift for your brother's wedding tomorrow.*

_____ *Setting up a filing system for the courses you're taking this semester.*

_____ *Searching your desk for an overdue insurance bill that must be paid today.*

_____ *Having the brakes in your car inspected after the "brakes" light comes on.*

_____ *Scheduling your car's 50,000-mile service.*

_____ *Taking a break from studying to swim for a half hour in the pool on campus.*

_____ *Asking your physician about a suspicious-looking skin mole.*

Writing quickly, make a list of activities that aren't urgent and might have long-term benefits for you. (This high-speed, non-stop listing process is called "brainstorming.") Put a check in front of any activity you plan to perform this week.

JOURNAL ACTIVITY: THE $25,000 IDEA

Use Lee's "$25,000 idea" to write three priorities at the beginning of each day this week. At the end of each day, write a brief evaluation of how the day went. Did you find it helpful to set priorities? Why or why not?

DAY 1

1.

2.

3.

The results:

DAY 2

1.

2.

3.

The results:

DAY 3

1.

2.

3.

The results:

DAY 4

1.

2.

3.

The results:

DAY 5

1.

2.

3.

The results:

DAY 6

1.

2.

3.

The results:

DAY 7

1.

2.

3.

The results:

EVALUATING YOUR JOURNAL ENTRIES

1. *As you reread your journal entries, do you find that some of your priorities appear several times? What conclusions can you draw?*
2. *Did you discover anything new about your priorities? Yourself? Your preferred style of time management?*
3. *Did you fail to accomplish any of your important priorities during the last week?*
4. *How does your time-management style (open-ended or closure) affect the way you handle your priorities?*
5. *Based on this journal experience, do you plan to make any changes in the way you manage your time?*

◆ HOW TO MANAGE YOUR TIME ◆

A pencil and a piece of paper are two of the most powerful tools of time management.
EDWIN C. BLISS

Whether you're an "open-ended type" or a "closure type," good time management requires self-knowledge, awareness, and a written plan. You don't have to follow a rigid schedule or rush madly from one task to another. A good time plan puts *you* in charge, allowing you to set your own priorities and make choices that suit your personality and lifestyle. On the following pages you'll find many suggestions for making a time plan that works for you.

Before you start planning, you should spend some time getting in touch with your needs and preferences. A good first step is keeping a time log—spending a week or so writing down your hourly activities. The log will help you see where your time is going, where your time-wasters are, and where there's room for change.

Where Does Your Time Go?

To find out where your time actually goes each week, follow this two-step plan:

Leave room in your time-management plan for relationships and activities you enjoy.

1. List your current priorities. Include academic, athletic, social, financial, community, family, or spiritual goals that are important to you. You may also find it helpful to list the *roles* you play: parent, son or daughter, friend, employee, student, and so on. Later you will use these lists to complete your time plan.

2. Photocopy the time log on the following page and carry it with you for a week, noting how you spend each block of time. (The sole purpose of the log is to help you track your time. Don't try to function like a robot every moment!)

EVALUATING YOUR TIME LOG

After you've kept a time log, you're ready to analyze and learn from it. Begin by spending a few minutes reviewing the entries you made. Then write responses to the three statements about time. Experts say these statements apply to almost everyone. Are they true for you?

1. *Much of our time is already planned for us—class schedules, jobs, family responsibilities, commuting.*

Your response:

2. *We often spend our time in unproductive ways.*

Your response:

3. *Much of our time is fragmented into short blocks, each less than thirty minutes long.*

Your response:

SETTING PRIORITIES AND MAKING CHOICES

Time is life! Now that you've kept a time log, you are more aware of where your time actually goes. Your next challenge is to set priorities and make choices about the time in your life. This does not mean you have to work or study every moment. It does mean investing your time in activities you find important and fulfilling. To get started, reread your Personal Mission Statement; then answer the questions below.

1. *From your time log, enter the total time spent:*

studying _____
attending classes _____
in employment _____
in child care _____

	Sunday	Monday	Tuesday	Wednesday	Thursday	Friday	Saturday
6:00–7:00							
7:00–8:00							
8:00–9:00							
9:00–10:00							
10:00–11:00							
11:00–12:00							
12:00–1:00							
1:00–2:00							
2:00–3:00							
3:00–4:00							
4:00–5:00							
5:00–6:00							
6:00–7:00							
7:00–8:00							
8:00–9:00							
9:00–10:00							
10:00–11:00							
11:00–12:00							
12:00–1:00							

Figure 2.1 Time Log

doing housework _____

running errands _____

commuting _____

preparing and eating meals _____

in personal grooming _____

having telephone conversations _____

taking part in other socializing _____

enjoying television and other entertainment _____

sleeping _____

exercising _____

participating in sports _____

practicing hobbies _____

2. *Note the time you spent on each priority listed in question 1:*

3. *Complete the statement that applies to you:*

   a. *Because I'm usually a "closure type," I* _____

   _____.

   b. *Because I'm usually an "open-ended type," I* _____

   I _____.

4. *Complete the following statements:*

   a. *I spent less time than I expected on* _____.

   _____.

   b. *I spent more time than I expected on* _____

   _____.

   c. *I'd like to make these changes:* _____

   _____.

   d. *My biggest challenge in managing my time is* _____

   _____.

   e. *I'm going to make this change starting today:* _____

   _____.

  f. *While keeping the time log, I realized* _____

  _____ .

  g. *Now that I've evaluated my time log, I feel* _____

  _____ .

COLLABORATIVE ACTIVITY: SET YOUR PRIORITIES

Meet with a group of other students to compare your responses to statements c, d, e, and f.

  1. *What similarities did you notice?*

  2. *What differences do you see?*

  3. *What time-management challenges do you share with other students in your group?*

  4. *How does your time-management style (open-ended or closure) affect your daily life?*

  5. *Share one strategy you have already used to handle the challenges of college life.*

  6. *During this group session, did you learn any ideas or strategies that will help you manage your time more successfully?*

Looking Ahead

Since time is life, this self-evaluation is worth repeating. Changes in your life will present you with new demands on your time. Plan to photocopy the time log in a few months and go through the process again. The time log and evaluation activity are excellent tools for discovering new ways to handle challenges.

As you learn more about planning, remember that *self-management*, not time-management, is your primary goal. Having a time plan is the beginning, not the end, of this process. The rest of this unit will offer you many suggestions for getting the most out of the twenty-four hours given to you every day.

Writing a Time Plan

Now you're ready to write a time plan. Here are the steps to follow:

1. Make a photocopy of the time log on page 49. Fill in all your obligations for the coming week—classes, commuting, work, doctors' appointments, meal preparation and so on.

2. Use a blank sheet of paper to write down roles, goals, and activities for the coming week. (Be sure to include study, recreation, adequate rest, and time for family and friends.) Wherever possible, write down specific days and times for each activity. (Rereading your responses to the earlier activity "Setting Priorities and Making Choices," page 48, may help you get in touch with the priorities in your life.)

3. On your blank time log, fill in as many of the activities listed in step 2 as you can. Be realistic: Don't overschedule yourself, and allow time for interruptions and emergencies. Although you may have to omit some activities listed in step 2, you should plan enough time to meet all your obligations. Make any adjustments needed until you have a workable plan.

4. Use the One-Minute Checklist on this page to evaluate and adjust your time plan; then make a final copy of the plan to use as a guide during the coming week.

5. Reread "Make Friends with Calendars" on pages 6 and 7 of Chapter One. Transfer items from your time plan to your pocket calendar and planning calendar.

One-Minute Checklist

These questions can help you evaluate your time plan:

_____ Does your plan address your priorities?

_____ Did you allow sufficient time for study (two hours for each hour of class) and college assignments?

_____ Are study periods short and varied enough to prevent boredom, but long enough for you to make progress?

_____ Is there time for errands, home upkeep, and personal tasks?

_____ Is there sufficient variety in your time plan?

_____ Is your plan flexible enough to let you make last-minute changes when necessary?

_____ Did you schedule time for fun, rest, relaxation, and relationships?

6. At the beginning of each day (or the end of the previous day), refer to your planning calendar to make a daily "to-do" list. Use your time plan as a guide; highlight your three priorities for the day to ensure that they catch your attention.

7. Evaluate your time-management plan—and your success in following it—each day. How many items did you cross off your "to-do" list? Did you attend to all three priorities? Do any items consistently remain undone at the end of each day? What did you learn about planning and time management today, and how can you apply that knowledge tomorrow?

---

1. Roles and related activities for the coming week (wherever possible, note days and times):

family - call Mom and Dad 8 p.m. Wed.
friend - buy Lisa's wedding gift Wed. after English
friend - racquetball Tues. aft 3:00 - 5:00 Greg
friend - lunch with Kathy noon Mon.
friend - movie with Greg Fri. eve
Sucessful student - anatomy study group,
           Eng. research paper, speech prep, ethics

2. My top goals for the next week (wherever possible, note related activities, days and times):

review for anatomy quiz -
                    Thurs. eve 7:30-9:00
                    (call Joan)
Lisa's wedding - gift
                    + wedding Sat afternoon
speech practice - 9:00 Wed, 2:00 Fri.
           (video? pronunciation?)
fitness - racquetball Tues., jog Sat. &
                    Sun.

Figure 2.2 Roles and Priorities Worksheet

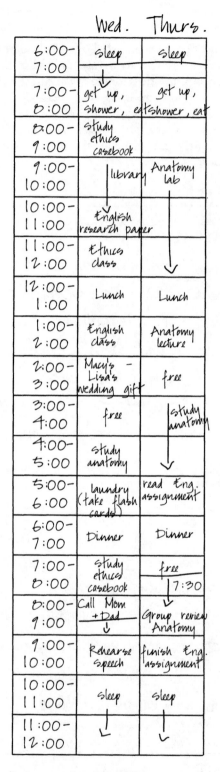

	Wed.	Thurs.
6:00–7:00	sleep	sleep
7:00–8:00	get up, shower, eat	get up, shower, eat
8:00–9:00	study ethics casebook	
9:00–10:00	library	Anatomy lab
10:00–11:00	English research paper	
11:00–12:00	ethics class	
12:00–1:00	Lunch	Lunch
1:00–2:00	English class	Anatomy lecture
2:00–3:00	Macy's – Lisa's wedding gift	free
3:00–4:00	free	study anatomy
4:00–5:00	study anatomy	
5:00–6:00	laundry (take flash cards)	read Eng. assignment
6:00–7:00	Dinner	Dinner
7:00–8:00	study ethics casebook	free 7:30
8:00–9:00	Call Mom + Dad	Group review Anatomy
9:00–10:00	Rehearse speech	finish Eng. assignment
10:00–11:00	sleep	sleep
11:00–12:00		

Figure 2.3 Part of a Student's Completed Time Plan

Making a Term Plan

For many students, daily and weekly planning aren't enough. Holidays, vacations, special projects, and scheduled events can disrupt even the best time plan. It's stressful to discover that you've promised to help decorate for a sorority party the night before an important exam—or to find that a term paper is due the week you're supposed to work overtime at your part-time job.

Making a term plan can help you avoid time conflicts, and the process is similar to the planning you've already done. Equip yourself with a college activity calendar and a list of upcoming events related to your friends, family, social life, community activities, and job. Reread your Personal Mission Statement to remind yourself of your top priorities.

1. Use your planning calendar to list dates when you expect to participate in college events; also list dates for exams, registration, and other college requirements.
2. On your planning calendar, select dates and times for any preparations you must make: purchasing tickets, clothing, or equipment; making reservations; telephoning friends; renting a car; and so on. Select dates for performing those tasks, and mark them on your planning calendar.
3. Use the same process to plan family, community, and job-related events.
4. Check your list against your Personal Mission Statement. Have you overlooked anything that should be included in your term plan?
5. During this planning process, evaluate the choices you're making. Are they realistic? Are you allowing enough time for study, sleep, and other basic needs? Over-scheduling can lead to stress—and it can take days or weeks to recover from one chaotic weekend. Don't forget to allow time for laundry, paperwork, cleanup, and other essential tasks.

◆ THE BENEFITS OF SELF-MANAGEMENT ◆

Discipline is making sure you do what is good for you.
                                        Bill Saks

Being in control of your time does not mean sacrificing spontaneity, fun, and friendship. Self-management—the ability to make thoughtful, deliberate choices—can actually help you reduce stress and enjoy life more. If you're an open-ended type, your choices can help you eliminate procrastination; if you're a closure type, time-management principles can help you overcome unnecessary perfectionism.

But no one ever said that self-management is easy. You'll need both awareness and courage, for you must constantly make decisions about where your time is going. The following ideas will help you make choices that work for you:

1. Apply the 80/20 Rule. In almost any situation, 80% of the benefits come from only 20% of the possibilities. If you checked your closet right now, you'd probably discover that you wear 20% of your clothing 80% of the time: If you have ten shirts hanging there,

you probably wear two of them most of the time. If your personal telephone directory lists fifty numbers, you dial only ten of them most of the time.

In time management, the 80/20 Rule means that you should *not* try to do every possible task. Instead you should look for the 20%, or one-fifth, of possibilities that contain most of the benefits.

Suppose, for example, you're preparing for a test on Shakespeare's *Romeo and Juliet*. It's not difficult to come up with five study tasks that might be helpful. You can review your class notes, reread the play, meet with a study group, research the play in the library, or watch a videotape of *Romeo and Juliet* in the college's learning center. But you can't do all five effectively. Instead you should choose the one possibility most likely to help you write an A paper. The best choice might be the study group, where you can share insights and information about the play with other students.

The 80/20 Rule has two important benefits. First, it encourages creativity: You're always generating a list of options and then choosing one. Second, it relieves your guilt about not doing *everything*. Because your time and energy are limited, the 80/20 Rule encourages you to choose the best option without worrying about the others. As a result, you're less likely to feel overwhelmed, and procrastination becomes less of a problem. While you're discussing *Romeo and Juliet* in your study group, for example, you don't have to feel guilty that you're not studying in the library or watching a videotape. With practice, the 80/20 Rule can be a powerful time-management tool.

2. Fight Parkinson's Law. This law states that a job usually fills up all the time available. If you set aside a whole weekend to study for a history test, you may not accomplish anything else during that time. Procrastination can eat up big chunks of your time: Since the whole weekend lies ahead, you may have trouble settling down and getting started.

But if you also have a math assignment, a date, and a pile of laundry, you may work in all three during the same weekend.

To make the best use of your time, set realistic limits for assignments and chores. Plan to switch activities occasionally to stay fresh and alert. It's depressing to spend a whole weekend on one task—and you won't be at your best while you're completing it.

3. Get control of your TV viewing. How much television time showed up on your time log? Like many Americans, you may do most of your relaxing in front of the TV. It's a great way to unwind—but it can also be a major time-robber. If you spend too much time in front of the TV, you may miss out on new experiences and new friendships. Your fitness level, relationships, and grades may deteriorate.

After evaluating their time logs, many students realize that they watch too much TV—and don't enjoy it as much as they thought. Much of their time is spent watching programs they don't really like, simply because they haven't discovered other enjoyable uses for their time.

To get control of your TV viewing, study the program listings at the beginning of each week and mark only the shows you really want to see. Plan other activities for the in-between times. Keep a chart of your progress, and remind yourself often of the benefits: better relationships, higher grades, a more interesting life. Above all, stand up and switch off the TV when your program is over.

4. Vary your recreational habits. Watch an occasional show on public television, and tune in the public radio station in your area—you'll learn a great deal. Buy a newspaper you're not used to, and pick up a magazine you've never read before. Watch a classic movie instead of a current feature, and experiment with other forms of recreation: a concert featuring music that's new to you, a new dance form, a different sport. You may become a lifetime enthusiast—and you'll benefit from a broader cultural background.

5. Make the most of the empty spaces in your day. Your time log may have revealed empty spaces that can be converted into productive time. You may wait in laundromats, reception areas, or bus stations with nothing to do. Standing in lines eats up time, as does commuting. Here are some tips for making those moments productive:

- Play educational audio tapes in your car. (You can buy them, borrow them from a library, or make them yourself by reading class notes into a tape recorder.) If your car doesn't have a sound system, buy an inexpensive portable player and an adapter that plugs into the cigarette lighter.
- Commute with another student, and use the time to talk about the subjects you're studying.
- Play audio tapes while getting dressed and completing household chores.
- Carry a paperback book to read when someone keeps you waiting. If you have too much to carry, buy a used paperback, tear it into sections, and carry part of it with you.
- Always keep a book in your car so that you have something to read if you're delayed during an errand.
- Review your flash cards (see Chapter Four, "Active Learning").
- Go over your memory devices (again, see Chapter Four).
- Practice a skill during free moments: dribble an imaginary ball, work on your dance posture, translate a sentence into French, or quiz yourself on new vocabulary words.
- Hang informative signs where you'll see them often. Post mathematical formulas, vocabulary words, historical dates, and other factual information. Use large print, and make the signs eye-catching: Add a colored border, for example, or paste on pictures from the Sunday comics. (Mirrors and clocks are great places for signs.)

Empty moments often mean boredom and fatigue. When you're waiting for your turn in the bathroom at night, for example, you may not feel like opening up your history book. You have only a few minutes, you're tired, and you certainly won't accomplish much in such a short time. But it pays to make a habit of doing one small extra task even when you don't want to. Read a paragraph or two in that history book, ask yourself what's likely to be on tomorrow's Spanish quiz, or review the steps in today's chemistry experiment. Often you'll surprise yourself by becoming interested in what you're doing, and you'll have a new burst of energy. And even if you don't, you'll have accomplished something—however small—towards a goal.

Quick study periods are no substitute for the large blocks of time needed to master college material. But these "quickies" are excellent ways to strengthen your memory. And skeptical students often report an additional payoff: dramatic improvement in concentration. If you study only when conditions are perfect, you'll never learn how to cope with noisy, chaotic surroundings. Start getting accustomed to concentrating during both short and long study periods.

READING THOUGHTFULLY: TIMESAVING HABITS

You're about to read excerpts from a chapter on habits from *Psychology. Briefer Course* written by psychologist William James (1842–1910). Before you begin reading, answer the questions in the following activity.

BEFORE YOU READ

Answer the following questions:

1. In what ways can habits be beneficial? How can they be harmful?

2. What connections can you see between habits and self-management?

3. List four or five positive habits that you have. Then list four or five that interfere with self-management.

---

from   **"Habit: Its Importance for Psychology"**
by William James (1892)

First, habit simplifies our movements, makes them accurate, and diminishes fatigue.

Man is born with a tendency to do more things than he has ready-made arrangements for in his nerve-centres. Most of the performances of other animals are automatic. But in him the number of them is so enormous that most of them must be the fruit of painful study. If practice did not make perfect, nor habit economize the expense of nervous and muscular energy, he would be in a sorry plight.

Second, habit diminishes the conscious attention with which our acts are performed. In habitual action, mere sensation is a sufficient guide, and the upper regions of brain and mind are set comparatively free. Habit is thus the enormous fly-wheel of society, its most precious conservative agent. The more of the details of our daily life we can hand over to the effortless custody of automatism, the more our higher powers of mind will be set free for their own proper work.

There is no more miserable human being than one in whom nothing is habitual but indecision, and for whom the drinking of every cup, the time of rising and going to bed every day, and the beginning of every bit of work, are subjects of express volitional deliberation. Full half the time of such a man goes to the deciding, or regretting, of matters which ought to be so ingrained in him as practically not to exist for his consciousness at all. If there be such daily duties not yet ingrained in any one of my readers, let him begin this very hour to set the matter right.

In Professor Bain's chapter on "The Moral Habits" there are some admirable practical remarks laid down. Two great maxims emerge from his treatment. The first is that in the acquisition of a new habit, or the leaving off of an old one, we must take care to launch ourselves with as strong and decided an initiative as possible. Accumulate all the possible circumstances which shall re-enforce the right motives; put yourself assiduously in conditions that encourage the new way; make engagements incompatible with the old; take a public pledge, if the case allows; in short, envelop your resolution with every aid you know. This will give your new beginning such a momentum that the temptation to break down will not occur as soon as it otherwise might; and every day during which a break-down is postponed adds to the chances of its not occurring at all.

The second maxim is: Never suffer an exception to occur till the new habit is securely rooted in your life. Each lapse is like letting fall of a ball of string which one is carefully winding up; a single slip undoes more than a great many turns will wind again. Continuity of training is the great means of making the nervous system act infallibly right.

A third maxim may be added to the preceding pair: Seize the very first possible opportunity to act on every resolution you make, and on every emotional prompting you may experience in the direction of the habits you aspire to gain. It is not in the moment of their forming, but in the moment of their producing motor effects, that resolves and aspirations communicate the new "set" to the brain.

No matter how full a reservoir of maxims one may possess, and no matter how good one's sentiments may be, if one has not taken advantage of every concrete opportunity to act, one's character may remain entirely unaffected for the better. There is no more contemptible type of human character than that of the nerveless sentimentalist and dreamer, who spends his life in a weltering sea of sensibility and emotion, but who never does a manly concrete deed.

After You Read

1. What new words did you encounter in this selection? How will you learn their meaning?

2. What questions do you have? How will you find answers to them?

3. What do you think is James's most important point?

4. What relationship does James draw between habit and the effective use of time?

5. Do you agree with James's three maxims? Why or why not?

6. Can you apply any of his ideas to your own habits and use of time?

7. What is one specific habit you would like to develop that would help you make more effective use of your time? What suggestions from this selection might help you develop that habit?

Persistence Pays Off

In *The Boys of Summer*, author Roger Kahn wrote about George "Shotgun" Shuba, an outfielder who was one of the best hitters for the old Brooklyn Dodgers baseball team. Kahn told Shuba, "I would have given anything to have had your natural swing." "You could have," Shuba said. When Kahn—himself a baseball player—looked bewildered, Shuba explained how he'd acquired his "natural" swing.

Years before, as a teenager, Shuba had devised a plan to develop the skills he'd need in order to be chosen by a major-league baseball team. From one of the beams in his basement he hung a length of string with knots representing the strike zone. Then he drilled out some of the wood in a baseball bat, replacing it with lead to make the bat heavy— forty-four ounces. Every night he swung the weighted bat six hundred times at the clump of knotted string, developing the strength and control that later made him a great hitter.

"In the winters," Shuba said, "for fifteen years, even when I was in the majors, I'd swing at the clump six hundred times. After sixty I'd make an X on a chart. Ten of them and I had my six hundred swings. Then I could go to bed. You call that natural? I swung a 44-ounce bat 600 times a night, 4,200 times a week, 47,200 swings every winter."

"I wish I'd known this years ago," Kahn said. Shuba's hitting practice, which took him thirty or forty minutes a night, culminated in a major-league baseball career. Can you invest the same amount of time in a dream of your own? Or can you find just five minutes to invest in that dream? And can you begin today? If the answers are "yes," read on.

Five Minutes a Day. You've probably seen TV advertisements for fitness equipment promising spectacular results in just a few minutes a day. If you're skeptical about those claims, you're right. No one can achieve an important goal—physical fitness, academic

Does Clutter Slow You Down?

Many people spend enormous amounts of time maintaining their possessions—finding, cleaning, repairing, labeling and storing them. If you're constantly pressed for time, consider disposing of some of the possessions you no longer need. There are many advantages: You'll spend less time searching drawers and closets; you'll save money on repairs; your living space will be more attractive; you may be able to recycle items for the benefit of others.

Some tips for reducing clutter:

1. Use the 80/20 Rule to decide which utensils, clothes, tools, and recreational items are important to you. Chances are you use and need only 1/5 of your possessions; why keep the rest?

Most students can benefit from storing or discarding unimportant items that clutter their lives.

success, mastering a foreign language—without a major investment of time and effort.

But those five minutes *can* help you make a significant start on any long-term goal important to you. When you're feeling overwhelmed, the plan can be a powerful weapon against procrastination. Once you've established the habit of plunging into a difficult task for five minutes a day, you'll be able to avoid much of the panic that paralyzes many students when they tackle a major test, research paper, or term project.

The plan can also help you make significant progress on any lifetime goal that's important to you: improving your communicating skills, understanding math, learning sign language, slimming down. You can evaluate goals, develop strategies, and keep yourself motivated. And it's great for memorization—for example, you can invest five minutes a day learning medical, literary, accounting, or sociological definitions.

2. Search for alternatives. If something has sentimental value, could you photograph it and throw away the original item?
3. Be realistic about the future. If you don't have time to use an item now, or it doesn't fit or suit your lifestyle, get rid of it. You can make appropriate purchases in the future, when new needs arise.

Your clutter-reduction project should include your desk. Searching for lost items can be tiring and time-consuming.

Follow these guidelines:

1. Have only one project on top of your desk at a time.
2. If important papers are waiting for your attention, keep them in a red folder. You won't have to worry about misplacing them in a pile of clutter.
3. Sort all incoming papers into two piles: those worth your attention (process them) and the rest (throw them away).
4. Time-management expert Alan Lakein has a useful rule for dealing with paperwork: After sorting, handle each piece of paper only once. Don't pick it up unless you're ready to work on it.
5. Avoid storing items in desk drawers, where they're likely to be misplaced or forgotten. File them or throw them away. (Some very productive executives refuse to have drawers in their offices.)

Getting Started. You can't master geometry, figure-skating, or French cooking in five minutes a day. But you can reap surprising benefits by concentrating on one small area persistently, day after day. Try spending five minutes pondering a mathematical theorem, or imitating phrases on a foreign-language tape, or practicing arm movements in front of a mirror, or reading about French sauces. Memorize vocabulary words, or practice a line of piano music, or look closely at a painting that impresses you. Read a page in a difficult book—even if you don't understand it well—or put yourself through a short exercise routine.

Be warned: At first you may feel that you're wasting your time. Be persistent, however, and remember that five minutes daily adds up to thirty-five minutes a week, over two hours a month. If you're still skeptical, ask what you would have accomplished by *not* investing that time each day.

Enjoying the Payoffs. This plan will teach you three important lessons about success. First, you'll learn that any significant achievement begins with small steps. Repetition and persistence are much more important than inborn talent. (If you need convincing, reread the story about baseball player George Shuba.)

Second, you'll learn how to make a workable plan. Successful people know how to divide a huge goal into manageable bits so that they build up momentum and enthusiasm in the early stages of a new project.

Third, and most important, you'll learn how to manage the anxiety that often accompanies a new undertaking. Many people lose courage when they begin a major project. The remedy is a workable plan that starts with simple, confidence-building tasks.

If you're really frightened about a new project, spend just five minutes a day overcoming your fears. Pull out a drawer in the library card catalog, or seat yourself front of a computer there. Be sure to spend the full five minutes doing *something*—anything—in that spot before you leave. If you've never learned how to swim, put on a swimsuit each day and stand near the pool, even if you don't have the courage to jump into the water. Spend just five minutes trying anything that scares you—but be sure to go back again the next day.

If you stick to this system, you'll gradually learn how to take advantage of the free moments scattered through even the busiest day. The five-minutes-a-day plan *doesn't* mean that you're supposed to be working on a goal every minute. You're still in charge of your time, and you can choose relaxation and recreation whenever you wish. But the plan will teach you how to concentrate and reap rewards during short spaces that might otherwise be wasted.

After you've tried the plan for a while, you'll discover the biggest payoff: an increase in your enthusiasm, so that five minutes suddenly isn't enough anymore. Now you can start setting aside longer blocks of time for your goal. When it's well under way, think about starting all over again—five minutes a day on a new learning adventure. Who knows what you'll accomplish by using this system all your life?

Suggested five-minute projects:

To earn higher grades:

- review a lecture with an A student
- turn your class notes into possible test questions
- summarize a reading assignment on an index card
- spend five minutes exploring a section of the library that's new to you
- at the end of a class, summarize on an index card everything important that was said

To build and strengthen relationships:

- listen to someone without turning away or interrupting
- introduce yourself to a person you'd like to know better
- quiz yourself on the names and interests of anyone new you met today

◆ PROCRASTINATION ◆

Almost everyone procrastinates—delays tackling a task—from time to time. The results are both predictable and unpleasant: frantic last-minute attempts to complete work on time, disappointing results, low grades, guilt, and turmoil.

Procrastination often occurs when students face tasks that seem overwhelming or unpleasant—writing a research paper, preparing a tax form, making an appointment for major dental work. Conflict can also lead to procrastination. If you and your spouse disagree about the spot for your next vacation, you may delay making plans until it's too late to get a reservation at the places you like.

Inner conflicts can slow you down when you're choosing a topic for a paper. And perfectionism can lead to procrastination. If you're worried about inadequate performance, you may have trouble getting started on a challenging task.

Many people mistakenly think that willpower is the only antidote to procrastination. As you'll see in the following pages, many other remedies are available. Some take only a minute or two! Once you've acquired a procrastination "toolbox," you're likely to find it much easier to start—and complete—the challenging work assigned in college.

GETTING IN TOUCH THROUGH FREEWRITING

In the space below, freewrite about your experiences with procrastination. The following questions may help you get started: When do you find it hardest to get started on a task? Are there any times you are particularly prone to procrastinate? What feelings do you have when you're procrastinating? What strategies have you used to overcome those feelings? How well have they worked for you?

Do you suffer from do-nothingism? Have you ever stared at a piece of paper without being able to write a single word? Do you ever watch a TV program you don't like because you're afraid to tackle a difficult assignment?

Dr. David Burns, author of *Feeling Good*, calls this problem "do-nothingism," and he says the solution is surprisingly simple: Just take one small step. Doing *something*, he says, always feels better than doing nothing. He recalls one depressed patient—an artist—who had lost faith in himself and given up drawing years before. Somehow the patient had convinced himself that he couldn't draw something as simple as a straight line. When the therapist said, "Prove it!" the line came out so straight that the patient began drawing again, and soon the depression was gone.

This is an extreme case, but "do-nothingism" paralyzes almost everyone from time to time. Be your own therapist by choosing a single "instant task." Write a sentence for an essay that scares you; complete one step in a difficult math problem (even if it's just a diagram); read a paragraph in a textbook that seems overwhelming. When you're finished, spend a minute or two thinking about the experience. How was it? Can you do it again? The second mini-task is usually easier than the first—and so it goes, until you surprise yourself with what you've accomplished.

COLLABORATIVE ACTIVITY: OVERCOMING "DO-NOTHINGISM"

Meet with a group of three or four other students to brainstorm a list of "instant tasks" for overcoming "do-nothingism." Generate the list quickly, without stopping to evaluate the entries: Anything goes. When the list is completed, each member should choose an "instant task" to apply to a project that seems difficult or unpleasant. If possible, meet again in a few days to discuss the results.

Good-by, Perfection!

If it's worth doing, it's worth doing badly.

ANONYMOUS

Perfectionism is one of the biggest causes of procrastination. Perhaps this sounds strange to you, for you may have been taught that every task should be done perfectly. But the truth is quite different. Since your time is limited, you *can't afford* perfectionism.

Get unimportant tasks out of the way quickly—and imperfectly—so you're free to concentrate on your priorities. When you've identified a goal that's important to you, make a strong commitment to achieving it. Share your dreams with friends and family; plan to invest significant time and energy in the pursuit of your goal; look within yourself for the dedication and passion you will need for success.

Most important, don't allow perfectionism to derail a project. For example, don't waste time looking for a ruler when you're underlining the important ideas in a text—a hand-drawn line is good enough. And don't be too fussy about laundry, cooking, cleaning and entertaining. This *doesn't* mean washing your jeans in the same load with a delicate lace dress, or serving unappetizing food. It *does* mean that you don't have to iron everything, that it's all right to serve simple meals, and that you can offer your friends store-bought refreshments rather than homemade ones. While you're in school, delegate chores to other family members even if they're not as thorough as you are. Give the "$25,000 idea" a chance to work for you by putting first things first, last things last.

Most important, don't allow perfectionism to develop into do-nothingism. If you're afraid your research paper or lab report won't be perfect, you may be too intimidated to begin writing. In the same way, you may miss out on an enjoyable sport or hobby because you don't think you can master it.

When you feel overwhelmed by a difficult assignment, ask yourself the following questions:

1. "What are the minimum standards I must achieve?" Instead of struggling to produce a brilliant English composition, start by attempting an imperfect first draft. Remember, it's easier to get started on a simple project than a hard one. You can redo it later, when you've gained some courage and momentum.

2. "What's the cost of my perfectionism?" The need to be perfect is a form of self-punishment—exactly what you *don't* need while you're in college. Even worse, perfectionism can create stress and procrastination. Have you ever spent a whole evening doing nothing because you couldn't get started on an assignment? Perfectionism was probably the culprit. When you give yourself permission to be imperfect, stress will be less of a problem, and you'll find yourself enjoying new challenges.

3. "Am I really afraid of lowering my standards?" Choosing to be imperfect doesn't lock you into anything. Once you've produced an average research paper, humanities project, book report or athletic performance, you can always go back and raise your standard. When you give up perfectionism, all you're really losing are guilt and self-criticism. Why not say good-bye to both right now?

4. "Why do I demand more from myself than from others?" You probably wouldn't force a family member or friend to meet an impossible standard. Why inflict such a negative experience upon yourself?

Do it Now! Many students have used the following suggestions to overcome procrastination:

1. Set the stage. Gather everything you need before you undertake a challenging task. Purchase needed supplies, such as index cards or computer discs. Organize a space for storing books and notes while you're completing your project.

2. Banish distractions. Find a spot away from the TV, radio, stereo, and telephone. Avoid locations that remind you of less-important chores: laundry, dirty dishes, unmade beds. "Out of sight, out of mind" is a useful motto for people who are easily sidetracked.

3. Do an "instant task"—the simpler, the better. Sit at your desk and turn on your computer. Open a notebook and take out a pen. Read a paragraph in a textbook; look up a word in your dictionary; draw a diagram for a math problem. Remain in the same place until the "instant task" is finished and you're ready to start another one.

4. Begin with a difficult step. If "instant tasks" don't work for you, push yourself to do the hardest part of an assignment or project. You may find that it's not as hard as you expected. And when you've completed the most challenging parts of a task, you won't have any trouble motivating yourself to finish.

5. Make a public commitment. Tell family and friends about the challenge you've taken on. Announce the date when you plan to finish it. They'll serve as a support group, and you won't want to let them down by procrastinating.

6. Make a progress chart. List the micro-steps you need to complete before you achieve your goal. Cross off each step as you finish it. The chart monitors your progress and motivates you to persist.

Resolving Time Conflicts

Time conflicts often cause procrastination. When it's difficult to choose between two or more possibilities, many people simply postpone making a decision at all. The result: procrastination and frustration.

At the beginning of this chapter you learned that "closure types" and "open-ended types" have different approaches to time management. Conflicts between people with different time-management styles can lead to procrastination. If two people can't agree on the guidelines for a project, they may postpone it or even give it up completely. Since you will spend the rest of your life working, socializing, and living with other people, you need to learn how to coordinate your time needs with theirs.

First, keep communication open. Explain your preferences to teammates, coworkers, and family members. Encourage others to do the same so that compromises can be worked out. Open-ended types may have to abide by a deadline they dislike, or closure types may have to adjust to an uncomfortable level of flexibility. Talking matters over always helps.

Remember that friends and family members may feel left out because you're busy with college. Talk about your dreams, hopes, and challenges. If you're frustrated about having to do too much for others, make a list of the responsibilities you're carrying. In a non-threatening way, show the list to family members or friends. Explain that your stress level is higher than you can handle comfortably, and ask if they can take over part of the list. Sharing your feelings—and showing concern for the feelings of others—strengthens and deepens relationships.

Second, make family and friends participants in your life. On a day when you're not attending classes, show your children or parents around the campus. Be enthusiastic about your new experiences, and tell them how much their support means to you.

Finally, remember that time is the greatest gift you can give another person. Think for a moment about the people who have been most special in your life. Chances are they are people who have freely shared their time with you. Don't allow your college responsibilities to isolate you from others. When making a schedule, always build in time for people important to you. A college degree is a great accomplishment, but it won't mean as much if no one is there to celebrate with you.

Meeting Your Time Needs—and Theirs. What happens when you and a friend or family member have a disagreement about time? Perhaps your mother wants you to help clean the garage, while you think it's more important to study for a humanities test. Or you want to take your date to a basketball game, but she's more interested in a concert. Because modern life is hectic, and time is often limited, conflicts like these arise frequently. If you don't know how to handle them, guilt and anger can harm—or even destroy—a relationship that's important to you. But if you're a skilled problem solver, you can often resolve conflicts like these so that each person's needs are met. Try one or two of the following solutions:

1. Make an alternative offer. Could you clean the garage next weekend, when you won't be studying for any major tests? Or could you skip a shopping trip this weekend to make time for the garage? Or do half the cleaning now, and half later?

2. Brainstorm other possibilities. Perhaps a friend could help with the garage in exchange for your help with another project later. You and your date might come up with an idea for Friday night that's much more fun than either the basketball game or the concert.

3. Discover and discuss underlying needs. Often time conflicts are a symptom of more serious problems with the relationship. If your spouse feels threatened by your new college friends and activities, he or she may cover up those feelings by making excessive demands on your time. Since the real (although hidden) issue is insecurity, talking about time conflicts won't eliminate the problem. But reassurance—and setting aside time for the two of you to rebuild your relationship—may end the conflict.

4. Be open and honest about your own needs. Don't expect automatic and instant understanding from others. They may not understand how difficult your organic chemistry course is, and it might be difficult for them to understand your needs for rest, recreation or study time. Talk about your feelings without blaming, shaming, or criticizing others. Share details about your schedule, assignments, thoughts, and feelings. As understanding grows, so does cooperation.

Cooperation is a learning process: Don't expect perfection right away.

EXERCISE 3: PLAN YOUR ACTIVITIES

1. *List the people most important to you right now.*

2. *Beside each name, list one activity that might help you get more enjoyment from your relationship with that person. (Strategies might include a shared meal, talking over a particular issue, writing an overdue letter, inviting the person to attend a campus event with you, and so on.)*

3. *Select three names and choose a time and place during the next week to perform the strategy you've chosen. (If you can't devise a workable plan, reevaluate your answers to step 2. It might also be helpful to ask a friend or family member for suggestions.)*

4. *At the end of the seven days, review your original plan. What parts were successful? What might you do differently next time?*

5. *Meet with a small group of other students to compare your experiences. What challenges are common to your whole group? Which are unique? What can you learn from one another?*

 ## USING WHAT YOU HAVE LEARNED

1. What is the most important discovery you made about yourself as you worked through this unit?
2. What is the biggest time-management challenge you face right now?
3. What specific strategy do you think will help you the most as you face this challenge?
4. What is the most important discovery you made during the time-log activity?
5. What goal is especially important to you right now?
6. What five-minute task, related to this goal, do you plan to complete today?
7. What are three specific strategies you plan to take to improve your relationships while you're in college?
8. What is one strategy you plan to use when procrastination becomes a problem?
9. What are your three most important priorities today?
10. Horace Mann wrote, "Habit is a cable; we weave a thread of it each day, and at last we cannot break it." Do you agree or disagree? Why?

 ## EVALUATING YOUR PROGRESS

1. As I look back on the past seven days, I've seen an improvement in these areas:

_____ organizing my life

_____ protecting my health

_____ planning my time

_____ concentrating

_____ taking notes

_____ active learning

_____ reading critically

_____ writing effectively

_____ thinking critically

_____ communicating with important people in my life

_____ enjoying my free time

_____ allowing myself to be imperfect

2. In the coming week, I plan to invest five minutes a day working towards this goal:

CHAPTER 3

Getting the Most Out of Class

Education has only one basic factor . . . one must want it.

GEORGE EDWARD WOODBERRY

 PREVIEW

1. Class attendance, effective listening, and skillful notetaking are important to your college success.

2. You can use class time to practice thinking and speaking skills that will be useful in your career.

3. Diversity—ideas, activities, and people new to you—can trigger personal and intellectual growth.

 IN-CLASS INTRODUCTORY ACTIVITY: YOUR CLASSROOM EXPERIENCES

Spend a few minutes thinking about a classroom experience you particularly enjoyed—a course, lecture, or activity that stands out in your memory. In the space below, freewrite about

the experience: when and where it happened, who was there with you, and what you par-
ticularly enjoyed about it. Then complete the activities that follow.

COLLABORATIVE ACTIVITY

1. *Why was this experience so enjoyable for you?*
2. *What was the instructor's role?*
3. *What was your role?*
4. *Meet with a small group of other students to share and compare the experiences you've described. On the basis of your discussion, what conclusions can you make about effective learning experiences?*

GROUP DISCUSSION NOTES:

◆ GETTING THE MOST OUT OF CLASS ◆

The memorable classroom experiences your group discussed probably had several features in common: The material was interesting; the subject was important to you; you were actively involved in some way—intellectually, emotionally, physically. Other factors might include humor, fun, a teacher with a rare gift for performing, and opportunities for sharing with other students. Experiences like these are an exciting part of the educational process.

Naturally, you can't expect the same level of excitement from every class. Not all teachers are skilled performers, and not every subject is going to intrigue you. Some courses offer minimal opportunities for interaction with the professor and other students.

Nevertheless, you have the power to make every class a worthwhile experience. This chapter will show you how active involvement in class—no matter who's teaching or what methods are used—is one of the keys to college success. How you listen, take notes, prepare, and participate can transform an ordinary learning experience into a memorable one. It's all up to you.

Students who take notes and think critically get maximum benefit from the hours they spend in college classrooms.

Twenty Reasons to Attend Class

Eighty percent of success is showing up.

WOODY ALLEN

1. The person who teaches the course usually assigns the final grade.
2. Concentration during class shortens your study time afterwards.
3. You can have your questions answered by an expert in the field.
4. Professors who know you well may use their professional contacts to provide you with references and other valuable career assistance.
5. You'll sharpen your notetaking and listening skills—both of which will be valuable in your career.
6. Classes are great places for developing new friendships.
7. Collaborative learning projects will help you develop social and leadership skills.
8. You'll get a return on your investment in college tuition.
9. You'll gain up-to-date, useful information not found in books.
10. You'll get clues about the material most likely to appear on tests.
11. Professors who know you well may nominate you for scholarships and academic awards.
12. A good lecture condenses and connects information that might take days—or longer—to acquire on your own.
13. You won't have to rely on secondhand information about assignments and test dates.
14. Your vocabulary will improve.
15. Your classroom experiences will reinforce the learning experiences you've had on your own.
16. Class lectures often contain the answers to test questions.
17. You'll start to feel more comfortable in an academic setting.
18. You'll observe skilled thinkers in action.
19. Intellectual discussions will sharpen your speaking and reasoning skills.
20. It's difficult, if not impossible, to get A's if you don't attend class faithfully.

COLLABORATIVE ACTIVITY: YOUR REASONS FOR ATTENDING CLASS

Place a check in front of the five reasons for attending class that are most important to you. Then meet with three or four other students to compare your checklists. Are your priorities similar, or different? What conclusions can you draw?

Individual Learning Preferences

Everyone—including you—has preferred ways of learning. Traditional college courses are designed for good listeners who enjoy studying independently. In a typical college classroom, students listen to a lecture, take notes, and study the course textbook after class by themselves.

But research shows that not everyone learns best that way. Some students experience success when they talk about what they're learning; others profit from being active while they learn—and there are other differences as well. By discovering your own preferences, you can choose the study techniques that work best for you. If traditional classroom methods—lectures, reading, and notetaking—don't suit your learning style, you can discover and adopt study methods that work well for you.

The learning experience you described at the beginning of this chapter probably reveals a great deal about your favorite ways to learn. You can learn more by discovering your preferred learning style.

DISCOVERING YOUR LEARNING STYLE

Record your answers to these questions; then follow the instructions for interpreting your answers.

PART I

1. *When you don't understand a concept, do you prefer to*

   a. look for an explanation in a book
   b. find someone to explain the concept to you

2. *If you're given a choice, would you rather*

   a. help prepare a group project
   b. prepare your own project

3. *In general, are you more interested in*

   a. new ideas and theories
   b. practical skills you can put to use

4. *When you learn something new, do you wonder*

   a. how you can use this knowledge
   b. whether this knowledge is consistent with what you've already learned

5. *When you're given a challenging assignment, do you*

   a. ask a friend to work with you
   b. face the challenge on your own

6. *Do you learn more from*

   a. listening to a lecture
   b. reading your textbook

7. *If a professor gave you a free hour for study, would you*

    a. read your textbook
    b. study with other students
    c. stop by the professor's office to discuss what you're learning
    d. investigate a subject that interests you but isn't part of a course you're taking

8. *Imagine that you're sitting in class when the professor begins talking about a new theory that he or she finds fascinating. Do you*

    a. want to hear more about it
    b. wish the professor would talk about something closer to the everyday reality you know best

PART II

Think of two successful learning experiences you've had in school. Use the space below to describe each one in a few words. Then check the three factors that were most important to each experience.

9. *Briefly describe your learning experience here:*

Check the three factors that were most important to you:

_____   *a.*   *learning with the help of others*
_____   *b.*   *freedom to learn in your own way*
_____   *c.*   *helpful information from a teacher*
_____   *d.*   *interesting material to read*
_____   *e.*   *exposure to new ideas*
_____   *f.*   *improving your ability to do something important to you*

10. *Briefly describe your learning experience here:*

Check the three factors that were most important to you:

_____ a. *learning with the help of others*
_____ b. *freedom to learn in your own way*
_____ c. *helpful information from a teacher*
_____ d. *interesting material to read*
_____ e. *exposure to new ideas*
_____ f. *improving your ability to do something important to you*

FIGURING YOUR SCORE

Read each category and give yourself one point for each of the answers you chose. Then add up the points in each category.

Visual learner: 1a, 6b, 7a, 9d, 10d
Auditory learner: 1b, 6a, 7c, 9c, 10c
Social learner: 2a, 5a, 7b, 9a, 10a
Independent learner: 2b, 5b, 7d, 9b, 10b
Conceptual learner: 3a, 4b, 8a, 9e, 10e
Pragmatic learner: 3b, 4a, 8b, 9f, 10f

Now find the categories with your three highest scores and circle them. These are your preferred ways to learn—your learning style. Write your three top choices here:

Understanding Your Learning Preferences. The explanations that follow will help you understand your learning preferences more clearly. Read the descriptions of your three top choices first. If they don't seem right for you, read the others to see if any of them fit better. Always trust your own experience more than the information given in a self-test or questionnaire.

Visual learners would rather read a textbook or study a diagram than listen to a lecture. If you're a visual learner, you may have trouble concentrating on an hour-long college lecture. The listening and notetaking skills in this chapter may be especially helpful to you. You can also ask friends to photocopy their notes for you so that you can fill in any gaps in your own set. Reading your textbook before you attend class, and supplemental reading afterward, may help you get more from a lecture.

Auditory learners would rather listen to an explanation than read it. If you're an auditory learner, you may learn a great deal during college lectures; studying a textbook may be more difficult for you. Group study can be helpful because students listen to explanations from one another. Talking to students, tutors, or professors interested in your subject can reinforce your learning. Films, videos, and audiotapes are useful learning aids.

Look for creative ways to use your auditory learning style. Author Marie Killilea, who describes herself as "ear-minded rather than eye-minded," discovered that rereading what she'd written was no help when she was revising a manuscript. Instead of giving up, Killilea hired a student to read the manuscript aloud while she listened and made corrections.

Social learners enjoy group projects and collaborative learning. If you're a social learner, you may have difficulty studying alone and tackling individual research projects. Whenever possible, make friends with other students and form study groups. Tutoring services and professors' office hours can be extremely helpful to you. Study partnerships can provide support and encouragement. Even if you and a friend are taking different courses, you can schedule study or library time together. Author Natalie Goldberg and a friend meet once a week in a cafe to write together. Although they always work on different projects and rarely offer each other direct help, their companionship makes writing less lonely.

Independent learners like the freedom of working alone. If you're an independent learner, you may feel frustrated by the give and take of group work. You may prefer courses and professors that emphasize individual projects. When you work with a group, you may be happiest volunteering for tasks that you can complete on your own. Be aware, though, that teamwork and collaboration are vital in many professions. Group projects in college can help you develop important social skills.

Conceptual learners enjoy theories and ideas. If you're a conceptual learner, you enjoy exposure to new information and may not care that a subject isn't useful. Pronunciation and grammar drills can be frustrating for you, and you may dislike hands-on learning experiences in laboratories and computer centers. Sometimes supplemental reading can add interest to courses that don't at first interest you. Talking to a professor or student who shares your interests can also be helpful.

Pragmatic learners are practical. If you're a pragmatic learner, you want to learn useful information, and you may feel impatient with theories and abstract explanations. Theory-minded professors sometimes forget to mention practical applications of material they're teaching: ask for examples and explanations. Field trips, use of computer software, laboratory experiences, work-study programs and study groups can make abstract subjects more real and enjoyable for you.

GETTING IN TOUCH THROUGH FREEWRITING

Use the space on the following page to freewrite about your learning preferences—or draw a picture of yourself learning in one or two of your favorite ways. Be creative! You can tell a story from your own school experiences, or make up a story that puts you in an ideal learning environment. Other possibilities are drawing cartoons, writing a song or poem, listing some of your favorite learning strategies, or inventing other ways to describe yourself. When you've finished, share what you've written or drawn with two other students. Discuss the similarities and differences in your learning preferences. What did you learn from this discussion? Jot down notes in the space below.

Using Your Learning Preferences. Your college experiences won't always match your personal preferences. You won't be excused from individual testing on the grounds that you're a social learner, and you'll have to work on group projects even if you prefer to work independently. You'll also find that some professors are more compatible with your learning style than others. If you're a down-to-earth pragmatist, you may have difficulty following a complex lecture about literary theory; meanwhile a conceptual thinker in the next row may be thinking your literature professor is the best teacher he's ever had.

Despite these difficulties, the flexibility of college life allows you to make several accommodations to your personal learning style.

1. Consider signing up for courses with professors who work well with your learning style. If you're a visual learner who has trouble following a lecture, a lively professor may make it easier for you to listen in class—or sign up for a class that emphasizes outside reading. Social learners may be happiest with professors who stress collaborative work; independent learners may enjoy classes built around individual projects. Ask friends about professors' teaching styles and favorite assignments.

2. Broaden your understanding by studying with other students. A professor's explanations may not always match the thought processes that work best for you. Dance instructor Gene Kallenborn says, "Sometimes there are five hundred ways to explain a concept—and only one works with each student." Even if you're an independent learner, group discussions may clarify points you didn't fully understand in class.

3. Be creative in devising study activities that match your preferred style. If you're a social learner, seek opportunities to interact with other students. Is there a campus organization that specializes in your major field? If not, could you help start one? If you're an auditory learner, find out where you can borrow videotapes and audiotapes from libraries; check the campus newspaper for talks by visiting experts in subjects that interest you.

Conceptual learners often enjoy reading the theories, philosophies, and principles underlying their fields of interest. Pragmatic learners can benefit from hands-on study aids in computer labs and study centers; working as a student assistant or volunteer can also enhance learning.

4. Adopt a positive attitude towards learning experiences that don't suit your style. An unpleasant task may help you develop hidden abilities that will serve you well later on. Successful people are versatile: They are skilled listeners and readers who can cooperate and compete, theorize and apply knowledge.

Get Involved in Class

Look around in your next class: How many students are spending the whole period in motionless silence? You'll probably see some who are barely involved at all in what's going on; they don't take notes—or even make the effort to listen. It's incredible but true: Despite the high cost of college tuition, many students aren't getting the learning experiences they're paying for.

The following suggestions will help you get maximum benefits from all your classes:

1. Prepare ahead of time. Many professors assume you have studied the text beforehand: They use class time for discussion and supplementary activities. If you don't know the material, your learning experience will be much less effective.

But what about professors who teach right from the book? Preparation still pays off. Because you've already studied the material, classroom time will be a review. You can concentrate better, you'll find it easier to remember the material, and the lecture will give you clues about the points most likely to show up on a test.

2. Arrive early. If you miss the directions for the day's activities, or you're late for the professor's opening statements, you may have missed the most important moments of that class. Be punctual, seat yourself front and center, and have everything you need in front of you—notebook, pen, text, and the day's assignment.

3. Attend every class. When you skip a class, you risk missing important information about assignments and tests. More seriously, you lose an opportunity to master the course content, ask questions, and participate in the learning process.

4. Use class time to get help from your professors. Many professors routinely ask for questions and feedback from students: Have we spent enough time on this chapter? What points need development? Are the explanations in the textbook clear enough? Do you understand the assignment? Prepared students write down their questions ahead of time; during class they can strengthen their understanding of course material and improve their grade.

5. Increase your ability to concentrate. Arrive rested; you're wasting time and money if you're too sleepy to be attentive. During class, practice letting go of distractions and worries. Don't berate yourself about them: just gently turn your attention back to learning. Avoid using class time to daydream about social or family activities. If worries and

uncompleted tasks are a persistent distraction, writing a "to-do" list before class may help you set them aside so that you're free to concentrate.

6. Improve your listening skills. The better you listen, the more you'll get out of class—and life. Practice focusing on what's being said, and train yourself to return to the subject at hand when your attention lapses (which happens to everyone!). You'll learn more about listening on pages 99 through 100.

7. Introduce yourself to other students. Class members can be a support group for one another. Exchange telephone numbers if possible; you'll be able to ask for help—and offer assistance yourself—when it's needed. Learning can be a lonely, painful process. A sense of community and belonging can keep you motivated during difficult moments.

8. Do more than is required. Earn a reputation for enthusiasm and hard work. Your efforts may pay off later in recommendations for jobs and scholarships. You'll also get more out of college if you're willing to invest time and energy in learning. Best of all, you'll be preparing yourself to excel in your career.

EXERCISE 1: YOUR BENEFITS FROM ATTENDING CLASS

A list of suggestions for getting more out of class appears below. Put a check in front of each suggestion that you already practice regularly. Then circle the ones you plan to use this week.

_____   *I prepare for class ahead of time.*

_____   *I'm punctual.*

_____   *I attend every class.*

_____   *I'm rested, alert, and ready to concentrate.*

_____   *I choose a seat right in front of the professor.*

_____   *I write down questions to ask during class.*

_____   *I'm working on my listening skills.*

_____   *I keep a written "to-do" list so that uncompleted chores won't distract me during class.*

_____   *I've made friends with other students in my classes.*

_____   *I do more than is required.*

Use Critical Thinking to Rethink Assumptions about Learning

In Chapter One you saw that becoming aware of your assumptions, and changing them if necessary, is an important critical-thinking skill. Applying this skill to your college classes can increase your enjoyment of college and improve your concentration.

Before class begins—and during class, as needed—check yourself for negative assumptions that might inhibit learning. Here are a few to watch for; you can undoubtedly think of others.

- I'm terrible at math.
- I'll never learn this.
- I'll never use this information.
- I'm not artistic.
- Science is a man's subject, not a woman's.
- Art is a woman's subject, not a man's.
- I'm too old to learn this.
- Abstract thinking isn't for me.
- I can't write.
- I don't like libraries.

COLLABORATIVE ACTIVITY: BREAKING FREE OF NEGATIVE ASSUMPTIONS ABOUT LEARNING

Have each person role-play a student whose learning is inhibited by a negative assumption. Another person should role-play a helpful friend who examines the assumption critically. Afterwards have the remaining group members give feedback, and repeat the activity until everyone has role-played both a troubled student and a helper.

When the group is finished, discuss what you learned. How can you act as "helper" for yourself the next time a negative assumption threatens your success in college?

◆ DEVELOP INTERPERSONAL SKILLS ◆

College is an ideal place to develop interpersonal skills. Whether you're in a laboratory, a lecture hall, or a seminar room, college offers you many opportunities to experiment with roles you may not have tried before.

British drama critic Kenneth Tynan, who attended Oxford University in England, recalls how much he benefited from opportunities to interact with students and professors. He says, "I had three years in which to experiment with any kind of eccentricity that appealed to me, and in which to learn how far I could go. Most people wait until they are grown up to spread their wings; by then it is often too late for them to do so without injuring others."

Some opportunities for experimentation are easy to spot. In speech class you'll soon learn the differences between informal conversation and talking formally to a group. If you participate in sports, you will learn that playing for a team feels different from competing by yourself. Campus groups offer opportunities to develop leadership skills—chairing a meeting, leading a discussion, helping a group achieve consensus on an issue, negotiating an agreement with other campus or community organizations.

The classroom itself can be an ideal place to develop new skills. Many professors design collaborative classroom projects that allow students to try new roles—learning manager, researcher, reporter, or facilitator for a group. And other college experiences may allow you to practice being a writer, scientist, literary critic, artist, and mathematician—to name just a few. It's hardly surprising that so many professional people are grateful for the challenges and growth they experienced in college.

Developing Your Speaking Abilities

Professors often encourage students to participate in class discussions. Unfortunately, many students miss out on these valuable opportunities for personal growth. Using the excuse that they're shy or uncomfortable in class, they spend their classroom hours in silence.

If you're reluctant to speak up in class, try changing your perspective. No matter what career you choose, public speaking will be an asset. Men and women in responsible, influential positions must have strong communication skills. Resolve to use every opportunity, no matter what subject is being taught, to let your voice be heard. In a surprisingly short time you'll start feeling more comfortable and confident with your new role.

Here are a few variations of the speaker role to try. Begin by stating the name of the person you're responding to—either the professor, guest lecturer, or another student. Speak slowly and loud enough so that everyone can hear you; don't block your mouth with your fist or hand. Be courteous, relevant, and brief. If you feel nervous, tighten your diaphragm—the large muscle under your ribcage—and take a deep breath before you begin.

1. Questioner. Ask for clarification or development of a point that interests you: "Dr. Johnson, could you say a little more about the recent DNA research that you mentioned?"

2. Affirmer. Describe in a personal way how you benefited from a particular point: "Jamal, I'm glad you told us how you handled that problem. I'm going to try that system myself."

3. Challenger. State why you disagree with someone else's viewpoint or belief: "Lisa, I have another explanation for Lady MacBeth's treatment of her husband."

4. Contributor. Share an idea, belief, or experience that confirms a point made in class. "David, your comment reminded me of my visit to the D-Day invasion sites in France with my family last summer. At Utah Beach I talked with a man who'd taken part in the invasion. He made the same point that you did—the invasion's success was a combination of expertise and luck."

JOURNAL ACTIVITY: PRACTICE SPEAKER ROLES

For the next week, practice the Speaker roles described on the previous pages: Questioner, Affirmer, Challenger, Contributor. Choose a role each day and make at least one appropriate statement. In the spaces below, record what happened and how the experience felt. (Remember that you can practice these roles before and after class—and outside of class as well.)

DAY 1

What role did you choose?

Briefly summarize what you said.

How did you feel?

DAY 2

What role did you choose?

Briefly summarize what you said.

How did you feel?

DAY 3

What role did you choose?

Briefly summarize what you said.

How did you feel?

DAY 4

What role did you choose?

Briefly summarize what you said.

How did you feel?

DAY 5

What role did you choose?

Briefly summarize what you said.

How did you feel?

DAY 6

What role did you choose?

Briefly summarize what you said.

How did you feel?

DAY 7

What role did you choose?

Briefly summarize what you said.

How did you feel?

READING THOUGHTFULLY: OVERCOMING NERVOUSNESS

You're about to read a reminiscence by George Bernard Shaw (1856–1950), one of the most influential writers, thinkers, and speakers of our time. He is probably most famous for his highly successful plays, including *Man and Superman* and *Pygmalion*. Shaw was a prolific writer, writing innumerable books and essays about social, religious, and political issues.

Although he was a memorable and powerful speaker, he insisted that his skill was acquired, not natural. After he became famous, he described the fierce struggle he endured to overcome his shyness. Shaw never attended college, but as a young man he found other ways to develop his speaking ability. The following selection describes them.

BEFORE YOU READ

Answer the following questions:

1. What kinds of experiences do you expect Shaw to describe?

2. What feelings do you think he had as he was learning to be a public speaker?

---

from **"Who I Am, and What I Think" and Sixteen Self Sketches**
by George Bernard Shaw

My marvelous gift for public speaking is only part of the G.B.S. legend. I learnt to speak as men learn to skate or to cycle—by doggedly making a fool of myself until I got used to it. As it is, I am simply the sort of public speaker anybody can become by going through the same mill.

[When I was young] I had never spoken in public. I knew nothing about public meetings or their order. I had an air of impudence, but was really an arrant coward, nervous and self-conscious to a heartbreaking degree. [At my first meeting of a debating society] I started up and said something in the debate, and then, feeling that I had made a fool of myself, as in fact I had, I was so ashamed that I vowed I would join the Society; go every week; speak in every debate; and become a speaker or perish in the attempt.

I carried out this resolution. I suffered agonies that no one suspected. During the speech of the debater I resolved to follow, my heart used to beat as painfully as a recruit's going under fire for the first time. I could not use notes: when I looked at the paper in my hand, I could not collect myself enough to decipher a word. And of the four or five points that were my pretext for this ghastly practice I invariably forgot the best.

I persevered doggedly. I haunted all the meetings in London where debates followed lectures. In short, I infested public meetings like an officer afflicted with cowardice, who takes every opportunity of going under fire to get over it and learn his business.

AFTER YOU READ

1. What new words did you encounter as you read? What strategies will you use to learn their meanings?

2. What assumptions did Shaw make about public speaking as a young man? Were they correct?

3. Do you agree or disagree with the assumptions you listed in the previous question?

4. Reread your answers to the questions in Exercise 1. Did the experiences Shaw described match your expectations?

5. What did Shaw see as his mission? What was his primary goal?

6. Did anything in this reading surprise you?

7. How can you use the ideas you learned from Shaw?

◆ DEALING WITH DIVERSITY ◆

This chapter has encouraged you to take risks and experiment with new roles in your college classes. While you're making discoveries about yourself and your hidden potential, you'll also be dealing with ideas, activities, and people new to you. The diversity of college life is one of greatest advantages of attending college.

COLLABORATIVE ACTIVITY: THINK ABOUT DIVERSITY

How do you feel about this statement by psychologist Haim Ginott?

Labeling is disabling.

Strongly disagree	Neutral	Strongly agree
1	5	10

Mark the point on the line that best represents your position. Then answer the questions below.

1. *What do you think the statement means?*

2. *In what ways do labels "disable" people?*

3. *In what ways are labels helpful?*

4. *List as many labels as you can think of that might be applied to you: male, American, first-year college student, Methodist, and so on. Include descriptive words as well: friendly, tall, soft-spoken, and so on.*

5. *Now exchange your list from question 4 with another student. Discuss and compare both lists. In what ways are the labels helpful in building your understanding of each other? What do the labels leave out?*

6. *Describe a recent time when you felt a strong sense of belonging to a group (the setting might be in your family or at college, among friends, a club or team, at the workplace, or somewhere else).*

7. *Describe a recent time when you had a strong sense of yourself as an independent individual. What were you doing, and where? What qualities about yourself were you aware of?*

8. *Meet with three or four other students to discuss labels and group membership. When is it helpful to see yourself and others as part of a group? When is it helpful to see yourself and others primarily as distinct individuals?*

The Benefits of Diversity

Recently the staff of Buckingham Palace, home of the Queen of England, made an embarrassing mistake. When a visually-impaired computer expert arrived to receive an award from the Queen, the staff insisted that her guide dog remain outside. Although no explanation for this insensitivity was ever offered, it seems likely that the staff had not experienced the diversity most of us now take for granted. Since they had never seen a guide dog, they could not imagine that a dog could be anything but a pet that obviously had no place at a royal ceremony.

Fortunately, most colleges boast a varied student body that can help students learn firsthand about the similarities and differences between human beings. Campus visitors and exchange students offer additional opportunities. In addition to the fun, warmth, and joy they bring to your life, these people can broaden and deepen your experience, preparing you for the diversity you are likely to encounter in your professional life.

As your friendships widen, you'll also increase your own self-awareness. Families, religions, political advocates, and ethnic groups may hold values different from yours—and you may find your own outlook maturing in new ways.

For example, some religious groups, like the Seventh-Day Adventists, emphasize personal health habits; others do not consider health a spiritual issue. Worship styles are another difference. Many religious groups worship only in large communal gatherings. But in Judaism, home religious observances are an important part of the religious calendar, with women and children taking significant roles.

If you're not a member of one of these religions, you might be surprised to hear a sermon about health, or to receive an invitation to a home religious ritual. But labeling these traditions "right" or "wrong" isn't helpful; what matters is your willingness to explore a perspective different from what you're used to.

Ethnic and political differences can also set you thinking. Some advocates of legalized abortion, for example, assume that opponents are motivated by religious intolerance. And some opponents assume that anyone who promotes the right to abortion must lack morals and respect for human life. If you spend some time getting acquainted with both groups, however, you're likely to find that people can't be classified that easily. And you might be stimulated to think about some abortion-related issues that had never occurred to you before. While you are formulating your own position about abortion, you will benefit tremendously from this input.

It's normal to have mixed feelings about diversity: Many people enjoy the stimulation of new personalities and experiences but feel apprehensive about having their own value structures challenged. Remind yourself that you don't have to accept every new idea you hear. Exposure to new possibilities, however, is essential to developing mature thinking habits.

Sometimes it takes courage to listen attentively to a different point of view. Strive to develop that kind of courage: It will enhance your college experiences immeasurably. Later on, you'll discover that open-minded listening is vital in the working world as well.

And there's a bonus. If you're an astute reader, you noticed that these ideas about diversity also involve critical thinking. Any time you become conscious of your assumptions, or look at an issue from a different angle, you're thinking critically.

College life offers you many opportunities to develop new friendships and explore new ideas.

 COLLABORATIVE ACTIVITY: DISCOVER YOUR ATTITUDES ABOUT DIVERSITY

PART I

If you agree with a statement below, write A in the blank; write D if you disagree. Then meet with three or four other students to compare and discuss your answers.

_____ *I had limited experience with diversity before I came to college.*

_____ *I can determine what people think and believe on the basis of their age.*

_____ *Most members of the same religious group think alike.*

_____ *Most members of the same ethnic group think alike.*

_____ *Most members of the same political group think alike.*

_____ *Most citizens of a country think alike.*

_____ *Male attitudes, beliefs, and skills are very different from female attitudes, beliefs, and skills.*

_____ *Any member of a group should be able to serve as a mouthpiece for that group.*

_____ *People who know what educational institution I attend can accurately predict my attitudes, beliefs, and behavior.*

PART II

List the ideas you heard about diversity during this group activity. Put a check in front of the ideas and attitudes that make sense to you.

PART III

Write a few sentences describing your participation in this activity. How freely did you share ideas and feelings with other group members? How did you handle any disagreements that arose? Did you feel a sense of belonging? What did you learn from this experience?

If You Feel Different

Feeling different—alienated, alone, isolated—can weaken your motivation to succeed. Many students feel uncomfortably different when they begin college—different either from others, or from the familiar person they used to be.

Perhaps education has become important to you for the first time; you're wondering what became of the carefree student you once were. You may have a disability, or you might be older than most first-year students, bi-cultural, or a member of a minority group. Perhaps you're a male in a traditionally female field, such as primary education, or a female in a male-dominated field, such as criminal justice or engineering. Shyness, homesickness, and the newness of college can make almost any student feel lonely or uncomfortable. These strategies can help you feel at home and enjoy your new experiences:

1. Don't let negative expectations hold you back. Edward de Bono, author of many books about thinking, uses the term "tethered thinking" ["limited thinking"] to describe the negative assumptions that trap many people in unhappy lives. If your thoughts about college are "tethered," you'll miss many enjoyable and enriching experiences.

Don't assume that you can't be class president because you're an international student, married, or a member of a minority group. Some students avoid sports and other campus activities for reasons that exist only in their imaginations: They think only superstars are welcome on college teams, or that they won't fit in, or that others will reject them. Be courageous in trying new experiences; they're part of the fun of college—as well as great opportunities for personal growth.

2. Think about the feelings of others. If you're nervous, you're not alone. Others who feel the same way you do may just do a better job of hiding their feelings—or perhaps they think you're someone who's incredibly competent and unapproachable. Smile, introduce yourself, and show a warm interest in others. Good icebreakers are asking other students where they're from or what courses they're taking. Seeking help is another winning strategy: conversations about math assignments, lab reports, and research papers often lead to satisfying college friendships.

3. Make a contribution to campus life. Join a campus organization, work for a cause you care deeply about, or offer to help other students with subjects you know well. Be open and accessible: Your willingness to talk about your background and lifestyle, hopes, and dreams, may encourage others to extend themselves in new friendships.

4. Regard other students as resources. You can learn a great deal by asking other students to educate you about their heritages. Worldwide markets are becoming more and more common today; you'll meet travelers from abroad even in small towns. The future may transform you into one of those travelers yourself. Avoid spending all your free time with groups of students just like yourself. In the cafeteria, student lounge, and library, seek out students who come from different backgrounds. Learn—and share—as much as you can.

5. Set ambitious goals for yourself. Sometimes students who are outside the mainstream mistakenly settle for less than what they really want from college. Don't let low

expectations push you into a college major or a career that doesn't interest you. When psychologist Dr. Joyce Brothers entered graduate school, the department chair tried to persuade her to withdraw so a man could take her place. At that time few women had advanced degrees in psychology, and some of her professors felt they would be wasting their time educating a married woman who would probably drop out to have children. Fortunately, she persisted and earned the psychology degree she had long dreamed of having.

Such problems are much less common today, largely because of the courageous women who challenged such stereotypical thinking. But prejudice and sexism still occur in our society, and you may encounter bias yourself. If so, resolve to keep your confidence high and to blaze a trail for others. Many colleges have staff members assigned to assist students with special needs, or you can make friends on your own with professors and staff members you admire. One good strategy is to visit them during office hours to discuss what you're learning, share your dreams, and seek advice.

GETTING IN TOUCH THROUGH FREEWRITING

In the space provided, freewrite about your own feelings about being on campus. In what ways are you different from other students? What do you have in common? Mention incidents, conversations, and feelings. Remember that you're writing to discover and express your own experience. Do not be concerned about spelling, usage, sentence structure, and organization.

◆ NECESSARY SKILLS ◆

Listening Skills

Perhaps you've already started experimenting with the activities described in this chapter: thinking critically, asking questions, joining in class discussions, taking thorough notes, continuing to discuss what you're learning after class is over. One common factor among all these activities is listening—an activity that, to many people, does not look "active" at all.

Although listening may look passive, it isn't. First, you must block out all the sights and sounds that distract you from what's being said. Second, you have to deal with a neurological problem: Your mind processes words faster than they come out of a speaker's mouth. As a result, there are countless empty milliseconds that your brain wants to fill up with other thoughts: the coming weekend, a problem that's bothering you, a tempting memory. Third, you have to set your ideas, personality, and mood aside in favor of someone else's. Finally, listening takes you out of the spotlight. Someone else has the floor, and you're doing nothing—or so it seems.

For all these reasons, many people simply give up trying to listen. During a conversation they think only about what they're going to say when it's their turn to speak. In class they daydream or doze.

The good news is that daily life offers you countless opportunities to improve your listening skills—and the rewards are well worth the effort. You can practice listening in every conversation and every class; TV programs, radio news reports, meetings, and other events provide other opportunities. Monitor your progress by trying to repeat what you

They've Pushed Their Limits

Heather Whitestone, Miss America of 1995, is deaf. Ballerina Alicia Alonso learned the difficult role of Giselle while she was almost totally blind.

Athlete Bobby Clarke excelled in the challenging sport of hockey despite his diabetes. "It's no big deal," he said. "I just take my medication, watch my diet and try to do my thing."

Civil rights leader Jesse Jackson turned down a football scholarship from the University of Illinois when he learned that black athletes had limited opportunities. He transferred to a college in North Carolina where he became a star quarterback.

Michelle Smithdas, blind and deaf, earned a master's degree in education from Teachers College, Columbia University, so that she could join the faculty of the Helen Keller Center for Deaf-Blind Youth. Her deaf and blind husband, Bob Smithdas, is a director at the center.

Jim Abbott, the eighth Yankee to pitch a no-hitter, has only one hand.

African-American contralto Marian Anderson was denied voice training and singing roles because of her race.

Joe Montana, superstar quarterback of the San Francisco 49ers, was born with scoliosis (irregular curvature of the spine). Injuries often kept him on the sidelines during his college years. What's holding you back?

heard; after a group discussion, see if you can recall what each person said. Your memory will begin to improve without inventing memory devices. Your efforts will pay handsome benefits both in school and your career, for you will have access to an impressive storehouse of useful information.

If listening seems too passive for you, make yourself active. Adjust your body language to show that you're interested in the speaker: Lean forward slightly, nod, and resist the impulse to look around. Make eye contact. Be mentally active as well: Check your understanding of what was said, and prepare any questions you need to ask. Think critically: What assumptions did the speaker make? Are they justified? Is the speaker's message consistent with your knowledge and experience?

Don't be discouraged by forgetful lapses and slip-ups; just keep listening. You'll soon discover that you remember more when you're actively involved in your learning experiences. Best of all, you'll be preparing yourself to be a powerful participant in professional and community life.

When Listening is Difficult. Experts agree that listening is vital to your academic and professional success. Unfortunately, however, listening isn't always easy. Many superb thinkers lack the sparkle and polish needed to enthrall their listeners (just as many entertaining speakers lack intellectual depth). And sometimes the problem lies within yourself: You're tired, distracted by personal problems, or simply unmotivated. A teacher who speaks rapidly or uses a sophisticated vocabulary can be difficult to listen to.

One key to meeting these challenges is preparation. Picture yourself walking into class with an imaginary framework inside your head, one that's organized with spaces and boxes for you to fill in. By giving yourself an interesting and worthwhile task, you've made listening much easier. Create the framework before class by completing any reading assignments and reviewing notes from previous days.

Additional Strategies for Better Listening.

1. Ensure that you're physically and mentally able to get the most out of class. Practice putting yourself into a frame of mind to get the most out of each learning experience. If sleepiness is a problem, get enough rest the night before and choose a front seat. Students in military academies are allowed to stand up and walk around when they feel sleepy in class; you can ask your professors if they'd allow you to use the same strategy.

Five-Minute Listening Task

At least once a day, spend five minutes listening to what others are saying. The setting can be a classroom, a table in the cafeteria, your dorm room, or the dining room in your home. Then evaluate how well you concentrated and how much you remembered from was said. Continue to practice listening to family members, friends, co-workers, professors, students, college staff, and community members. After each five-minute listening task, identify one change you could make to listen better next time.

Teach yourself to let go of distracting thoughts. If your attention wanders to other tasks you have to do, write them down before class so that you don't have to worry about them.

2. Use class time to formulate thoughtful responses to what you're hearing. Critical thinkers look for connections to information learned in the past, personal experiences, and other subjects. If you're taking a psychology course and a literature course in the same semester, try to connect them. You could ask yourself how the family in O'Neill's *Long Day's Journey into Night* is similar to the dysfunctional families in your psychology text.

3. Let go of your judgments about teaching styles. It's natural to look forward to classes with personable, lively instructors. But don't assume that entertaining lecturers are always great teachers—or that less gifted speakers aren't. Many people say that they didn't realize who their best teachers were until college was over. A professor who spoke in a monotone may stand out for his love of learning and depth of knowledge. A disorganized teacher may be remembered for the insights and humor that flashed through her lectures.

If you find yourself distracted by negative feelings about a professor, make a list of positive features to look for the next time you attend class. Rereading page 77, "Twenty Reasons to Attend Class" may spark some ideas. Reread your list before each class, and listen for positives during the lecture. These strategies pay off in two ways: You'll feel better, and you'll learn more.

4. Ask study partners and study groups to help you supplement your notes. After each class sit down with three or four other students to answer this question: What did each of us get out of today's class? Meet with study partners to supplement your notes and fill in any gaps.

5. Be open to new ideas and approaches. Some students stop listening when they discover that a professor or classmate holds a different religious belief than theirs, or votes differently, or disagrees with their ideas about abortion, capital punishment, or another issue. You may have trouble concentrating when someone disagrees with facts or values you learned in school, at church, or at home.

Although it's natural to want to be around people who think the way you do, don't allow yourself to be turned off. Part of the college experience is being exposed in a personal way to ideas very different from your own. You can expect to encounter many startling viewpoints during college and afterwards, in the professional world. If these differences keep you from concentrating, turn them into a mental exercise: Pretend that you're a scientist who's trying to learn as much as possible about minds very different from your own. As time passes, you'll get better and better at this game, and you'll learn a great deal from it. (The strategies in Chapter Eight, "Critical Thinking," will be helpful to you as well.) Most important, don't let a clash of ideas prevent you from having a powerful learning experience at college.

6. Visit the professor during office hours to clarify confusing points. Professors usually enjoy talking about their subjects, and most genuinely like students; that's why they chose the teaching profession. Professors often welcome visits during office time. The benefits for you are obvious: You'll learn more, and you'll make a positive impression on the person who assigns your final grade. Find out each professor's office hours and make use of them.

The Thinker

This is a role you can assume even in a large class when only the professor is speaking. Labeling yourself a "thinker" makes you an active participant rather than a mere onlooker. It's especially helpful to visual learners who have trouble following lectures; it can also improve your notetaking skills.

Imagine you're an expert who's evaluating the information delivered to you. What points seem most important to you? Most useful? What connections can you make to information and experiences you've already had? Write your ideas and reactions in your class notes to ensure that you'll remember them later: Professors often welcome your reactions to what's being taught.

After class, look for an opportunity to continue practicing the Thinker role with at least one other person. Visit the professor during office hours, or have a dialogue with a study partner, or meet with a study group. Discuss your ideas with family members, co-workers and friends.

"The horror of that moment," the King went on, "I shall never, never forget!"

"You will, though," the Queen said, "if you don't make a memorandum of it."

LEWIS CARROLL,
THROUGH THE LOOKING-GLASS

Notetaking

Think for a moment about the special classroom experience you discussed at the beginning of this chapter. How much more would that experience mean if you had complete notes about it?

Effective notes are much more than scribbled words on a page. First, they're a storehouse of information you want to keep close to you. Even a stimulating lecture can fade from your memory, causing a disappointingly low grade on a test. Second, you can't expect college professors to drill you on new information the way many high-school teachers do. College professors generally see their role as presenting and explaining new material: The act of recording and memorizing it is up to you.

Most important, notes can capture the unique outlook of a gifted teacher you once had, the framework of a central concept in your major field, or the vital details an intellectual breakthrough that reshapes your life. Ask a few professional people whether they value their old notebooks. You'll learn an important lesson about the shortness of memory and the value of writing down an experience.

But many learning experiences are going to seem less important to you. Why take notes? Here are nine reasons:

Why Take Notes?

1. Professors often share information that doesn't appear in textbooks, handouts, or other resources. Professors can draw upon their own experiences to make abstract ideas come to life (especially important to pragmatic learners). They can introduce you to new concepts by making connections between two subjects that seem unrelated—literature and psychology, for example, or sociology and history.

2. Information in class notes often appears on tests. Your class notes may contain important clues and facts about examinations. There's a good chance that anything your professor repeated or explained at length will appear on a test.

3. Many learning experiences increase in importance as time passes. A college education is not just an accumulation of knowledge; it can also be a catalyst for vast personal changes. In future years you may often refer to your college notes on writing, public speaking, personal health, business, psychology, or other subjects.

4. You can use college notes to refresh your memory when you take advanced courses later on. If you're an English major, your poetry notes could be invaluable in graduate school. If you're studying nursing, your pharmacology notes could help you pass a licensing exam later in your career. The same is true of accounting, education, and many other fields.

5. You'll remember course content longer if you write it down. Research shows that your memory improves when you're an active learner. Because notetaking activates your mind, eyes, ears, and fingers, it's an effective way to learn new material.

6. Notetaking encourages you to think critically about what you're learning. In a large lecture hall, discussion must usually be held to a minimum. But you can use your notebook to practice the Thinking role described on page 102. Allow space in the margins of your notebook to jot down questions, comments, associations, and feelings that occur during class. After class, find another person who's willing to hear your reactions and talk about them, or visit your professor to talk about them. This kind of critical thinking will help you take good notes because you'll be listening for key information. And you'll remember more of what you hear in class because you're listening actively.

7. A good set of notes is a personal statement of what you've learned. Everyone perceives the world differently. Your personality, special strengths, past experience, and goals set you apart from everyone else—and your learning process is unique as well. By personalizing your notes—including questions, associations, and reactions—you are actually creating a personalized guide to the course content.

8. Your notes may be the only record you have of your best classroom experiences in college. The intellectual legacy of the Greek philosopher Aristotle has come down to us chiefly in notes kept by his pupils. In the twentieth century, most of our information about Ferdinand de Saussure, the founder of modern linguistics, has come from student notebooks. Your favorite professors will be as special to you as these giants were to their pupils. Good notes can keep an experience alive years after your college graduation.

9. Notetaking is a skill you'll use the rest of your life. You will be taking notes at meetings and conferences in both your professional and community life. Now is a perfect opportunity to develop the ability to select what's important and write it down clearly enough so that you can understand your notes later.

Notetaking Techniques. Notetaking is an art, for you are creating a personal library of facts and ideas from your college experience. To practice this art effectively, you need to condense what you're hearing in class, respond to it, and record it clearly enough so that the notes continue to make sense to you as time passes.

Effective notetaking begins with a mental picture of the product you want to create. If the word "notetaking" automatically prompts you to think of a formal outline, you need to think again. Professors don't always lecture in a systematic way—points A, B, C and subpoints 1, 2, 3. A formal outline can be frustrating when a lively class discussion is going on. The stimulating ideas that fly through the air may not fit tidily into your outline.

What, then, does a good page of notes look like? It should include all the following:

- the date, course title, and professor's name
- the topic for the day
- the most important statements you heard in class (you can use a colored pencil or marker to underline them after class—an excellent review technique)

- facts and other information you want to remember
- question marks and blank spaces to remind you of points you might have missed that will need clarification after class

Consider using the Cornell format, which has served many college students well. It's a simple system that encourages you to think critically when you review your notes. Draw a vertical line about one and one-half inches from the left side of each sheet of notebook paper. Draw a horizontal line about two inches from the bottom of the page.

During class, leave the left margin blank; you'll use it for key words, questions, or comments later. Record your notes as usual on the right side of the line. Leave the two-inch space at the bottom empty as well; you'll write a summary here later.

During class, write down facts and ideas for later review (page 108 lists "signals" that professors often use when they're sharing important information). Listen intently so that you don't miss anything significant. But don't be discouraged if you can't always keep up, or if a distraction causes you to miss a point. Put a question mark or blank line in your notes to mark places that you want to fill in later. You can get the missing information from the professor after class is over, or another student may help you fill in any gaps.

Later, when you review your notes, think critically about what you heard in class. Can you make connections between today's notes and other information you've heard? Does a personal experience come to mind? What points need clarification? Use the left margin to make notes about these points; that space can also be used for key words and review questions to help you prepare for testing. Think of that space in the left margin as a personal learning log—a daily record of your reactions to what you're learning.

Before your study session is over, reread the notations in the left margin and choose a follow-up strategy if needed. For example, you might call your study partner for a discussion, or ask your questions during class the next day, or visit your professor during office hours.

Review your notes within twenty-four hours—the period in which most forgetting takes place. Use this review time to rewrite or type any notes that are incomplete or hard to read—your memory will be fresh enough to supply most of the missing information. This is also a good time to write a summary of the most important points—or the main idea of the lecture—in the space at the bottom. Later, when you're preparing for testing, you can cover or fold over everything on the page except that bottom space. Then you can try to recreate what was on the page, using the bottom summary as a prompt. This strategy is a superb way to build your confidence before a test.

Don't try to make your notes picture-perfect and publishable: You have other priorities too. No matter how good they are, notes aren't everything, for they can't learn the course material for you. Notetaking is *not* the same as studying. Depending on the course, you may also have to practice new skills, invent memory devices (Chapter Five) and quiz yourself on new material.

Other learning activities can supplement what you learned in class. Activities might include outside reading in books and journals, practice in a learning lab, watching videotapes, discussions with friends, and trips into the field.

You can also ask a professor for permission to tape-record a class. (Some professors don't mind; others prefer not to be taped.) Tapes are good study devices, and they also

3/10/94

Humanities 1412   African American Music

origins	Africans brought drumming to American
def. polyrhythm	polyrhythm - multiple rhythms at once
def. syncopation	syncopations - shift of accent to weak beat
musical expression	"Field hollers," spirituals, folk music
	community entertainment
ragtime era	1899 - 1917 ragtime era
importance	African rhythms + sophisticated Western
	harmonic tradition + musical forms
influenced Eur.	influenced Brahms, Dvorak,
composers	Dubussy, Stravinsky
	crossing of racial lines
3 "classic	"classic ragtime" 3 composers
ragtime" composers	- Scott Joplin 1868 - 1917 "King of
	Ragtime" black Texarkana-born
	educated in Western musical tradition
dates	- James Scott 1886-1938
birthplaces	black Missouri born
	- Joseph F. Lamb 1887 - 1960
	white New York City
Joplin most	Joplin was his mentor.
important	

origins of African American music
crossing of racial lines in ragtime
3 "classic ragtime" composers
importance of ragtime

Figure 3.1 The Cornell Notetaking System

prevent you from overlooking or misunderstanding what happened in class. A few warnings are in order, however:

1. Tape recorders can malfunction when you need them most.
2. If you use an inexpensive cassette, background noise can overpower most of what was said in class.
3. Tapes can make you overconfident because the content is recorded only on the cassette, *not* in your head. You still have to concentrate to learn class material.
4. Listening to a tape-recorded lecture takes much longer than rereading a good set of notes.
5. Cassettes don't record your questions, reactions, and associations. You still need notes about your role in your learning experience.

EXERCISE 2: YOUR NOTETAKING EXPERIENCES

Answer the questions below:

1. *Which of the advantages to notetaking on pages 103 through 104 are most important to you? Why?*

2. *Does the notetaking system you used in high school work well for you in college? Why or why not?*

3. *How do you expect to use your college notes after your courses are completed?*

4. *Explain this statement: Notetaking is not the same as studying.*

5. *What do you find hardest about taking effective notes? What do you find easiest?*

The Signals Game. If you have trouble concentrating in class, play a mental game with yourself: How many notetaking "signals" can you hear? These signals are words and actions that alert you to possible test questions. The following suggestions will get you started; you'll discover many more yourself.

1. Some words emphasize important points, like these: *important, crucial, remember, vital, critical, notice, central, essential, make sure*

2. Anything an instructor repeats is worth noting. Signals include: *in other words, to put it differently*

3. Transition words let you know that another idea—often an important one—is being introduced: *the following points, on the other hand, in addition, next, furthermore*

4. Summary words signal that the professor is restating the central point of the lecture (this is a good time to check your understanding: Does your idea of what was most important today match your professor's idea about it?): *in conclusion, finally, summing up, the main point*

5. Some actions are notetaking signals as well. Pay close attention when your professor: writes on the board, stops lecturing to read a statement from a book, stops to ask if the class needs more help with a concept, tells you that particular information will appear on a test, mentions that many students have difficulty with the concept or skill under discussion

Keeping Up with Assignments

Completing your college assignments is vital to your academic success. The fast pace of most college courses requires students to learn much of the content on their own: Many professors consider assignments important enough to use as part of the final grade for the course.

Daily and weekly assignments reinforce what you're learning in class, help you master course content, and prepare you to acquire new information; they also provide opportunities for you and the instructor to give one another feedback.

The following suggestions will help you get the most benefit from college assignments:

1. Write down all assignments in a convenient place where you can find them easily. Some students have a special assignment notebook. Make sure you've copied them accurately and completely.

2. Make sure you understand each assignment. Ask for clarification in class, or visit your professor during office hours. If your professor has an office telephone number, record it in your assignment notebook; you can call to ask questions during office hours. Make use of any handouts distributed in class that contain information about the assignment.

3. Break lengthy or complex assignments into small steps: research, writing a rough draft, visiting the learning center. Select dates and times for each step and record them on your calendar.

4. Exchange telephone numbers with other students in each class: You'll be able to help one another with difficult assignments.

5. Fight the temptation to procrastinate. Use an "instant task" (page 68) when an assignment seems frighteningly large. Time-management expert Alan Lakein recommends telling yourself "Do it!" when you're facing an unpleasant task.

6. Have faith in the learning process. An assignment that has little meaning now may reveal its benefits later on. (Samuel Scudder, remember, was bewildered at first by the command "Look at your fish!") Most assignments have hidden benefits: improvement in reading comprehension, speed, or vocabulary; developing skill at following directions, organizing ideas, or critical thinking; gaining greater insight into your major field; becoming familiar with resources . . . the list goes on and on. Don't become discouraged if you don't reap instant benefits from every assignment.

7. Do your best on every assignment. Some people complain about their "poor memories" when actually they have a totally different problem: They never learned the material in the first place. Almost any assignment will help you improve your memory, concentration, time-management skills, and critical-thinking ability.

One-Minute Checklist

How effective was today's class experience? These seven questions will help you get more out of your classroom experiences. After each class, answer yes or no to each one:

_____ I completed the assigned work before class.

_____ I reviewed my previous notes.

_____ I concentrated and refocused my mind when my attention wandered.

_____ I took an active role in today's class by speaking (when practical), taking notes, and thinking critically.

Escapes and Excuses

Many students are easily distracted by "escapes"—low-priority activities that tempt them away from assignments. Would you rather study an economics text or talk on the telephone with a friend? Because most students prefer the conversation, a ringing phone is an automatic "escape" from study.

To avoid the lure of escapes, monitor your own behavior during study periods. Most tasks and interruptions that pull you away from your desk are actually "escapes"—housework, drop-in visits from friends, routine paperwork, hobbies, and chores. A good time-plan can help you resist escapes. It's easier to stick to a task if you've scheduled pleasurable activities for yourself later in the day or week. Rereading your Personal Mission Statement can also help you avoid escapes.

Excuses are statements inside your head that draw you away from your responsibilities. Here are ten classic ones; perhaps you can think of others:

This is boring.

This isn't important.

I'm tired.

I'm hungry.

I've been sitting too long.

It's late. I'm working too hard.

I shouldn't have to do this.

This is unreasonable.

I'll never use this.

The "instant tasks" described in Chapter Two are excellent weapons against excuses. Once you've started a task, and perhaps found it interesting, excuses lose their power. Another helpful strategy is to answer each excuse with positive self-talk about the importance of success in college:

This is important to me.

I can do this.

This task has benefits for me.

Later I'll be glad I persevered with this.

This may be more interesting when I get involved in it.

I'm looking forward to finishing this.

I can break this task into small, manageable steps.

I can keep going a little longer.

Since my professor thinks this is important, I'm going to give it my all.

_____ I read my notes after class and filled in any missing spaces.

_____ To minimize forgetting, I reviewed my notes within twenty-four hours after class.

_____ I sought answers to any questions I had about today's class.

EXERCISE 3: OVERCOMING ESCAPES AND EXCUSES

Answer the questions below:

1. *What is an "escape"?*

2. *What are three of your favorite escapes to avoid studying?*

3. *What is an "excuse"?*

4. *What are three of your favorite excuses to avoid studying?*

5. *List three strategies that might help you resist giving in to an "escape" or an "excuse."*

USING WHAT YOU HAVE LEARNED

1. Which of the Speaker roles on pages 86 and 87 is most enjoyable for you? Describe three times when you've played this role.
2. List three people of interest to you whose backgrounds are different from yours in some significant way. (They can be people you know or have only heard about.) What common experiences could you draw upon in a conversation? What differences would you find interesting to discuss?
3. List the behaviors you might observe in a student who's an active learner. Circle the behaviors you practiced yourself during the previous week. Then choose two others you plan to start practicing now.
4. Ask another student to be your notetaking partner for one course this week. Take notes as you usually do and make a photocopy for your partner. At the end of the week, sit down together to compare your notes. Fill in any gaps, and discuss any questions and remarks you wrote during class. Then evaluate this partnership experience. If it worked well for you, consider having a study partner for other courses you're taking.

EVALUATING YOUR PROGRESS

1. As I look back on the past seven days, I've seen an improvement in these areas:

   _____ organizing my life

   _____ protecting my health

   _____ planning my time

   _____ concentrating

   _____ taking notes

   _____ active learning

   _____ reading critically

   _____ writing effectively

   _____ thinking critically

   _____ communicating with important people in my life

   _____ enjoying my free time

   _____ allowing myself to be imperfect

2. In the coming week, I plan to invest five minutes a day working towards this goal:

CHAPTER 4

Managing
Stress

Great emergencies and crises show us how much greater our vital resources are than we had supposed.

WILLIAM JAMES

 PREVIEW

1. Stress is a normal—and sometimes positive—feature of college life.

2. You can choose from a variety of strategies to reduce the physical and emotional effects of stress.

3. Critical thinking can help you overcome negative thought patterns.

4. Painful emotions can stimulate you to make positive changes in your life.

5. You can reduce stress levels by putting yourself in charge of your life.

 IN-CLASS INTRODUCTORY ACTIVITY: WHAT ARE YOUR STRESS FACTORS?

Chances are that your college life includes a number of "stress factors"—elements in your everyday experience that cause emotions like tension, anxiety, and frustration. "Stress fac-

tors" can include academic challenges, time pressures, family difficulties, financial worries, and a host of other issues.

COLLABORATIVE ACTIVITY

Using the scale below, meet with two or three other students and compare your responses.

How does stress affect you?

Little effect	A serious problem
1	10

Meet with a small group of other students and compare your answers to the following questions:

1. *Do you think you're experiencing more or less stress than you had in high school? Give reasons for your answer.*

2. *What are some stress factors that are outside your control?*

3. *What are some stress factors that you can control?*

4. *How do you know when you're experiencing stress?*

5. *What are some ways you've tried to reduce your stress levels? How effective are they?*

◆ STRESS: CAUSES AND EFFECTS ◆

Stress is an inescapable feature of modern life, and college is no exception. Time pressure, academic challenges, an unfamiliar environment, loneliness, changes in sleeping and eating patterns, financial problems, job-related problems, complex relationships—all can lead to elevated stress levels.

Because human beings are a combination of mind and body, stress has both physical and emotional effects. Stress releases additional amounts of the hormone adrenaline, increasing your strength so that you can run from danger or resist a physical attack. But the adrenaline serves no purpose if you're not in physical danger. Instead, the adrenaline intensifies emotions. If you're worried about a test, stress can increase your tension, confusion, and anxiety—exactly what you don't need to earn a high score.

In moderate amounts, stress is not harmful and can even be beneficial. Low levels of anxiety, commonly called "butterflies," include the fluttering stomach, sweaty palms, and dry mouth that often accompany important events. Most successful people learn to cope with this kind of anxiety, and some even enjoy the stimulation it adds to their lives. When you're performing in public or competing in a sport, low levels of anxiety can stimulate your body to produce extra adrenaline, helping you do your best.

Intense stress, on the other hand, can decrease your ability to think and perform effectively. Fortunately, you can learn to manage stress and minimize some of its negative effects.

How to Manage Stress

1. Monitor your own stress levels. For most people, irritability is an early sign of stress-related problems. Watch your own emotions and behavior for danger signs, including excessive fatigue, apathy, or anger. Act quickly to bring stress down to a manageable level. Many students find these suggestions helpful: Take an exercise break, talk to a trusted friend, get more sleep, adjust your study or work time, schedule an activity you enjoy, ask a tutor or professor for tips about difficult assignments.

2. Keep your expectations realistic. Frustration is a major cause of stress—and a sign that you may need to revise your expectations about college, friendships, your job, or your family. No college is perfect; no relationship can be satisfactory all the time, and no family or job can meet all your needs. Discussing your feelings with a trusted friend can help keep your expectations at a realistic level.

3. Accept your own limitations. Expect mistakes, forgive yourself, and keep going. Most successful people experience failures, obstacles, and errors (as you'll see on pages 119 through 120). Don't let guilt and negative thoughts hold you back. If negative thoughts are a persistent problem, discuss them with a friend or counselor.

4. Find a stress-reduction activity that works for you. Hobbies, sports, and other recreational activities are powerful weapons against stress. Vigorous physical movement—dancing, bowling, walking, swimming—discharges negative energy, relieves tension, and reduces the negative effects of adrenaline. Experts agree that regularly having healthful

fun is a powerful stress-reducer. Find activities you can enjoy both alone and with others, and set aside time for them often.

5. Build a support group. Nurture relationships with friends and family; rely on them for encouragement, affirmation, and trust during difficult moments—and be there for them when they ask for the same kind of help.

6. Use campus resources. Tutoring, computer-assisted instruction, support groups, counselors, and administrators can help you overcome difficulties. Ask for help early: The accumulated stress from a series of minor annoyances can make a small problem feel like a major crisis.

Team sports can help you manage the day-to-day stress of college life.

7. Guard your health. The freedom and social life on campus can tempt you with dangerous lifestyle choices: inadequate sleep, unhealthful eating habits, cigarettes, excessive fast food, experimentation with alcohol and other dangerous substances. Make a commitment to your own well-being during college.

8. Think positively. Psychologist William James believed that most people use only about 10% of their potential. In spite of their unpleasantness, negative experiences can boost your self-esteem by putting you in touch with your hidden strengths and unknown gifts.

9. Find out which stress-management techniques work best for you, and use them often. The "Who's In Control?" section beginning on page 138 is a helpful resource for students who want to stop feeling like victims. The Success Journal described on page 121 is an effective tool for strengthening courage and self-esteem. Other parts of this chapter may help you meet your special needs.

10. Monitor your attitude. Human-potential experts say that 90% of experience is what goes on in our minds. Often it's not an event that's awful or wonderful—it's how we define it. If you expect to feel overwhelmed, frustrated, confused, or anxious occasionally during college, you won't panic when one of those emotions hits you. The reverse is true as well: If you're excited and happy about attending college, you won't be unnerved by minor crises and disappointments.

11. Focus on your goals. Stress is easier to manage if you're working steadily to make your dreams come true. Build your confidence by reviewing your personal mission statement regularly. Keep a list of day-to-day goals and cross them off—even the small ones— as you achieve them; celebrate your successes, both major and minor. Review the goal-setting advice in Chapter One for more suggestions about goals and motivation.

EXERCISE 1: YOUR STRESS-MANAGEMENT STRATEGIES

Answer the questions below, referring to the list of strategies above:

1. *List the numbers of any strategies you're already using to manage stress.*

2. *List the numbers of any strategies you intend to try.*

3. *Make a list of goals for the next two days, and plan a small celebration afterwards.*

4. *Describe the attitude you have today towards attending college. Is it different from the way you usually feel? Do you see a need for any changes? If so, what strategies might you try?*

Are You Afraid of Failure?

The higher up you go, the more mistakes you're allowed. Right at the top, if you make enough of them, it's considered to be your style.
Fred Astaire

Telling yourself an upbeat story about a successful person can help you recover from a disappointment or painful experience. (The "successful person" can be anyone—a teenager who landed his first job, a senior citizen who ordered a meal in French for the first time, a college student who passed organic chemistry, or you at some happy moment in your life.) To get you started, here are a few stories of people who turned failure into success.

Jan Carlzon, president of SAS Airlines, says he's grateful for all the mistakes he made in his first management job. Four years after he started the job, he says, he'd learned enough to start doing things right for a change. Alan Lakein, a pioneer in time management, feels the same way about his business errors. After each one he said, "That's another mistake I won't have to make again."

Florence Nightingale struggled for years to break away from her controlling Victorian parents, who believed women belonged at home. Finally, she defied their wishes and headed a small group of women who nursed wounded British soldiers in the Crimean War. After becoming a national heroine, she opened the first nursing school in England and laid the foundations for the modern nursing profession.

Barbara Jordan, first African-American governor of Texas, lost her first two elections in 1962 and 1964. President Bill Clinton grew up in a troubled family: His father died before he was born, and his stepfather was an alcoholic who abused his mother.

During World War I, humanitarian Albert Schweitzer was confined to a prison camp with no books or medical equipment (Schweitzer was a scholar, musician, and physician). His fellow inmates were workers with far less formal education than he had. Schweitzer asked the inmates to teach him everything they knew about their jobs—furnace repair, shoemaking, cooking, and other skills. Later, he said this informal education was a tremendous help in running his African hospital.

The Beatles were failures the first year their records were sold in the United States. Stevie Wonder's first two records were also failures. Dr. Seuss, author of *How the Grinch Stole*

Continued

Continued

Christmas and many other children's books, was rejected by twenty-three publishers when he tried to sell his first book.

Athlete Florence Griffith Joyner was defeated in high school track meets by another student, Valerie Brisco, who defeated her again in the 1984 Olympics. Joyner persisted and later set world records in the Seoul Olympics in 1988.

Belgian author Georges Simenon was frustrated because a prestigious French publication rejected all his short stories. The editor, a famous French writer named Colette, advised him to change his style. Simenon followed her advice, began writing for the publication, and became one of the world's best-selling writers; his fictional detective, Inspector Maigret, has been portrayed on television many times.

Walt Disney's early animated film business, Laugh-O-Grams, ended in failure and thousands of dollars in unpaid bills. Disney sought work as a Hollywood director but was turned down by every major studio.

Composer Ludwig van Beethoven had a hearing impairment that kept him from listening to some of the magnificent symphonies he composed. What if he'd given up?

What if *you* give up?

The Beatles were failures when their recordings were first marketed in the United States.

JOURNAL ACTIVITY: MEETING YOUR CHALLENGES

If you feel overwhelmed every time you face a new challenge, a Personal Success Journal can boost your courage by reminding you of obstacles you've overcome in the past. You can get started by trying this journal experience for the next seven days.

Begin by recalling a time when you overcame your doubts and successfully met a challenge. Examples might include learning to ride a bicycle or passing an algebra test. Record a few details about the event—you need not write complete sentences—and add any comments you wish to make. Continue to recall one such event from either past or recent experience to record in your journal each day.

After you've used up the spaces below, you may want to continue making entries to reread when your motivation or courage need recharging. Many students buy a separate notebook for this purpose; others record entries in a special section of their looseleaf binders.

DAY 1

The challenge you met:

Your comments:

DAY 2

The challenge you met:

Your comments:

DAY 3

The challenge you met:

Your comments:

DAY 4

The challenge you met:

Your comments:

DAY 5

The challenge you met:

Your comments:

DAY 6

The challenge you met:

Your comments:

DAY 7

The challenge you met:

Your comments:

COLLABORATIVE ACTIVITY: SHARING YOUR SUCCESSES

Meet with three or four other students to share some of your past successes. (You need not show anyone your journal entries, but be ready to describe an experience or two.) The group discussion may remind you of other successes you've had—or put you in touch with suggestions for ways to achieve success in the future. Record any helpful ideas you've heard, along with remembered past successes, in the space below.

GROUP DISCUSSION NOTES:

READING THOUGHTFULLY: LEARNING FROM PAINFUL FEELINGS

Emotional pain can be a catalyst for change. When strong feelings arise, look for the lesson that might be hidden underneath. The suffering you're going through may be a sign that an important value of yours has been threatened, or that you need to alter your thinking or behavior. The reading selection below contains suggests several valuable lessons you can learn from painful feelings. Before you start reading, complete the activity below.

BEFORE YOU READ

Answer the following questions:

1. List as many negative feelings as you can.

2. What does each feeling signify? Write a few words describing the causes or meanings of each feeling you listed. (For example, the cause of sadness could be disappointment or loss.)

3. Most people have a few dominant feelings that they experience more often than others. Put a check next to the feelings you listed in Question 1 that you know best.

---

from ## Do It! Let's Get Off Our Buts

by John-Roger and Peter McWilliams

Beneath hurt is caring. The depth of the hurt indicates the depth of the caring. The anger that hides the hurting shows the degree of caring, too. We only hurt about things we care about. Yes, when anger covers the hurt we say, "I don't care about them; I *hate* them." That's part of the caring, too.

Hurt feelings are a reminder to find A, refocus on A, feel the caring you have for A, and find alternate ways to get A, even if B, C, D, E and F get in the way.

Another word for caring, of course, is love. Love is powerful. Keep it directed toward your goal. Most people use hurt as a reason to stop. Then you truly *are* hurt; you hurt yourself—you keep yourself from attaining your heart's desire.

Feel the *passion* of caring. Put that behind your goal. If you feel *anger*, remember this is the energy for change. *Use* it; *do* something with it. What you do may not work. If it does work, great. If not, you've learned something—probably lots of things. If nothing else, you've learned one more thing that won't work. Even if you can't do anything physically, use the energy to *imagine* success.

AFTER YOU READ

1. Reread your answers to the questions in Before You Read. How similar (or different) are your answers from what you've just read?

2. Did any sentences in this selection have particular meaning for you? Circle one or more idea that you found powerful.

3. What did you learn from this selection that you can apply to your own life?

GETTING IN TOUCH THROUGH FREEWRITING

In the space below, freewrite about the connection between painful feelings and values. The following questions may help you get started:

What negative feelings affect you the most? What triggers them? What do you think the feelings mean? What solutions have you experimented with? How well have they worked for you? What other solutions might you try?

◆ TAKING CHARGE OF YOUR FEELINGS ◆

Since you have a great deal of power over both your thoughts and behavior, you frequently have the option of choosing your response to a situation. This does *not* mean that you have to go through life as an unfeeling robot, or that you can (or even should) always avoid negative emotions. It does mean that sometimes—perhaps more often than you'd think—you can make choices when things go wrong.

Test scores are a good example. Imagine four first-year students discussing a test they've failed. The first is feeling guilty: "I should have studied harder. I let myself down. I don't deserve to be in college. Here my parents are sacrificing for my education, and I let them down." The second student is angry. "I never had a chance with that test. It was nothing like I expected. Why didn't the instructor give us some warning ahead of time? I hate college. They enjoy making life miserable for students." The third student is apathetic. "I don't care. It's just one test. I'm not even going to study for the next one—it never does any good." Finally, the fourth student is depressed. "I'm hopeless. I'll never make it. It's the same old story. I studied hard, but I can't do it. I'm not like the others."

If you questioned these students about their feelings, they would probably say that their feelings were the only "natural" response they could have to the situation. They might be surprised if you pointed out that all four of them reacted differently to the same problem—a low test score.

Many people resign themselves to feeling guilty, angry, apathetic, or depressed when a problem arises. They've always responded that way, and it doesn't occur to them to seek other possibilities. But the four students who failed the test have a number of options: analyzing the test to see where the problems lie, planning new strategies to prepare for the next test, talking to the professor, visiting the learning center, or forming a study group. They could also experiment with lifestyle changes to see if fatigue, poor nutrition, or insufficient study time was a factor. Still other choices include asking for extra-credit work to raise the test grade, dropping the course in order to make a better start next semester, and hiring a tutor. Making a plan is always a more useful response to a problem than sinking into negative feelings.

Quite possibly *you*, like many people, often respond to different problems with the same negative emotion—guilt, anger, apathy, or depression. Monitor your feelings to see if you can find a recurring pattern—or ask close friends and family members if they've noticed one. (Usually they have!) When a negative feeling starts to overpower you, start looking for other ways to think, feel and—most importantly—act.

Leaving the "Comfort Zone"

If my curve is large, why bend it to a smaller circle?

HENRY DAVID THOREAU

Sometimes we misjudge stress, assuming that it's a warning that our lives aren't working, when actually it's an indicator that growth and new possibilities are at hand. According to John-Roger and Peter McWilliams, the writers you met on page 124, "Anything we haven't done (or thought) often enough to feel comfortable doing lies outside the comfort zone. When we do (or think) these things (basically, anything new), we feel uncomfortable."

If you've been forcing yourself to live in ways that don't suit you, change can be liberating and exhilarating. Attending college can be an important step in creating the kind of life you've always dreamed of living. But your plunge into the academic world may trigger a stressful period when almost everything you do feels wrong. Your success depends on your ability to tolerate elevated anxiety and other negative feelings until your new choices feel comfortable. Ralph Waldo Emerson once offered this useful advice: "Do not be too timid and squeamish about your actions. All life is an experiment."

a) analysis

Katie keeps interrupting me when I'm studying. I get irritable with her and feel guilty afterwards. She's only four and doesn't understand why she can't have all my attention. She's having trouble getting used to having a mom in college.

b) test a solution

I'm going to try a couple of things. She and Dan could do son father-daughter things together. I'll ask him to plan something — maybe play a video game together. Also I'm going to bring Da and her to campus Saturday to help her understand what my studying is all about.

c) assess the results

Both solutions helped. Dan didn't want to play a video game — took her out for ice cream instead. Katie can't have ice cream every time I study, but he can figure out something else for them to do. She was excited about seeing the campus on Saturday. (Dan enjoyed the visit too) Sunday afternoon when I was studying, and Dan watching football, she played by herself. First she said, "You're getting ready for your school, Mama."

d) make any changes needed

I'm going to ask Dan to talk to Katie about other activities. I'm going to ask Katie to make a list of activities she can do by herself too.

Figure 4.1 Problem-Solving Plan

Three Magic Words: "Make a Plan"

When you find yourself worrying about money, relationships, academics, or other issues, rechannel that energy into planning. What actions would improve the situation? What can you do about the problem right now? Doing *something* constructive almost always feels better than worrying about it. As soon as you begin working on a solution, you're likely to experience less stress.

How do you get started? Experts suggest following these four steps:

1. Analyze the situation
2. Test a solution
3. Assess the results
4. Make any needed changes and begin the process again until the problem is solved

These steps are powerful stress reducers, for three reasons: First, by putting you in charge, they empower you to find workable solutions. Second, they challenge you to think critically. If you've been feeling stuck and hopeless, searching for new solutions can put you in touch with new reserves of energy. Most important, this problem-solving model stimulates you to take positive action. Surprisingly often, a small first step propels you much closer to a solution than you'd dreamed possible. Speech-language pathologist Janet Rafenski says that many times her clients' stuttering disappears after only one therapy session. When they find the courage to talk honestly about their problem, it ceases to exist.

What challenges are you facing? What one step could you take that might make a big difference in your life?

Signs that you may be leaving the "comfort zone" include guilt, anxiety, fear, depression, and anger. Since negative emotions can have many meanings, you can't always determine what message a stressful period is trying to convey. If you've recently made some alterations in your goals or lifestyle, consider the possibility that your symptoms are a predictor of positive changes, with more to come. And use the stress-management techniques on pages 116 through 118 to sustain your courage and motivation as you leave a familiar "comfort zone" and grow into a new one.

Managing Stress in Relationships

People change and forget to tell each other.

LILLIAN HELLMAN

Like you, friends and family members have "comfort zones" that may be disrupted by your new interests, activities, and friendships. If tensions arise, avoid attacking friends and family members, and don't become defensive. Here are some strategies that can be helpful:

1. Use "I-messages" to communicate your feelings. Instead of blaming others—"You always play the radio too loudly"—focus on your needs and feelings: "I can concentrate

Often you can choose how to respond to a negative situation.

Thirteen Problem-solving Tips
from *The Art of Clear Thinking* by Rudolf Flesch

1. Write the problem down.
2. Translate the problem into plain English.
3. If possible, translate the problem into figures, symbols or graphs.
4. Don't rely on your memory but use written or printed sources.
5. Know how to use a library.
6. Take notes and keep files.
7. Discuss the problem with others.
8. Try turning the problem upside down.
9. Don't be afraid of the ridiculous.
10. If you feel frustrated, don't worry. Relax; turn to other work; rest; sleep.
11. Take time to be by yourself. Free yourself of trivial work; rest; sleep.
12. Know the time of day when your mind works best and arrange your schedule accordingly.
13. When you get an idea, write it down.

better when the radio is lower." Whenever you need to deal with a problem, try to start your sentences with the word "I":

Negative message: "How can you ask me to run an errand when you see how busy I am?"

"I-message": "I'm trying to figure out how to do this assignment, so this isn't a good time for me to run an errand."

Negative message: "You never cooperate with me."

"I-message": "I need cooperation so I can finish writing my essay and we can go to the movie together."

Finding fault with others can provoke defensiveness and a return volley of blame. "I-messages," on the other hand, foster understanding and teamwork. They won't magically transform relationships that aren't built on mutual cooperation: That kind of change is a long-term project that may even require a few sessions with a professional counselor. But "I-messages" often work surprisingly well—and they're always better than blaming.

2. If you want others to respect your priorities, show respect for theirs. Build trust by showing friends and family members that their needs are important to you. This principle does not require abandoning your goals to help others pursue theirs. It does mean factoring the wishes of others into your plans. A five-year–old's feelings are as real to him as yours are to you. Whenever possible, discuss issues and seek at least a partial compromise.

3. Reassure those around you that they're as important to you as ever. Words aren't everything, but at the right moment they can be a powerful healing tool. (A quarter isn't much either, but it's more valuable than a hundred-dollar bill when you desperately need to use a pay telephone.) Say "I love you" and "I care about you" often.

4. Practice patience. Any change can disrupt a cherished relationship. Over time, however, adjustments can be made and harmony restored. When stress hits you, temper your negative emotions to avoid permanent damage to others. If you expect friends and family members to overlook an occasional stress-related lapse on your part, extend the same privilege to them. Don't allow the inevitable stresses of college life to erupt into discord that may be impossible to heal.

5. Be an effective listener. Learn the skill of "reflective listening"—restating the idea or feeling you're hearing rather than advising, judging, blaming, interrupting, or changing the subject. If your best friend tells you she's having a math test tomorrow but doesn't understand binomials, a reflective response would be, "You sound worried." Instead of criticizing her or telling her what to do, you can encourage her while she explores possible solutions: an emergency meeting with her study group, a visit to the learning center or professor's office, a study session with a computerized math program.

Life is full of stressful moments. Relationships become deeper and stronger when friends and family can talk openly about their thoughts and feelings. Reflective listening isn't always appropriate, of course: Often you'll need to share information, state opinions, and solve problems assertively. But reflective listening is a useful tool that you can learn easily and develop with practice.

COLLABORATIVE ACTIVITY: REFLECTIVE LISTENING

Meet with two or three other students. Allow a few minutes for each group member to share a short story about a recent incident, positive or negative, such as a flat tire or a telephone call with good news. Group members should practice appropriate responses: "You must have been frustrated" or "You sound thrilled." Make sure everyone has opportunities both to speak and to listen.

Non-judgmental listening strengthens relationships and encourages others to make choices that work for them.

EXERCISE 2: PRACTICE "I-MESSAGES"

Think of ten negative statements a student under stress might want to make to friends or family members. Then write each statement as an "I-message." When you're finished, discuss your list with another student. What similarities do you notice? What are the differences? Could any of the "I-messages" be rewritten to make them more effective?

◆ SOLVING COLLEGE PROBLEMS ◆ THROUGH CRITICAL THINKING

The significant problems we face cannot be solved at the same level of thinking we were at when we created them.

ALBERT EINSTEIN

When stress levels rise, thinking tools can help solve problems and recharge your motivation. A useful first step is to freewrite about a difficult situation. Don't worry about grammar and spelling, and don't hold anything back; you can always destroy the paper after you're finished with it. When you're finished, start writing a rebuttal. If you can't think of any positive thoughts to counter your negative ones, pretend that you're writing to a friend who's dealing with the situation, not yourself. We rarely treat others as harshly as we treat ourselves during low moments.

More ammunition against negative thoughts appears below in thinking strategies that can help you conquer five common self-defeating beliefs.

Five Self-Defeating Beliefs.

1. I'd be happier if I quit college.

Thinking Strategy: Ask yourself "What if?" and then answer the question honestly. This is a good activity to do with a trusted and supportive friend, but if necessary you can go through the process alone. (Be sure to *write* about the situation as well as *think* about it. Psychologists emphasize the importance of writing as a problem-solving tool: Moving the pen or pencil prompts your mind to move more effectively towards a solution.)

Begin by filling in the blank space in the following question: "What will I accomplish if I *don't* _____ [finish the semester, pass my math course, graduate from college, etc.]?" Then go on to answer the question you've set for yourself.

Expect some of your answers to be positive: My spouse will be happier; I won't have to struggle with algebra; I'll get a full-time job. But other answers will be negative: I'll never achieve my dream of becoming a nurse; I'll miss this opportunity to fulfill my potential; I'll let myself down.

This question is useful because it quickly puts you in touch with the motivators that brought you to college in the first place. Remember that a college education has been an unattainable dream for countless people: Just by enrolling in college you took a giant step denied to many others.

After thinking about the "What if?" question, many students realize that what they'll accomplish if they don't finish the semester—or college itself—is . . . nothing. Try this process yourself the next time you're discouraged. As soon as you're in touch with your motivators again, spend another minute planning a positive step towards fulfilling your college goal.

2. I can't possibly do all that's expected of me.

Telling yourself "I'm overwhelmed" is an *overgeneralization*—thinking a problem is a single, massive lump instead of a combination of small, interrelated parts.

Thinking strategy: Break down the task into the smallest steps you can think of. Make sure your list is complete. Then choose the smallest step and get started on it immediately. Post the list in your study area and cross items off as you complete them.

3. I'll never get this right.

There's a perfectionistic fallacy hidden within this statement: I have to be perfect, or all my efforts are worthless.

Thinking strategy: Once you uncover the hidden falsehood, you can easily defeat it. Anyone can accomplish a great deal without coming close to perfection. You probably don't do any single thing perfectly, and you probably don't know anyone else who does, either. Yet you—and the people you know—are worthwhile human beings. (More ammunition against perfectionism appears on pages 66 to 67 in Chapter Two.)

4. I'm a hopeless case.

Guilt can be a useful motivator for change, but it can be also the result of faulty reasoning. What you're really telling yourself is that you can make up for past mistakes by dwelling on them and feeling miserable. Guilt can also be an excuse for avoiding an unpleasant task. Finally, psychologist Fritz Perls—founder of Gestalt Therapy—notes that guilt can be a cover-up for resentment.

Thinking strategy: Think, write about, or talk to a friend about the possible meanings of your guilt. Do you really think that feeling miserable makes up for work you haven't done? You can probably dispel that mistaken idea very quickly. If you're using guilt to avoid work, do an "instant task," as described in Chapter Two—spending one minute doing *anything* productive to get a fresh start on the project that scares you.

Always check your attitude for hidden resentment as well. Perhaps you need to spend a few moments focusing on the real reasons you're in college. If family or friends are pushing you to study, and you're annoyed by their interference, try an attitude adjustment. Develop the habit of thinking of your education as a gift *to* yourself, *from* yourself, rather than an obligation to others.

5. A college education isn't that important anyway.

This is an example of the "tethered thinking" you read about earlier. Negative thoughts are preventing you from expanding your thinking in a positive direction. Your college experience seems worthless because you're trapped in the frustrations of the immediate moment and can't see the rewards ahead.

Thinking strategy: Unleash your creativity to visualize as powerfully as possible your future as a college graduate. Dare to daydream and to share your daydreams with at least one friend.

COLLABORATIVE ACTIVITY: SOLVE LEARNING PROBLEMS

With a group of three or four other students, role-play the five learning problems you just read about. Begin by having two students role-play the first problem. Student 1 complains about feeling overwhelmed; Student 2 acts as a helpful friend who explains the thinking strategy that will solve the problem. Then go to the second problem—"I'll never get this right"— with other students role-playing Student 1 and Student 2. If possible, keep switching problems and roles until everyone has had a chance to act as both a concerned student and a helpful friend.

Are You Asking the Right Questions?

Sometimes asking a simple question can help you reduce stress—if it's the *right* question. Although there are no absolute guidelines for deciding which questions are *right*, the following suggestions can be helpful.

First, it's often better to ask *what* rather than *why*. *Why* puts you into the past, dealing with circumstances that can't be changed. Good problem-solvers usually avoid trying to find out who's at fault: Instead, they ask *what* can be done to solve the problem. Don't waste time asking why the dry-cleaner doesn't have your clothes ready; work out a solution instead. Can you wear something else? Could your bill be reduced to compensate for the delay?

Second, aim for positive questions rather than negative ones. Instead of asking whether you're getting any benefit from your algebra class, ask what changes would make your learning experience more effective. (There's the *what* question again!) Negative ideas, doubts, punishments, and blame don't work nearly as well as positive thinking.

Finally, look for questions that focus on you rather than on other people. Instead of asking why the college doesn't have a secure place to park your bicycle, ask what *you* can do about the problem. (Notice again the switch from *why* to *what*.) Some *who* questions are attempts to assign blame: "Who decided that the learning center would be closed all weekend?" A better question would be: "Since the learning center is going to be closed, where can I get help with my math assignment?" "Who might I talk to about revising the schedule next semester?"

These three guidelines won't apply to every situation. But after you've tried them for a while, you'll see that they're often a powerful problem-solving tool.

EXERCISE 3: ASK THE RIGHT QUESTIONS

Rewrite the following questions according to the guidelines above:

1. *Why is scholarship money so hard to get?*

2. *Who locked the keys inside the car?*

3. *Why is the format for research papers so different from what was required in my high school?*

4. *Who overcooked these pancakes?*

5. *What are the reasons for closing the learning center on Sunday mornings?*

6. *Who decided that math tutors are available only two evenings a week?*

7. *Why doesn't the college offer more free cultural events?*

8. *Why can't librarians make change for the copy machines?*

9. *Who decided that all English compositions have to be typed?*

10. *Wouldn't it be safer if parking spaces for evening classes were closer to the Science Building?*

Just Say No

I hate housework! You make the beds, you do the dishes—and six months later you have to start all over again.

JOAN RIVERS

Some of the stress you'll experience in college is the result of having too little time and too much to do. The "just-say-no" skill is a useful adjunct to the lessons you've already learned about time management. To apply this skill, simply ask yourself: What would happen if I "just say no" to this task? If the answer is "nothing," consider doing exactly that— "just say no" and release some time for activities that have a higher priority for you.

The "just-say-no" skill is useful because it helps you rid yourself of tasks you've been performing because of guilt or habit. Although it sounds negative, it has a positive side too: You're free to discover better ways to perform routine tasks—or you can substitute something totally different.

Suppose, for example, that you've always cooked Thanksgiving dinner for your extended family. Yours is the only dining room big enough for everyone, and relatives look forward to the event all year. But you're dreading it because you'll be working on a humanities project and an economics paper right around then. To discover alternatives, ask yourself: "What would happen if I just said no?" Family members might be willing to do some of the cooking themselves—and might even enjoy showing off their culinary skills. Or everyone could meet at a restaurant, with the added bonus that there would be no cleanup chores afterwards. Or you could rent a church hall or community room. Now you've generated some possibilities that can be discussed with other family members.

"Just say no" doesn't mean that it's okay to be selfish, blunt, or rude. It does mean that you—and others—are entitled to explore the option of saying no and to evaluate its consequences.

Former First Lady Rosalyn Carter recalls that early in her marriage she spent hours searching for special holiday and birthday gifts for close friends and family members. As she and her husband Jimmy became more involved in politics, she had much less time for shopping. The big surprise, she notes, is that people seemed to like her gifts just as much.

The "just-say-no" option is often most useful with obligations you impose on yourself—as Rosalyn Carter did with her extensive shopping trips. If housework burdens you, ask "What would happen if I 'just say no' to a fourth of the housework?" If the answer is "Nothing," feel free to cut back—and to question the importance of other tasks in the same way.

Aimee's Just-Say-No List:
-coach the gymnastics team at the Girls Club (I'll offer to spend three afternoons helping the girls with the balance beam instead)
-Chair the Halloween Dance committee (but I'll help put up decorations)
-tutor Frank in Spanish (he can find someone whose Spanish is better than mine)

Karl's Just-Say-No List
-carpool with Greg and Andy (inconvenient for me—if they keep looking, they'll find other students who live in their neighborhood)-fix Sandy's VCR (I don't want to be an unpaid electronics technician anymore)

Figure 4.2 Just-Say-No Lists

EXERCISE 4: WHEN CAN YOU SAY NO?

Make a list of routine tasks you perform during a normal week. Then reread each item, asking yourself "What if I 'just say no' to this task?" Circle any tasks on the list that you'd consider delegating to others, performing less often, cutting back, or eliminating.

Your list:

Reread the items you circled. Which ones are you ready to delegate, postpone, or eliminate this week? List them here:

After seven days have passed, write a few sentences describing how you carried out your resolution and how it worked for you:

Who's In Control?

Asking yourself "Who's in control?" can help you get in touch with your own power to make effective choices. When you're tempted to blame others for a situation you don't like—or you start making an excuse for a mistake—ask yourself "Who's in control?" The question works equally well in study groups and class discussions.

The question, "Who's in control?" can also improve your family life and other relationships. Avoid making statements like these: "She always makes me angry when she does that" or "I just lose control when he talks to me that way." Is another response possible? Could you walk away, ask a friend or family member to mediate, write a letter explaining how you feel, or react in some other way? When you have a large repertoire of problem-solving behaviors, you're likely to have satisfying relationships with family members and friends.

Although you can't always change your thoughts and feelings, putting yourself in control can help you work through stressful situations. South African leader Nelson Mandela spent twenty-seven years in a government prison for advocating racial equality. Instead of becoming hopeless and bitter, he kept believing that a better life was possible for blacks in South Africa. After he was freed, he put his prison years behind him, was elected president of the Republic, and encouraged both races to work together to build a new South Africa.

Listen to yourself as you talk about daily challenges. When you make a statement from List A, you are putting others in control; List B puts you in control:

List A (Others Are in Control)

It's not my fault.

They talked me into it.

They made me do it.

I have no other choice.

This always happens.

I never got around to it.

I have too much to do.

If they'd stop annoying me about it, I'd do it.

I didn't think I could say anything.

List B (You're in Control)

I'm in charge.

I can make my own decisions.

I don't have to please others all the time.

I can think of several ways to handle this situation.

I don't have to repeat the mistakes of the past.

I'm in control of my time.

I can decide what projects to undertake.

Even when others annoy me, I can make my own decisions.

I'm not afraid to say what I think.

EXERCISE 5: WHO'S IN CONTROL HERE?

Place a check in front of each statement that shows that the speaker is in control; use an X to show that the speaker is placing responsibility on someone else:

_____ *My two-year–old never lets me study.*

_____ *I go to the library when my house gets too noisy.*

_____ *When I'm feeling blue, I call a friend who has a positive outlook on life.*

_____ *I don't know how anybody can be expected to understand the diagrams in this physics book.*

_____ *I inherited my poor attitude towards math from my parents.*

_____ *I've stopped feeling guilty about leaving my son with a baby-sitter when I'm in class.*

_____ *Penmanship wasn't emphasized when I was in grade school, so I've never been able to write neatly.*

_____ *It isn't always easy, but I stick to my study schedule even when my wife wants me to do something else.*

_____ *I'd rather study engineering than nursing, but my parents say that I would make a terrific nurse.*

_____ *If a professor can't get me interested in a course I'm taking, I don't do well.*

One-Minute Checklist

Asking yourself the following questions can help you take control of a stressful situation. A "yes" answer suggests you need to take more responsibility for finding a solution.

_____ Have I made someone else's opinion more important than my own?

_____ Am I allowing another person to make my decisions for me?

_____ Am I relying on someone else's help instead of handling the situation myself?

_____ Am I wasting time blaming instead of looking for a solution?

_____ Have I been complaining instead of taking charge of the situation?

_____ Have I been afraid to tell others what I really want?

_____ Have I been afraid to seek cooperation from others?

EXERCISE 6: STRESS REDUCTION STRATEGIES

List the stress-reduction strategies you would recommend to the students in the examples below. Generate as many strategies as you can for each person.

1. Anne signed up for three courses in her first semester at college. Each professor assigns about two hours of work for each hour spent in class. Anne commutes from home to save money and works twenty hours a week at a store selling athletic equipment. She can't keep up with her assignments and has trouble following the lectures. Her parents have never been to college and don't sympathize with her difficulties.

2. Greg is a second-semester student. Although his floor in the dorm was quiet last semester, new students have moved in who play music late at night. He's having trouble concentrating on his studies and doesn't sleep well. Because he's a pre-med student, he is determined to earn superior grades and has given up racquetball, which he used to enjoy in high school. He says he feels lonely, but he considers studying more important than seeking out friends.

3. Kecia, a first-semester student, is a divorced mother of two children in elementary school who sometimes demand attention when she's trying to study. Because she has never studied a foreign language before, she's struggling to keep up with the other students in her French I class. None of her friends are studying French, and she can't afford a private tutor: The money from her scholarship and child-support payments doesn't go very far.

4. Alex is a second-semester student from the Middle East. He is active in the International Students Association and works part-time in a local restaurant. Friends from the association and his job take up a great deal of his time. They've discovered a pub that serves alcohol to underage students. Alex would like to cut back on his social life and raise his slipping grades, but he feels out of place on campus and relies on the emotional support he receives from his friends.

USING WHAT YOU HAVE LEARNED

1. Think of a time when you experienced low-level stress—"butterflies." How did that experience feel? How did you handle the "butterflies"? Can you think of any positive experiences in the future that may trigger similar feelings?
2. T. H. Huxley once wrote, "There is the greatest practical benefit in making a few failures early in life." Do you agree or disagree? Why?
3. Imagine that you'd like to "just say no" to a task that friends or family expect you to do. What strategies would you use to win their cooperation?
4. Devise a four-step plan for a large or small problem you're facing right now.
5. Make a list of enjoyable activities that could help you reduce stress. Choose one you haven't tried lately and schedule a time to do it.
6. List two unrealistic expectations you once held about college. Then describe two realistic expectations you hold now.
7. Choose one of the five self-defeating beliefs from this chapter (pages 132 through 134). Imagine that while a friend was discussing a college problem, you realized that this self-defeating belief was present. What would you say to build your friend's confidence?
8. Write two "I-messages" and two positively worded questions that you might use in a stressful situation.
9. Write a short dialogue between two college students. Have one describe a college problem while the other offers reflective-listening responses.

EVALUATING YOUR PROGRESS

1. As I look back on the past seven days, I've seen an improvement in these areas:

   _____ organizing my life

   _____ protecting my health

   _____ planning my time

_____ concentrating

_____ taking notes

_____ active learning

_____ reading critically

_____ writing effectively

_____ thinking critically

_____ communicating with important people in my life

_____ enjoying my free time

_____ allowing myself to be imperfect

2. In the coming week, I plan to invest five minutes a day working towards this goal:

CHAPTER 5

Active Learning

Attention, attention must be paid.

LINDA LOMAN IN ARTHUR MILLER'S
DEATH OF A SALESMAN

 PREVIEW:

1. Remembering is easiest when learning experiences are meaningful.

2. Concentration is one of the keys to a better memory.

3. Active involvement in a creative learning experience can boost your memory power.

4. You should plan intensive studying during the times of the day when you're most alert.

 IN-CLASS INTRODUCTORY ACTIVITY: FACTS VERSUS GENERAL LAWS

In Chapter One you read Samuel H. Scudder's account of his first lesson as a naturalist. Professor Jean Louis R. Agassiz told him, "Facts are stupid things until brought into connection with some general law" (page 18). Think about this statement and write a sentence or two explaining what it means to you. Then complete the activities that follow.

Your explanation of Professor Agassiz's statement:

ACTIVITIES:

1. *Give an example of a "fact" and a "general law."*

2. *Which do you find easier to learn: isolated facts, or facts that mean something? Why?*

3. *Give an example of a "fact" you encountered in a college class recently that is related to a "general law."*

4. *In Chapter Three you were introduced to six learning styles: auditory, visual, social, independent, conceptual, and pragmatic. What learning styles suit you best? What are your favorite learning activities?*

COLLABORATIVE ACTIVITY:

Meet with a small group of other students to share your answers to Question 3. Then discuss how finding relationships between "facts" and "general laws" can help you remember information in the courses group members are taking now.

◆ ROTE MEMORIZING VERSUS ACTIVE LEARNING ◆

Rote memorization—learning solely through repetition—can be sheer drudgery. You sit alone, staring at your notes or text, trying to repeat exactly what you've read and hoping it will stay with you until the next exam. The core of the difficulty lies in the dictionary definition of "rote"—memorizing "without full attention or comprehension."

Active learning, on the other hand, is a more natural process. You can probably recall in detail thousands of facts about interesting experiences you've had, and you probably have a wealth of information about subjects that interest you, such as popular music, sports, and hobbies. Your active involvement made this information easy for you to learn and remember. And you'll learn best if you consider your learning style when you're planning a study session: Will you work alone or with others? Will you emphasize reading or listening? Will you focus on practical, hands-on activities, or are you more interested in abstract ideas?

Some learning experts say they've never met a student who suffers from a "poor memory." But they've met many students who don't concentrate enough to absorb new ideas and information. For example, many people say they have a poor memory for names—at least that's a popular excuse for not remembering them. But notice how much easier the learning process becomes when you show an interest in someone's name. How did their parents chose the name? Did they disagree? Is there a special spelling or does an unusual story go with the name? After you've talked about a name for a few minutes, you'll have little trouble remembering it next time. Obviously your memory is much more powerful than you think. "Attention and comprehension"—the factors mentioned as lacking in rote memorization by the dictionary—are the keys to genuine remembering.

If you still think you have a "poor memory," ask yourself how long it takes you to learn an advertising jingle you've heard on TV or radio. You can probably learn the whole thing in two or three repetitions—perhaps only one. Success in college is determined not by the size of your brain or the strength of your will power (although your determination to succeed is an essential factor). Vital factors are practice, motivation, and meaningful learning experiences.

You have more memory power than you think. Start looking around you to see what the human mind is capable of doing. One college student earned low grades in French because she "just couldn't remember all that grammar." Later she became a teacher in a school for mentally handicapped children—including one who had grown up in France, moved to the United States with his family during the sixth grade, and promptly learned to speak fluent English. After getting to know him, she stopped making excuses about "all that grammar" and signed up for a night-school French class.

To tap into your own brain power, start transforming yourself into an active learner. Instead of memorizing a mathematical rule, use your imagination to make the rule come to life. "The fraction gets smaller as the denominator gets larger" is too abstract to be helpful to most students. Hands-on experiences with fractions, on the other hand, create a depth of understanding that will stay with you for life—especially if you work in a group. Cut an apple into halves, fourths, eighths, and sixteenths, and you'll never forget the rule. This kind of active learning builds your confidence when you're preparing for a test.

Last-minute cramming can create anxiety about forgetting. Because "crammed" information lacks organization and meaning, it's not going to stay with you for long. Even if you manage to get through a test with a passing grade, the information you forced into your memory won't be of much use to you later on.

This chapter will offer you two important strategies for better remembering. First, you'll learn psychological principles about the human memory that you can apply to your special needs. Second, you'll learn study techniques that make learning meaningful and allow you to manage your time effectively.

GETTING IN TOUCH THROUGH FREEWRITING

The following freewriting activities will help you gain insight into your own feelings and beliefs about the learning process.

1. List the skills, subjects, and types of information you know well. Cover as many areas as possible: car repairs, radio stations in your area, academic subjects, recipes, computer knowledge, public transportation routes, job skills, and so on.

2. Freewrite about the ways in which you learn best. Some (perhaps all) of the following activities will probably appear on your list: listening, reading, observation, asking questions, trial and error, research.

3. Reread your answer to the previous question. What conclusions can you make about your favorite learning activities? Can you apply those preferences to your college studies?

◆ THE READING AND WRITING CONNECTION ◆

Writing is making sense of life.

NADINE GORDIMER

Reading . . . is thinking that makes what we read ours.

JOHN LOCKE

Although reading and writing seem very different, understanding the connections between them can be important to your education. Writing activities can help you read better, and reading skills can serve you well in writing assignments.

Both reading and writing challenge us to "make meaning," as Ann E. Berthoff, an authority on the writing process, describes it. Chances are you've experienced this principle in your own writing. You may have discovered that you have the power to make a story from your past seem sad, funny, or embarrassing. Research papers, lab reports, and other writing assignments also challenge you to "make meaning": You, the writer, must gather facts and ideas, organize them, and make the final decision about what this information will mean to the reader.

But how do readers "make meaning"? Reading often looks like a passive act—absorbing information written by someone else who has already "made meaning" for you. Ultimately, however, it is up to you to use life experience, reading skills, and critical thinking to decide the meaning of a reading selection. Have you ever found that an essay or story meant something quite different to you the second time you read it? If so, you've seen that both readers and writers construct the meaning of a book, article, essay, poem, or story.

Your awareness of how you "make meaning" through language can enhance your learning in many ways. (You'll learn more about reading in Chapter Seven and language in Chapter Nine.) Here are two suggestions that many students have found helpful:

1. Take notes to increase your awareness of how you create meanings when you read and write.

Jot down your thoughts in the margins while you're reading and writing. Express yourself freely, without trying for correct sentence structure, spelling, or punctuation. No one will see these notes but you.

Here are samples of notes you might make while you're writing:

- Need a good example in this paragraph. Readers should feel what it's like to be homeless.
- I can't decide what my main point will be. Am I against student marriages, or just saying think about it first?
- Want to show how movies explore women's choices. *Newsweek* has something about Winona Ryder I can use.

Here are the kinds of comments you might write in the margins while you're reading:

- What's the point?
- Reminds me of Grandma's story about arriving at Ellis Island.
- Doesn't agree with what Prof. Anaya said about the Depression. Must ask her.
- Good argument!

This notetaking habit helps make you a more active thinker and, as a result, a more effective reader and writer.

2. Learn about your favorite writers.

Browse through books about writers and writing; read a biography of a favorite author. Books can give you an intimate look at how professionals use their own experience to generate ideas, gather information, and "make meaning" for their readers. Experiment with their methods in your own writing projects.

Keeping a "Learning Log"

A "learning log" is a kind of diary that supplements your class and lecture notes. Use it to write informally about the subjects you're studying: ideas, discoveries, questions, problems, solutions, feelings. You can also make connections between what you're learning and your life experience, and you can note topics that you'd like to investigate more deeply. Because you're the only person who will read your entries, punctuation and spelling are unimportant.

The log records not *what* you learned—that information goes into class notes—but *how* your learning experiences feel. Recording your progress this way has three important advantages. First, it helps you "make meaning" of what you're learning. Second, it's

Record how your learning experiences feel in a learning log.

an excellent tool for discovering and solving learning problems. Most important, it gives you practice in expressing yourself through writing. Because you probably spend much more time talking than writing, making regular entries in a learning log can have a significant effect on your writing skills.

Here are sample entries from two learning logs:

From Maria, who's majoring in nursing:

Lots of trouble following the pharmacology lecture. Dr. Chan covered the material very fast. I though I was ready for the lecture but wasn't. Julie, Luis and Dana also had a hard time. Next time I'll read the text more slowly, several times. The four of us will meet before the lecture to get each other ready. One victory to report. Dr. Chan asked us to write from memory ten facts from Tuesday's lecture. He really liked my list.

Psychology Learning Log
10/3 Need to spend more
time reading the textbook
before class. Having trouble
keeping up with the
notes during lecture, esp.
vocabulary.
10/5 Interesting discussion
today about "projections."
Prof. said projections are a
big issue in dating.
Want to think about dating
experiences— talk to Liz and
Aaron about them.

Figure 5.1 Learning Log

From Marc, who's taking first-year English composition:

Started planning my composition. Used the planning activities in my notes. They worked! I have lots of ideas. Had trouble with my opening paragraph. Reread handbook suggestions about intros—good ideas. Greg in the Learning Center promised to read my first draft tomorrow. I think this is going to be my best paper so far.

What to record in your learning log. Here's a list of possible topics; perhaps you'll think of others.

> problems
>
> solutions
>
> resources
>
> doubts
>
> plans
>
> breakthroughs
>
> feelings
>
> questions
>
> goals
>
> "real-life" connections to subjects you're studying
>
> conversations with students and professors
>
> topics you'd like to explore more deeply
>
> experiences with tests
>
> your progress with assignments
>
> what works
>
> what doesn't work

Learning Log Activity

1. Start with one subject. If you attempt too much in the beginning, you may get discouraged and lose the benefits of keeping a learning log. Later, when you're accustomed to making log entries, you can add other subjects.

Some students choose a favorite subject for their first log; others choose a subject that they find particularly difficult. For example, many students with math anxiety say that a math log helps them deal with their fears and build confidence. The choice is yours.

2. Use a divider to designate a section of a course notebook as a learning log. A spiral-bound stenographic notebook can also be a good choice because of its convenient size.

3. Date every entry. When you reread your log, the dates may give you important clues to your learning style. How long does it take you to master new concepts? to study

Ten Reasons for Keeping a Learning Log

1. You'll have a record of questions and interesting topics that can be used for research papers and term projects.

2. If you take a related course later, rereading the log will help you remember how this course felt—and what to expect next time.

3. You'll have a record of learning problems that might cause problems on tests.

4. You'll know how you prepared for each test, and how well your study plan worked.

5. You'll have a safe outlet for negative feelings.

6. You'll have a safe place to celebrate and brag about your progress.

7. You can record what happens in your study group—what works, what needs improvement.

8. You'll have an accurate record of how long it took you to master a difficult concept. (Although it may seem as though you've been struggling with square roots for months, your log may reveal that you started solving problems successfully after only five days.)

9. Rereading your log can help you discover your unique learning style. You may realize that visiting the learning center *always* helps, or that reading a Shakespearean play is difficult unless you watch a video first, or that you always overreact to tests. Knowing *who* you are is one of the first steps to success.

10. Rereading entries about your struggles and successes can give you courage when new challenges arise.

for a test? Are there special times during the semester (mid-terms, for example) when you tend to feel discouraged?

4. Write freely. No one is going to read your log but you: Use it as an outlet to express frustrations and doubts—as well as a place to congratulate yourself and celebrate your achievements. Having a record of both negative and positive feelings about your learning experiences can bolster your courage later, when those feelings surface again: You'll have proof that you've met challenges successfully—and can do so again.

5. Save your log. This record of your experiences may be valuable if you have to take a related course, a refresher, or a licensing examination later. It may also help you decide which professors to ask for recommendation letters.

6. Reread your log from time to time. In the margins note (and date) any additional comments or discoveries. Expect learning experiences to look different as time passes. The log may show you that a course that has proved valuable to you seemed meaningless at the time, or that it took half a semester to get used to a professor who is now a close friend. Most important, you'll be able to relive some of the breakthroughs and victories you'll be experiencing during your college years.

More Writing Strategies for Better Learning

People seldom see the halting and painful steps by which the most insignificant success is achieved.

ANNE SULLIVAN

The writing techniques that follow have helped countless students strengthen their memories and perform better on tests. Resolve to try them all this semester. The more strategies you have available, the more success you'll enjoy in college.

1. Mind-mapping

This is a favorite strategy for three reasons: It allows you to learn actively, it's loosely structured, and it encourages you to make connections between the facts and ideas you're studying. When you look for relationships within the information you're studying, your confidence builds—and you'll avoid the unpleasant feeling of having your head crammed with random pieces of information.

To make a mind map, you need a blank sheet of paper, a pen or pencil, and the information you're studying—notes, handouts, textbook. Write your topic in the middle of the page and draw a circle around it. Then draw a line outward from the circle and write a related idea or fact on it. Keep adding branching lines, each with an idea or fact. If needed, draw branching lines around these subordinate points, and keep going.

Feel relaxed and spontaneous as you make your mind map. It can't be done "incorrectly"—or "correctly," for that matter. It's up to you how you want to arrange the material you're studying.

For additional review, try drawing the map again from memory, or see if you can arrange the same information differently. Post a mind map on a wall (a great way to stimulate conversations with friends and family members!), or embellish it with cartoons and illustrations. One student, worried about a biology final, laminated her mind map and used it as a place mat at the diner table until the exam was over. (She made an A.)

Mind-mapping is a particularly effective study technique because it requires you to distinguish between main ideas and supporting points—an important critical-thinking skill.

2. Index-card outlines

Professor Max Brandon, who teaches social sciences at Polk Community College, shows his students how an index card can lead to meaningful learning. Students are permitted to bring a three-by-five index card to tests as a memory aid. He reports that most students quickly realize that jotting down facts won't improve their test grades much. They soon begin using the index card for an outline of the most important information presented in class.

This index-card idea is an excellent supplement to the flash cards described earlier. When you're trying to memorize relationships and principles, arrange them in outline form on an index card. Because outlining is a critical-thinking skill, you'll have begun the learning process before you even finish filling out the card. Then carry the card with you to study during your free moments. When you're reviewing right before a test, put the card out of sight and see if you can recreate it from memory.

Figure 5.2 Mind Map

3. Do-it-yourself test questions

In Chapter Three you learned to listen for words and actions that signal the importance of a particular piece of information. For example, the words "important" and "essential" are good clues to possible test questions.

Use this knowledge—and your own creativity—to make up your own test questions, answer them, and then grade them (with the help of your notes and textbook) as if you were the instructor. Do-it-yourself testing is an excellent active strategy because it encourages you

1860s J. immigration began
   suspicion + prejudice
1908 "Gentlemen's Agreement"
1913 calif. Alien Land Bill
12/7/41 Pearl Harbor
internment camps
   442 Regimental Combat Team
      High honors
   no JA ever charged with
            disloyalty
   6,000 JA linguists "saved
         1 million lives" (Gen'l
               Willoughby)
1952 Japanese born could
      be naturalized citizens
Issei = 1st gen. Nisei = 2nd gen.
Sansei = 3rd gen.
   S.I Hayakawa - scholar, senator
Minoru Yamasaki -architect
   Kristi Yamaguchi- figure skater

Figure 5.3 Index Card Outline: Sociology Lecture, Japanese Americans

to prioritize the information you're learning, and to evaluate your own understanding of course material.

READING THOUGHTFULLY: ARE YOU A GENIUS?

In the following reading selection, botanist David Fairchild (1869–1954) offers a definition of the word "genius." Before you begin reading, complete the following activity. As you read the selection itself, write down any questions that come to mind.

BEFORE YOU READ

1. Make a list of "geniuses" you've known or heard about.

2. Write your own informal definition of "genius."

3. Read a definition of "genius" in a dictionary. Is it similar to yours, or different?

---

from **The World Grows Round My Door (1947)**
by David Fairchild

When Galileo[1] was in prison, he looked out through the bars and watched the clouds. He may have scratched a bit when the fleas bit him or shuddered when the rats annoyed him, but that did not keep him from wondering about the various kinds of clouds he could see, and he made a classification of them that lived long after his death. He refused to allow the moments of his life which remained to him—and he could not tell how many his enemies would permit him to have—to be filled with a monotony of recurring human events when outside in the sky he could see a passing show which fired his imagination, already awakened by his new conception of this planet as a revolving ball. Galileo rose to the higher levels of his existence. He really lived among the clouds, even though his body was tied to a prison cell.

---

[1] Galileo Galilei (1564—1642), Italian astronomer and physicist, was imprisoned for claiming that the sun, not the earth, was the center of our planetary system.

It is this ability to rise into the clouds that we call genius, and we are pretty sure, most of us, that it is inborn; that it cannot be acquired; that it is not like other habits; not something which by effort we can learn and, once learned, make into a fixed unconscious attitude towards the world around us.

Personally I am not so sure whether watching the clouds intelligently, regardless of one's surroundings, may not be made into a habit. It is certainly true that there are immense differences between people in the ease with which they can become oblivious to a hubbub around them.

There appear to be quite different kinds of solitude. There is the solitude of Walden Pond[2] where no human being is in sight, and there is that which comes to one in a big city, knowing nobody and feeling lost and lonely as one makes one's way through a throng.

But that is not the point I wish to make. Whether you seek solitude in a crowd or in a tropical jungle matters little if the solitude takes you "into the clouds." These clouds can be made of all sorts of stuff, for I do not mean the actual clouds we see on a summer day.

I have known mathematicians who find in the world of numbers and their relationships a dream land that is of surpassing beauty. I know chemists who by means of proteolytic[3] enzymes are splitting the protein molecules with their thousands of imaginary atoms, and who live in a "cloud world" where I am lost before they have said three sentences. I see such men disappear into some brilliant white cloud mass and I envy them their ability to wander where perhaps no human imagination has ventured before.

AFTER YOU READ

1. What new words did you encounter in this selection? How will you learn their meaning?

2. What questions did you record about this selection? How will you answer them?

---

[2] American writer Henry David Thoreau (1817—1862) built a cabin near Walden Pond in Massachusetts to live alone and observe nature; he described his experiences in *Walden* (1854).

[3] Referring to a process that breaks proteins into simpler substances.

3. Is Fairchild's definition of "genius" different from the one you wrote earlier? from the dictionary's?

4. Do you think you might be (or become) a genius?

5. Can you draw any connections between Fairchild's ideas about genius and your college life?

◆ THE PRINCIPLES OF ACTIVE LEARNING ◆

Here are seven principles that can help you become an active learner:

1. Use as many senses as possible.

Begin by looking for opportunities to listen, look and write while you're learning. But don't stop there: Try to employ all your senses. Make yourself aware of smells during a science lab or a field trip. Practice your German in a German restaurant, or try cooking from a German cookbook. Talking about geography or history while you and friends are enjoying an ethnic meal can sharpen your memory.

2. Be as active as possible.

While studying his fish, Samuel H. Scudder drew pictures of his specimen and stuck his fingers into its mouth. Sitting down to read and memorize is only the beginning of learning: Use your creativity to invent other techniques. Draw political cartoons about historical events, act out an incident from a novel you're studying, listen to a recording of a famous speech, visit a museum . . . the possibilities are endless.

3. Utilize the "transfer of learning" principle.

You enhance your memory when you transfer, or apply, a skill in varied situations. Practice thinking, speaking, and listening both inside and outside of class—an effective transfer of learning. Remember that you don't have to stop reading critically when you close your textbook: magazines and newspapers work just as well. Even an advertisement can trigger critical thinking: Do you believe the product will deliver what it's promising?

Make a game out of discovering opportunities to apply what you learned in class. For example, think about biology when you look at the plants on campus; look for psychological issues in TV shows; practice using new vocabulary words in conversation.

4. Look for learning experiences in unexpected places.

If you went to Mexico to study Spanish, almost every waking minute would be a learning experience. Street signs, overheard conversations, newspaper headlines—everything would improve your Spanish *unless* you had an American roommate, watched English-language TV shows, and shopped in American-style stores.

Start looking for ways to convert ordinary experiences into opportunities to learn. Carpool with other serious students, and use at least part of your travel time to talk about what you're learning. Look for TV shows related to your college studies; lay a science magazine on your coffee table. Apply the principles you're learning about physics, chemistry, or biology to everyday experiences like driving across a bridge, cooking a meal, or petting your dog.

5. Seek ways to make new information meaningful.

You already know that meaningful learning is easier and more enduring than rote memorization. When you're studying philosophy, it helps to know that philosophers have long argued about the relationship between language and reality. With that insight, the differences between Plato and later philosophers are easier to understand. In history, a particular battle in the War of 1812 will make more sense when you have a general picture of the war itself—its causes, major events, and results.

An informal talk with your professor during office hours can help you see these connections; discussions with other students are useful too. Reading an encyclopedia article or a children's book about your subject can be helpful too. For example, a summary of the War of 1812 can give you an overall picture that you can later embellish with facts and ideas from your college course.

6. Keep your motivation high.

If you were riding in a private plane and suddenly had to take over the controls via radio directions, you'd quickly learn how to land the plane. Motivation is a powerful learning tool! Because college is a long-term project, you can't expect to maintain a high level of excitement and enthusiasm every minute. But you can recharge your motivation by visualizing the future you're aiming for, reminding yourself of your goals, and staying in touch with your intellectual and personal growth.

One of the best motivational strategies is to write a brief journal entry each day about your college experience. Record at least one experience you enjoyed, or a new insight that came to you, or a moment when you savored the feeling of success. Writing about college will help you focus on your positive experiences—and rereading the journal will help you keep your perspective when you feel tired or discouraged.

7. Share new information and ideas with family and friends.

You'll increase your studying efficiency (and enrich your relationships) if you involve family and friends in your studies. Teaching another person is one of the best study strategies ever: Try sharing new ideas and information with others.

If you live on campus, you can usually find another student who's interested in the courses you're taking. Off campus, friends and relatives of all ages can be drawn into your schoolwork. You'll learn a lot trying to explain new ideas and information to others. In addition, you'll strengthen the bonds of family and friendship, which need extra attention anyway while you're intensely involved with college. Make a game of teaching your children—or a neighbor's children—the names of everyday items in the foreign language you're studying. Get friends and relatives involved in discussions about history and psychology; most people have some familiarity with these subjects and may enjoy discussing the new perspectives you're gaining from college. If you're working a word problem in math, and someone asks what you're doing, read the problem aloud and explain the steps you plan to use in solving it.

EXERCISE 1: LEARNING ACTIVITIES

A list of learning activities appears below. Which activities could help you succeed in the courses you're taking now? Next to each activity you've selected, write the subject for which it would be helpful and the way you plan to use it. For example, next to "sing" you could write "French I: Learn a French folk song." Next to "visit" you might write "Art history: Visit the campus art gallery."

draw

write

taste

smell

touch

listen

ask

discuss

teach

explain

sing

dance

Experiment with new learning experiences in college: the results may surprise you.

move

walk

visit

browse

role-play

perform

recite

play

◆ **THE POWER OF CONCENTRATION** ◆

In *The Art of Loving*, psychologist Erich Fromm noted that many people "have never seen a loving person, or a person with integrity, or courage, or concentration." This sentence has puzzled many readers, who can well understand the importance of love, integrity, and courage, but aren't sure why concentration is included in the list.

But when you think about your relationships with others, you begin to see the importance of concentration. How often do you feel that people simply aren't there with you when you're talking? It's both flattering and rare to have someone remember a few days later what you said—to ask how your biology test went, or to recall that you were looking forward to a sports event or concert.

Concentration is vital to college work. Insufficient attention is the number-one cause of forgetting: Much "lost" information was never learned in the first place. You have probably seen the results in many areas of your life and the lives of others. Time is wasted learning material overlooked in class; assignments are completed incorrectly because instructions were missed; test grades are low, and reading retention is poor. Many "careless errors" in math and writing are actually the result of poor concentration. Even athletic performance can be hurt: The inability to focus can negate superb coaching.

Good concentration, on the other hand, pays handsome benefits. Samuel H. Scudder said he learned a great deal by sitting and looking closely at his fish for several days. Many people who take memory courses report that they're remembering more without applying the techniques they were taught: They're simply focusing their attention better. Students in every academic area have seen their test grades improve dramatically when they began monitoring their own levels of concentration. The only requirements are practice and motivation: let distractions go, concentrate on the present moment, and start looking for the payoffs.

Your mental capacity is so huge that you're unlikely to tap more than a fraction of your brain's potential during your lifetime. The key to this powerhouse is a rule taught by Alan Lakein, a time-management expert: "Work smarter, not harder." This unit will teach you many ways to "work smarter." The first and best way, however, is one you've already heard: develop your ability to concentrate.

GETTING IN TOUCH THROUGH FREEWRITING

Spend a few minutes writing about the word "concentration." The following questions may help you get started: How easy (or difficult) is it for you to concentrate on a task? a lecture? a reading assignment? a conversation? Have you ever tried to improve your concentration? What was the result? Would you like to improve your ability to concentrate?

A, B, and C Concentration Time. Because you're already familiar with time management, you're ready to apply a study system aimed at making the best use of your time all day long. The key to the system is to label each day's blocks of study time either "A," "B," or "C."

Use "C" time for low-concentration tasks, like reviewing a chapter you've already studied.

"A" time is for maximum concentration: You feel alert and can focus clearly. Because most students have busy schedules, "A" time is limited and should be reserved for difficult assignments and complex information.

"B" time is for less demanding tasks, such as review and routine assignments. "B" time is usually more plentiful since it doesn't require quite as much alertness.

"C" time—used for repetition and reinforcement—is usually abundant. A typical day is full of odd moments that can be used for "C" tasks: waiting for a lecture to begin, sitting at a bus stop, standing on line in the bank.

By identifying your A, B, and C time, and scheduling appropriate tasks for each one, you can increase your concentration and memory dramatically. Here's how it works. If you have a free hour between classes, label it "A" time and go to the library to work on high-concentration tasks, such as taking notes from your history text or completing a physics assignment. Later, while you're waiting in the noisy student lounge for your ride home, you can review your notes from history class and write them as questions on flashcards: "B" time. In the evening, when your laundry is going through the spin cycle, you can reread your history text or review your flashcards: "C" time.

This system allows you to get maximum benefit from all your study time. Unfortunately, many students (and perhaps you) have been taught to manage their time differently. They save intensive studying for evenings, which often constitute "C" time because friends or family members are present, noise levels are high, and fatigue is building. Even if you're unusually alert at that time of day, you may not be able to concentrate on one subject for long periods. Looking for smaller blocks of "A" time throughout the day will keep you fresher and improve your memory.

If your only free time comes in the evening, do "A" tasks first and switch subjects frequently. Even then, you should consider an alternative: Could you go to bed an hour earlier and spend an extra morning hour studying? Mornings are usually the quietest time of the day, and you're probably fresh enough after a night's sleep to concentrate better.

Remember that your study area is also a factor in determining "A," "B," and "C" time. Choose quiet settings (the library is probably ideal) for high-concentration "A" tasks. Noisier settings are suitable for "B" tasks, and only "C" tasks—repetition and drill—should be done in loud areas. Sometimes you can also enrich your study time—even changing it from "C" time to "A" time—simply by eliminating noise.

If you must study late in the day, when your energy is low, spend a few extra minutes walking or driving to a quiet place, like the library. Even though you're shortening your study time slightly, you're doubling or tripling your efficiency. And a quiet walk or drive is "A" time too. Although it can't be used for reading (unless you listen to a tape-recording of a book), you're free for intensive thinking about the subject you're studying.

A Skater Learns to Concentrate

When Olympic gold-medalist Dorothy Hamill was working on her "school figures"—elaborate patterns that give "figure skating" its name—her coach, Carlo Fassi, taught her an important lesson about concentration. Dorothy Hamill went on to become both an Olympic gold medalist and a World Champion.

from Dorothy Hamill On and Off The Ice
by Dorothy Hamill with Elva Clairmont

Sometimes, when I just couldn't seem to get a jump right, Carlo would come over and shout at me, explaining that I was holding back—hesitating. "You can't keep anything back," he said. "You have to believe you can do it or you never will. You have to put everything into it."

One morning I was skating a figure when I saw Carlo, my coach, watching me intently. Finally he called me off the ice and asked me what I thought I was doing. I looked at him blankly. "Practicing figures," I said.

"But what were you *thinking* about?" he persisted. "It wasn't the figures."

"I—I was thinking about the movie I saw last night," I stammered.

He made a gesture of impatience and said, "If you are going to do good figures, you don't ever *think* while you are skating. You think only of the blade on the ice. Okay?"

It wasn't okay. I told him I didn't think I could get through these sessions if I couldn't daydream. It would be too boring.

He drew in his breath. "Then give it up, Dorothy. Just give it up. Either you do it right, or you don't do it at all—okay?"

"Okay," I said finally. This was obviously lesson number one—be total. I decided to give it a try.

JOURNAL ACTIVITY: IDENTIFYING "A" TIME

For the next seven days, identify a block of "A" time each day. Plan a study task that requires concentration, and carry out your plan. In the spaces below, identify the "A" time block and the task you chose, and evaluate your study experience.

DAY 1

"A" time block:

Study task:

Your experience:

DAY 2

"A" time block:

Study task:

Your experience:

DAY 3

"A" time block:

Study task:

Your experience:

DAY 4

"A" time block:

Study task:

Your experience:

DAY 5

"A" time block:

Study task:

Your experience:

DAY 6

"A" time block:

Study task:

Your experience:

DAY 7

"A" time block:

Study task:

Your experience:

FOR GROUP DISCUSSION:

How effectively did this system work for you? How do you plan to use "A," "B," and "C" time in the future?

◆ SHORT-TERM AND LONG-TERM MEMORY ◆

Knowing how to transfer information from short-term to long-term memory is another key to successful remembering. "Short-term" memory includes anything from a few seconds to twenty-four hours—remembering a new phone number long enough to dial it once, or recalling the name of a painting you saw in your humanities class. After twenty-four hours, it's much more difficult to retrieve memories without hypnosis or other special methods. Psychologists estimate that after a day we will virtually forget 80 percent of what we've learned.

This tendency to forget has both advantages and disadvantages. The major advantage is that we don't clutter our thinking with nonessential information that won't be used again—the price of today's lunch, a dry cleaner's phone number, an advertisement in the evening paper. The disadvantages are obvious: We have to make a special effort to move information from short-term to long-term memory. Reading, listening, notetaking, and studying won't do the job by themselves. Here are some practical ways to transfer information into your long-term memory. Notice that they will also help you improve your concentration.

1. Review and expand your notes within twenty-four hours after class.

If you wait longer, you may not remember what some of your notations are about. Expanding your notes is important because you may refer to them much later, when you may have forgotten even more. Entries like "Thomas Jefferson story—good illustration of ingenuity" will be meaningless if you can't retrieve the story from your memory.

2. Overlearn difficult material.

Short-term memory can fool you into thinking you know more than you really do. Keep reading your text and notes, and work with your flashcards even if your memory seems solid. When you're taking a test you'll appreciate the extra review.

3. Seek meaningful contexts and connections.

As you saw earlier, meaningful information is much easier to store and retrieve from your memory. In addition to reciting and reviewing Latin grammar, try writing sentences that use this information. Because you've created a meaningful context, you'll remember the grammar longer. When you read, look for examples of grammatical principles; take notes on them. Copy sample sentences onto flash cards and keep reviewing them.

4. Take advantage of the notetaking strategies you've learned.

The Cornell format is ideal for review, since it encourages you to write questions in the left margin, and to include a summary at the bottom. Never underestimate the value of writing as a learning tool. Research shows that you absorb information more efficiently, and retain it longer, when you write it down.

5. Schedule sufficient study time to learn new material.

Every hour of class should be followed by two hours of study (reading your textbook and notes and completing homework assignments). Investing less time in your college courses may mean a low grade at the end of the semester—and an unsatisfying learning experience.

6. Spread similar subjects apart.

If you're taking two math courses, or two language courses, study them on different days—or at least different times of the day. Keep flash cards separated so that you're not reviewing both subjects at the same time.

7. Choose study techniques that match your learning style.

If you're an auditory learner, read notes aloud—or have a study partner read them to you. If you're an independent learner, work alone in a quiet place; if you're a social learner, schedule frequent review sessions with other students.

8. Choose appropriate settings for learning.

Students who say radios and TVs improve their performance are usually talking about low-level learning: completing simple math computations, reviewing material for the third or fourth time, sorting and organizing notes. If you can perform these tasks in front of a radio or TV, that's fine. But don't attempt even a moderately challenging assignment when outside distractions are present. Intensive learning often requires solitude and silence.

What are the Best Places for Study?

What should you do if you have a demanding assignment and no quiet place is available? Find one. Betty Friedan wrote her best-selling book *The Feminine Mystique* in a typing room at the New York Public Library; she said she could not have written the book amid the distractions of home. Novelist Madeleine L'Engle wrote in the library at an Episcopal cathedral in New York; since she couldn't afford to rent a room for typing, she served as the cathedral's volunteer librarian in exchange for writing privileges there.

Be creative (a critical thinking skill). Playwright Jean Kerr discovered an unusual writing area that worked beautifully for her. Besieged with interruptions when her four children were small, she did much of her writing in the family car. She explained, "Out in the car, where I freeze to death or roast to death depending on the season, all is serene. The few things there are to read in the front-seat area (Chevrolet, E-gasoline-F, 100-temp-200) I have long since committed to memory. So there is nothing to do but write." Studying in a car may not work for you—but how about a friend's house? a quiet coffee shop? an empty classroom?

EXERCISE 2: SELECT MEMORY STRATEGIES

1. *Choose one of the six suggestions on the previous pages that you'd like to use yourself. Write two or three sentences explaining how you will apply the suggestion to one of the courses you're taking now. Write another sentence describing the results you expect. Date your entry.*

2. *After a week has passed, reread your answer to the previous question. How did the suggestion work for you? Do you plan to continue using the suggestion? Why or why not?*

3. *What other suggestions appeal to you? How do you plan to use them?*

Improve Your Memory with Flash Cards

Some information must be remembered through sheer repetitive drill—the verb endings in French, the bones in a human skeleton, the rhyme scheme in a sonnet. Staring at a book until you've learned the material is neither efficient nor effective. Even if you memorize the information, you can't be sure you'll remember it for a test weeks or months later.

Flash cards are much more effective. Because you can carry them with you and study throughout the day, you won't have to schedule long periods of drill for rote memorization. And their convenience makes flash cards an ideal way to use the spare moments you read about in Chapter Two. You can purchase flash cards to use as study aids in many subjects—or you can create your own.

Do-it-yourself flash cards have three important advantages. First, they cost less. Second, they're custom-made to suit your special needs. Third, the steps you follow in making them—selecting material, turning it into questions, and writing down the questions and answers—are excellent learning strategies in themselves. Often you'll permanently learn a piece of information just by putting it onto a flashcard. A fourth advantage applies to parents who are enrolled in college. Children who are old enough to handle scissors can help make the flash cards—and feel proud that they're contributing to mom or dad's success.

How to Use Flash Cards.
1. Purchase a key ring or shower curtain ring to hold cut-up index cards with a hole punched near one end.
2. Stick a paper reinforcement around the hole to make the cards durable—a bonus if you hope to go to graduate school or take a licensing exam and plan to use the flash cards again.
3. Put a question on one side of each card and the answer on the other side. You can also write lines of poetry, quotations, and formulas to reread until they're memorized.
4. Each morning take a ring of study cards with you when you leave home. Take them out for review any time you have a spare minute. Don't underestimate the value of short study periods—for example, the moments when you're waiting for a class to begin.
5. Every few days remove from the ring any cards that you've mastered. Wrap a rubber band around them, store them in a box, and add new cards to the ring. Once a week, review the cards stored in the box; add any you've forgotten to the ring for a refresher.

You may wonder whether such a simple system can significantly improve your performance on tests. Be assured that it can. Many student are won over when they see how well flash cards work for a friend.

Other Memory Aids

Mnemonic devices. The term "mnemonic" is derived from a Greek word meaning "mindful." A "mnemonic device" is a study aid—often a rhyme or a silly sentence—that helps you recall facts. Countless students of astronomy have learned the planets of our solar system, in their order from the sun, by memorizing this sentence: "My very earnest mother just served us nine pies." "My (Mercury) very (Venus) earnest (Earth) mother (Mars) just (Jupiter) served (Saturn) us (Uranus) nine (Neptune) pies (Pluto)."

Mnemonic devices are fun to invent, and they can help you learn difficult subjects that require extensive memorization. Students in music courses often write their own lyrics (with the name of the piece and the composer) to the melodies of classical music to make identification easier. The first two lines of Beethoven's "Ode to Joy" from his Ninth Symphony, for example, could be sung this way:

> Number nine, number nine,
> "Ode to Joy" of Ludwig van. . . .

Do-it-yourself mnemonics can be created for any subject and shared with your study group for everyone's benefit.

But mnemonic devices have disadvantages. Most students forget them quickly after tests are over—a huge problem if you'll need the information later on for a licensing exam, or for your career. Even worse, mnemonics encourage superficial, "instant" learning. If you're really steeped in classical music, you won't need a gimmick to recognize

Figure 5.4 Flash Cards

Beethoven's Ninth Symphony. A serious student of astronomy is likely to know so much about the solar system that memorizing "My very earnest mother. . ." isn't necessary.

College is more about in-depth learning and critical thinking than quick memorization. Use mnemonics when you think they're appropriate—but always make meaningful remembering a higher priority. If you review material thoroughly, quiz yourself often, and practice other active learning strategies, you probably won't have to rely much on mnemonics.

Tape recordings. You can enhance your learning by listening to both commercially-produced and do-it-yourself learning tapes. Many auditory learners enjoy learning through listening in this way. Libraries are good places to find appropriate tapes; many bookstores also sell them. Most colleges have listening devices called "speech compressors" that make listening to tapes easier by eliminating the spaces between words.

You can also try making your own learning tapes. High-quality cassettes work best; cheaper cassettes usually have too much background noise. At home, you can play cassettes while you do routine tasks that don't require concentration, such as housework and other home upkeep. If you drive a long way to class, try listening to tapes in your car.

If study time is limited, consider listening to a learning tape while you're exercising or commuting.

EXERCISE 3: PRACTICE "ACTIVE LEARNING"

Practice "active learning" by performing these activities.

1. *Use your notes from a recent class or reading assignment to make a mind map.*
2. *Make a set of ten or more flash cards for a course you're taking now. Spend a day carrying them with you for study.*
3. *Invent a mnemonic device to help you memorize information for a course you're taking now.*
4. *Evaluate your experiences with the three previous activities. Did making these learning aids help you learn the material? Do you plan to use any (or all three) learning aids again?*

5. *How might a tape recorder help you learn in other ways besides recording lectures? List as many possibilities as you can. If you can, try at least one technique and evaluate the results.*

Combating Day-to-Day Forgetfulness

You'll probably never be tested about the whereabouts of your keys, eyeglasses, and wallet. But searching for these items can be a frustrating waste of time, especially when you're in a hurry. And other kinds of forgetfulness—with assignments, instructions, and other college requirements—can seriously harm your academic progress.

The solution, surprisingly enough, is to rely as little on your memory as possible. Keep two up-to-date calendars—one for detailed planning, one to carry with you—as explained in Chapter One. Take thorough notes about assignments, and establish a central storage place for all materials related to your studies. Make sure your name, address, and telephone number appear inside all your books and notebooks. Self-sticking address labels are a wise investment. Always leave your keys and eyeglasses in the same spot. (Some students purchase a small basket especially for that purpose and place it on a table or desk near the door.)

A durable bookbag or briefcase is essential for keeping college materials together. Invest also in large manila envelopes to take to the library with you. Label each with your name and telephone number so it will be returned if you lose it; the envelopes are invaluable for storing research information and computer disks.

If "loose and disorganized" has always been your style, you may need some time to adjust to this new system. But once you've mastered it, life will become easier. Instead of struggling to overcome the forgetfulness that plagues almost everyone, your system will do your remembering for you. And you mind will be free to concentrate on more important issues, including your education . . . and your life.

ONE-MINUTE CHECKLIST

The following checklist can help you determine how well your study techniques are working. Use it weekly (or daily if your courses are particularly challenging) to uncover trouble spots before they develop into serious problems.

_____ 1. I've scheduled about two hours of study time for each hour in class.

_____ 2. I stick to my study schedule as much as possible.

_____ 3. During study periods I keep my attention focused on the content I'm learning.

_____ 4. I often use my knowledge of my learning preferences to select study activities.

_____ 5. I discuss what I'm learning with friends or family members.

_____ 6. I've invented memory devices (such as mnemonics) for content that must be learned by rote.

_____ 7. I've been using study aids (such as flash cards, mind maps, sample test questions, and index-card outlines).

_____ 8. I review my notes soon after class.

_____ 9. I seek help when I'm learning difficult material.

_____ 10. I have a study partner or meet regularly with a study group.

_____ 11. I'm keeping a study log for at least one subject.

_____ 12. I know the best times of the day for intense study and use them wisely.

_____ 13. I consider myself an active learner.

 USING WHAT YOU HAVE LEARNED

1. Teach something you've learned recently to a child, friend, or family member. If you and your "student" enjoy the experience, plan to repeat it in the future.
2. Write down the subjects you're studying now. Next to each subject, make a list of activities and learning aids that might help you master the content. Underline the items on your list that you plan to use immediately.

3. For one day, keep an informal list of all the "active learning" strategies you used. Examples might include asking a question in class, underlining an idea in a textbook, or writing a list of vocabulary words in a notebook. Review your list at the end of the day. Is the list longer (or shorter) than you'd expected? Do you plan to make any changes in the future?

4. Reread "How to Form a Study Group" on pages 8 and 9 in Chapter One. Then use your group to learn and review the "Principles of Active Learning" on pages 159 through 161. Assign each group member one principle to present to the rest of the group. Have group members take turns acting as chair and notetaker. When all the presentations are finished, have a group evaluation to evaluate the experience. Did group study help you learn the material? Would you like to continue working with a study group? What did you learn from the experience that might make the group activity more effective in the future?

5. Meet with two or three other students who are keeping a learning log to discuss your experience. Here are a few topics to consider: How does the experience feel? When do you write in your log? What do you write about? On the average, how long do you usually spend writing your entries? What benefits do you expect? What similarities and differences do you observe among the members of the group? What has this discussion taught you about individual learning preferences?

6. Explain the difference between an "active learner" and a "passive learner" to someone who has not taken this course.

▶ EVALUATING YOUR PROGRESS

1. As I look back on the past seven days, I've seen an improvement in these areas:

_____ organizing my life

_____ protecting my health

_____ planning my time

_____ concentrating

_____ taking notes

_____ active learning

_____ reading critically

_____ writing effectively

_____ thinking critically

_____ communicating with important people in my life

_____ enjoying my free time

_____ allowing myself to be imperfect

2. In the coming week, I plan to invest five minutes a day working towards this goal:

CHAPTER 6

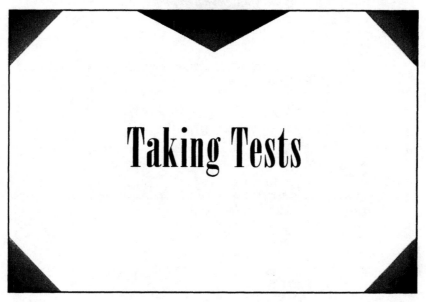

Taking Tests

We have nothing to fear but fear itself.

FRANKLIN D. ROOSEVELT

PREVIEW

1. A positive attitude and thorough preparation are your best weapons against test anxiety.

2. You can choose from many practical strategies to perform better on tests.

3. Critical-thinking skills can help you overcome negative attitudes and enjoy greater success on tests.

IN-CLASS INTRODUCTORY ACTIVITY: HOW DO YOU PREPARE FOR TESTS?

How do you usually prepare for tests? Choose the statement that best describes you. Then complete the activities that follow.

1. *I usually postpone studying and cram right before a test.*

2. *Because I study every day, I don't do much special preparation before a test.*
3. *In the past I haven't cared much and didn't study hard.*
4. *I study regularly, but I still have to cram for tests.*

ACTIVITIES:

1. *Describe how you usually feel when you take a test—your emotions (positive and negative) and level of confidence.*

2. *If you usually experience negative emotions when you take a test, describe how you'd like to feel instead. Be as specific as you can.*

3. *How effective were your study habits in high school?*

4. *Do you think you need to make any changes in your study habits for college? What changes do you think you'd like to make?*

COLLABORATIVE ACTIVITY

Meet with a small group of other students to compare and discuss your answers to Question 4. Write down any changes mentioned in the discussion that you'd like to try yourself.

◆ HAVE A POSITIVE ATTITUDE TOWARD TESTS ◆

Like many students, you may have experienced test anxiety—the shaky, queasy feeling that often accompanies college testing. The good news is that you can learn strategies that build confidence and help you improve your test scores. This chapter will help you develop a realistic attitude towards testing, prepare thoroughly ahead of time, and master several vital test-taking skills.

Put Tests into Perspective

Sometimes students overestimate the importance of tests, thinking the score is a measure of their worth. Nothing could be farther from the truth! A test is simply a measurement (sometimes a highly inaccurate one) of what you know about a subject at a particular time.

A low test score may be the result of insufficient study—but it could have many other causes as well. Perhaps you didn't read the test directions carefully enough, or you didn't understand what the professor wanted, or you didn't allot your time properly while you were answering the questions. A low test score might also be a warning that you're carrying too heavy an academic load, or you need to work with a tutor—or it could point to a totally different problem. What failing a test does *not* mean is that you're a failure as a human being.

Think about all the photographs of yourself that you've seen. Do they really represent what you look like? Of course not. They're two-dimensional, while you're living in

Remind yourself that a test is a measurement of what you know about a subject; it's not a statement about your self-worth.

"A" is for Attitude

American figure skater Debi Thomas was expected to win a gold medal in the 1988 Olympics. All she had to do was skate well in the final freestyle competition.

As often happens in Olympic competition, she made a mistake in the beginning of her freestyle program. The mistake wasn't serious; her competitor Katarina Witt, who was in second place, hadn't skated perfectly either. But more errors followed, and Debi Thomas barely qualified for the third-place bronze medal. Later she said, "Once I missed, my heart wasn't in it."

three dimensions; and they record what you looked like at one moment frozen in time, while you're moving through an ever-changing reality. Tests have similar limitations.

If you find yourself worrying about test scores, start changing your thinking. Ask yourself what will happen if you earn a low score on a test, and formulate a "just-in-case" plan. Could you take the test again? raise your average by doing well on a later test? submit additional work for extra credit? Even important professional tests can usually be retaken. Putting tests into perspective this way prevents the "all-is-lost" panic that paralyzes many students.

Teach yourself to view disappointments as temporary setbacks and useful learning experiences. This kind of positive thinking isn't always easy, but it's such a powerful success tool that it's worth the effort. Learn to take a deep breath, ask "What can I learn from this?" and formulate a new plan.

READING THOUGHTFULLY: SHE DIDN'T GIVE UP

You're about to read about Jacklean Davis, an African American woman who has been called the most successful homicide detective in New Orleans—a remarkable achievement in a field traditionally dominated by men. But Davis is exceptional for other reasons as well: She had difficulty meeting the entrance requirements for the police academy, and she didn't pass the academy course the first time she went through it. In addition, she was a single parent on welfare. Before you begin reading, answer the questions in the following activity.

BEFORE YOU READ

1. Suppose you were the director of a police academy. A young woman wants a career in law-enforcement but keeps failing the entrance test; you've also learned that she's afraid of weapons. What advice would you give her?

2. How do you handle setbacks? Think of at least two examples from school or other experiences.

---

from   **"One of New Orleans' Finest"**[*]
by Michael Ryan

Detective Jacklean Davis describes herself as "a very insecure child" who grew up wanting to make something of her life. Although she had a young daughter—she became pregnant at sixteen—she forced herself to finish high school. "Then I was on welfare," she said. "I knew that if I didn't do something right away, I would probably be on welfare for years."

Davis decided to go into law enforcement, took the examination for the police academy, and failed it. She took it again and failed. And again and again. On her fifth try, she finally made it; "I barely passed, but that didn't matter. What was important was that I passed."

Life wasn't any easier at the academy. "I went through it twice," she said. "This time, it wasn't because I failed—it was because of my fear of guns."

Davis overcame her fear of guns after many hours of practice, shooting repeatedly at targets until she became used to handling weapons. On her second attempt, she graduated from the academy.

Her goal was to become a homicide detective. "Homicide is considered the cream of the crop," she said. But getting there was tough. "On the majority of homicide units I've seen," she said, "recruitment is not always fair. You have to get past the stigma of being a female—let alone a black female." Rebuffed several times, she finally was placed on the elite squad when her work on a rape case helped lead to the capture of a serial killer.

Norman Pierce, a veteran homicide detective, praises her work. "If you needed anybody to go with you on a homicide, all you had to do was ask her. She was always eager to work, always eager to help you." Using contacts from neighborhoods she had patrolled, Davis followed up on leads others might have missed. The results were spectacular. Of the ninety cases assigned to her, arrests were made—or a suspect was identified—in eighty-eight. Her platoon cleared nearly eighty percent of its cases.

What keeps Jackie going? "When I was young, I was always told that I was not going to accomplish anything," she said. "I felt that, if I give up or if I screw up, it's going to be on Jackie's account, not because anybody else made her give up."

---

[*]Reprinted with permission from Parade, copyright © 1993.

AFTER YOU READ

1. List any words that are new to you. What strategy will you use to learn them?

2. Did any questions occur to you while you were reading? If so, how will you find the answers?

3. What character traits helped Jackie stay motivated during her struggle to become a police officer?

4. List the choices Jackie has made in her life. How effective were they?

5. What is Jackie's philosophy?

6. What challenges do you face in your college life?

7. What is your philosophy concerning facing challenges?

Set Realistic Academic Goals

Some students want so much to achieve perfection on tests that they increase their stress levels and set themselves up for failure. Are you one of them? To find out, answer these questions:

1. Do you take pride in forcing yourself to meet high standards?
2. Do you believe that you should always perform perfectly?
3. Do you fall into despair when you don't meet your own high expectations?

A "yes" answer to two of these questions can mean you're too hard on yourself. Of course there's nothing wrong with striving to do your best. But forcing yourself to meet impossibly high standards can lead to anxiety, depression, and even suicide. Even worse, it can weaken your courage, causing you to avoid new experiences and new challenges. If you tend to overemphasize the importance of success, now is the time to start changing your attitude.

First, realize you can't always predict what will appear on a test, how a professor assigns grades, or how well you'll perform a particular task. Successful people learn not to dwell too long on setbacks: They quickly pick themselves up and start working towards their next goal.

Second, ask whether you really want to spend the rest of your life allowing others to determine your self-worth. You don't have to be depressed and unhappy because someone else didn't like your work. College is a good time to teach yourself how to handle negative feedback effectively. Ask: Have I learned anything that will help me reach my goals? Some types of feedback are useful; others aren't. Learn to discriminate between the two, and to dismiss whatever feedback isn't helpful to you.

Don't be fooled into thinking that this change of attitude is a form of weakness. It takes strength and courage to say, "I'm proud that I followed my study plan, even though I didn't earn the grade I wanted." Successful people know how to congratulate themselves for following through on a program they set for themselves, even when evaluations from others are disappointing. You'll develop confidence and poise by following their example.

How Much Satisfaction Are You Experiencing? In *Feeling Good*, Dr. David Burns described a physician who became depressed whenever he had to face his own shortcomings. Burns taught him how to use a "satisfaction scale" that changed the physician's attitude and banished his depression. After each task the physician completed, he was told to grade *both* his effectiveness and his level of satisfaction. The physician quickly discovered that he could feel excited and happy even about a household task he had done clumsily and inefficiently. Fixing a kitchen sink one Saturday morning, for example, was disastrous. He made many mistakes and needed a great deal of help from a neighbor. But he still experienced a thrill when he turned on the faucet and saw that the plumbing was working.

How many times have you had a wonderful time doing something inefficiently or ineffectively? Can you have fun roller skating, baking a pie, or singing even if you're not the world's best at it? If the answer is *no*, it's time to change your thinking. Keep reminding yourself that "A" is for attitude, not achievement.

◆ HOW TO PREPARE FOR TESTS ◆

Thorough preparation is a powerful weapon against test anxiety. The time-management and active-learning strategies you've already learned can help you feel confident when you take a test. Another benefit is that thorough preparation helps you retain much of what you're learning.

"Cramming," by contrast, increases anxiety levels because of the pressure to learn a great deal of information quickly. Even worse, it results in only short-term learning—if, indeed, the information is absorbed at all. Putting yourself on a study schedule early in the term helps you avoid the stress and frustration of last-minute cramming sessions. The following suggestions can also build your confidence when you're preparing to take a test:

1. Ask your professor what the test will be like. Some professors are happy to tell students what to expect from the test—how long it will be, what information will be emphasized, and what kinds of questions will be asked.

Two Famous Failures

Recent British literary history records the stories of two famous men who started their careers as failures. The first, playwright George Bernard Shaw, began his writing career by producing five novels, all of which were rejected repeatedly. "I was a complete professional failure," he wrote. "The more I wrote and the better I wrote, the less I pleased the publishers. . . . Fifty or sixty refusals without a single acceptance forced me into a fierce self-sufficiency. I became undiscourageable, acquiring a superhuman indifference to praise or blame which has been useful to me since. . . ." The novels were finally published after Shaw became famous, and he received warm praise from many readers and critics.

The second "failure" was C. S. Lewis, a great British scholar of English literature, who couldn't pass the mathematics entrance exam for Oxford University. He had been well instructed in math but always made careless errors. While he was deciding what to do about his future, World War I broke out; Lewis enlisted in the British Army and served honorably. After the war, Great Britain showed its gratitude to the veterans by allowing them to skip some entrance requirements for universities. Lewis was finally admitted, excelled in his studies, and became one of Oxford's most distinguished graduates. Moral: Don't be too impressed by failure—in others and in yourself.

You'll learn more efficiently if your study plan includes a variety of settings and activities.

Write down the information you're given and use it to design your study plan (explained on page 190). Then try writing a practice test based on what you were told about the test. Taking this test a few times is excellent preparation; you can also exchange student-made tests with study partners.

If your professor prefers not to give advance information, do some detective work on your own. What topics were emphasized in lectures and readings? What have you learned about the professor from previous tests? Do not, however, rely too much on hunches. One art student failed an important test because she studied the work of only one painter—Claude Monet, her professor's favorite Impressionist. Be as thorough as you can in reviewing course material.

2. Check your mastery by testing yourself on your notes and other study aids. In Chapter Three you saw that the Cornell notetaking format can be used for test preparation. Fold back or cover up the large area on the right where you wrote your class notes. Then, using the key words and questions in the left margins as prompts, recite your notes from memory. An alternative is to cover up your notes so that only the bottom area is showing. The summary you wrote there can also be a prompt for recitation.If you've been making mind maps for information you've been studying, try drawing them from memory: You'll quickly be able to tell how thoroughly you know the material.

3. If you need help, get it beforehand. Make use of campus tutoring services, the library, and the college learning center. Find a study partner who can help you with mate-

rial you don't understand; ask your study group to schedule a review session. Any time you encounter material that might cause you difficulty on a test, find a way to conquer it. Creativity and determination are important factors in academic success.

GETTING IN TOUCH THROUGH FREEWRITING

Freewrite for three or four minutes about the test-taker you'd like to be. How would you like to feel, think, and act when you're taking a test?

Now freewrite about changes you could make to transform yourself into the test-taker you've just described. Let your imagination work freely; you don't have to make every change you write about here.

Reread what you've just written, and underline any change (or changes) you're willing to work on today. In the space below, describe specific steps you want to take immediately.

What's the Worst that Could Happen?

When you find yourself worrying about a challenge that lies ahead, ask yourself: "What's the worst that could happen?"

Suppose you're worried about a math test. The worst that could happen might be getting a D in the course. You don't want a D because it would lower your grade-point average and your parents would be disappointed. Think: Would those consequences significantly diminish the quality of the rest of your life? Unlikely! And you could retake the course, and maybe your parents would understand. . . .

Asking yourself this question puts fears into perspective so that you can concentrate on the present, rather than the future, and do something positive to prepare for that math test. You can also use this question to help friends and family members handle their fears in a positive way. Whenever you help another person in this way, you're strengthening your own ability to handle negative emotions.

Planning for Success on Tests

Opportunity is missed by most people because it is dressed in overalls and looks like work.

THOMAS A. EDISON

Planning is essential to effective test preparation. If tests worry you (as they do many students), decide right now to convert your worries into something more constructive—a plan. Worrying does nothing positive for you, and its negative effects can be severe: high stress levels, mental paralysis, anxiety, irritability, insomnia.

Planning, by contrast, has several important benefits. First, a plan gives your mind something positive to think about instead of worrying. You can practice gently turning your attention to the plan whenever worries begin to form. This kind of mental discipline is important to success in any field.

Next, a well-designed plan almost guarantees that you'll be well prepared for testing. By managing your time wisely and making a thorough list of study tasks, you can feel confident that you've learned the material thoroughly.

A good study plan also reduces stress. When an important test is coming up, you can allow yourself a break from studying for some guilt-free fun with your friends. Non-stop, last-minute cramming is no guarantee that you'll improve your test performance—and it won't be necessary if you've followed your plan.

Most important, planning enables you to use a variety of strategies to get ready for tests. You can go over your flash cards and notes, meet with a study group, design a practice test for yourself, and spend a few minutes daily on positive self-talk (explained later in this chapter).

Students who *don't* have a plan tend to fall into one of two traps. Some begin studying enthusiastically but lose momentum before they've learned all the material. Others procrastinate until it's too late to learn more than a fraction of what they need to know.

If you've ever had to cram for a test, you're probably familiar with one (or both) of these mistakes. Now's the time to switch to a more productive system.

How to Make a Study Plan. Here are the steps to follow as you make a study plan:

1. List the material you need to cover before your test. Check your notes, class hand-outs and textbook assignments to make sure your list is complete.

2. Choose a study strategy (or several, if needed), for each item on your list. Estimate how long each strategy will take. Be creative: include reading, flash cards, mind-mapping, listening to tapes, study groups, practice testing, and any other techniques that will help.

3. On your planning calendar, block out time for each strategy. You may want to write your entries in pencil so you can modify them while you're working out your plan.

4. Evaluate each day's schedule to make sure it's practical, and build in time for rest and recreation. Include flexibility in your plan as well: Delays and unforeseen events happen to everyone.

5. Plan a small celebration after your exam—or a larger one if you're taking exams for a whole week. *Don't* delay celebrating until you get your grades; you want to con-

Plan a small celebration after a test to reward yourself for following your study plan.

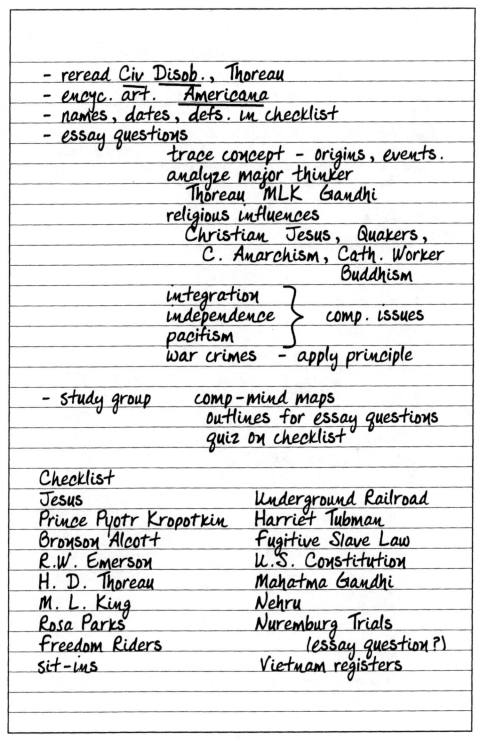

- reread Civ Disob., Thoreau
- encyc. art. Americana
- names, dates, defs. in checklist
- essay questions
      trace concept - origins, events.
      analyze major thinker
          Thoreau MLK Gandhi
      religious influences
          Christian Jesus, Quakers,
            C. Anarchism, Cath. Worker
                        Buddhism
      integration ⎤
      independence ⎬ comp. issues
      pacifism   ⎦
      war crimes - apply principle

- study group   comp-mind maps
                  outlines for essay questions
                  quiz on checklist

Checklist
Jesus   Underground Railroad
Prince Pyotr Kropotkin   Harriet Tubman
Bronson Alcott   Fugitive Slave Law
R.W. Emerson   U.S. Constitution
H. D. Thoreau   Mahatma Gandhi
M. L. King   Nehru
Rosa Parks   Nuremburg Trials
Freedom Riders   (essay question?)
sit-ins   Vietnam registers

Figure 6.1 Study Plan: Issues in World History—Civil Disobedience

gratulate yourself on your study strategies, not your scores. High performers in every field learn not to wait for external results to feel good about themselves. Instead they teach themselves to feel good about meeting their own goals successfully. You can do the same.

JOURNAL ACTIVITY: CARRY OUT YOUR STUDY PLAN

For the next seven days, carry out the study plan you've designed for yourself (page 190). In the spaces below, briefly note what part of the plan you carried out each day; then add comments about the experience. Was your plan for that day realistic? effective? Is there any feature of the plan that you'd do differently next time?

DAY 1

Tasks you performed from your study plan:

Your comments:

DAY 2

Tasks you performed from your study plan:

Your comments:

DAY 3

Tasks you performed from your study plan:

Your comments:

DAY 4

Tasks you performed from your study plan:

Your comments:

DAY 5

Tasks you performed from your study plan:

Your comments:

DAY 6

Tasks you performed from your study plan:

Your comments:

DAY 7

Tasks you performed from your study plan:

Your comments:

How to Talk to Yourself about a Test

In Chapter Four, you saw that there's a right way and a wrong way to talk to yourself. Statements like "I had no other choice" put others in control; statements like "I'm in charge of this situation" put you in the driver's seat. You can use the same positive self-talk to help yourself feel more confident about test-taking.

Start noticing what happens inside your head when you think about a test. Then practice substituting positive statements for the negative ones you're hearing. Here are some examples:

Change "I hate tests" to "I'm looking forward to doing well on this one."
Change "I'm stupid" to "I'm excited about learning."
Change "I always mess up" to "I'm successful in many areas in my life."
Change "This is hopeless" to "I'm doing something positive about it right now."
Change "I'll never learn this" to "I have a good study plan."
Change "I've always done poorly" to "I'm looking forward to success in college."

This positive "self-talk" can reduce your anxiety, spark you to study harder, and help you score higher on a test.

When you start trying to change your self-talk, you may find that the negative thoughts keep coming back. That's normal in the beginning because old thinking habits are hard to break. Accept what's happening and reinforce your new habit with a positive statement: "I'm learning to talk to myself in a positive way." You can also read from your Success Journal for a few minutes each day. With persistence, you'll find yourself taking tests more confidently—and you'll be able to teach others this valuable skill.

EXERCISE 1: PRACTICE POSITIVE SELF-TALK

In the space below, write ten positive statements you can say to yourself before a test.

ONE-MINUTE CHECKLIST

These questions will help you evaluate your preparations for testing. "Yes" answers mean that you're probably well prepared; "no" answers suggest a need to alter your preparations.

_____ I asked the professor for information about test format, types of questions, and material to be covered.

_____ I made a complete list of test topics.

_____ I selected study strategies for the information I need to learn (making mind maps and flash cards, listening to tapes, meeting with a study partner or study group, reading, visiting the learning lab).

_____ I made up and used a practice test based on the information I expect to find on the test.

_____ On my planning calendar, I set aside time for specific study tasks: reading, review, practice testing, relaxation, and positive self-talk.

_____ I reviewed my plan to make sure it is flexible, realistic, and thorough.

_____ I carried out my study plan each day.

_____ When I had negative thoughts about the test, I changed them to positive ones.

_____ I learned test-taking strategies (explained later in this chapter) for the kind of test I expect to be taking.

_____ I planned a post-test celebration—not for earning a high grade, but for sticking to my study plan.

◆ HOW TO TAKE TESTS ◆

You've already seen that thorough preparation and a positive attitude are powerful tools against test anxiety. A third important tool is skill at test-taking itself. The information on the following pages will help you avoid careless errors, understand test questions, think critically, and use your time effectively when you take a test. (Additional suggestions for science tests appear in Chapter Ten; information about math tests is given in Chapter Eleven.)

Objective Test Items

Although there's no substitute for thorough preparation, these test-taking strategies can increase your chances of scoring well on objective test items (true-false, multiple choice, matching, fill-in-the-blank questions).

True-False Questions. Remember that it takes just one word to turn a true statement into a false one. Qualifying words like *always, sometimes, never, only, often, occasionally, no, not* can be important clues. Try these examples:

1. The Electoral College decides which presidential candidate will take office. True or false?
2. American Presidents are always chosen by the Electoral College. True or false?
3. Composer Scott Joplin incorporated African-American syncopation into his distinctive piano compositions. True or false?
4. Composer Scott Joplin used only African-American syncopation to create his distinctive piano compositions. True or false?

Although 1 and 2 are similar, 1 is true while 2 is false. The Electoral College does decide which presidential candidate will take office (Statement 1). But the United States has had a president—Gerald Ford—who was never elected. Richard Nixon named him to replace Vice President Spiro Agnew, who resigned from office. Later, when Nixon himself resigned, Ford—who hadn't run for either office—became president (Statement 2). (The statement is false for another reason as well: The Constitution directs the House of Representatives to choose the president if no candidate wins a majority of the electoral votes.)

Similarly, questions 3 and 4 are similar, but 3 is true, while 4 is false. Joplin indeed used African-American syncopation in his compositions (Statement 3). But Joplin also used Mexican rhythm (in "Solace") and German waltz form (in "Bethena"), making Statement 4 false.

True-false questions can be tricky. Sometimes a statement will combine a fact with information that's false, like this:

5. During Ramadan, the tenth month in the Muslim calendar, devout Muslims fast from sunrise to sunset. True or false?

This statement is false. Although the information about fasting is correct, Ramadan is the *ninth* month (not the tenth) in the Muslim calendar.

In spite of their difficulties, true-false questions have two advantages. First, they're usually shorter than multiple-choice questions. Second, you have at least a fifty-fifty chance of being correct. If you have to guess, improve your odds slightly by assuming that long statements, with lots of qualifiers, are probably false. Remember too that teachers usually write "true" questions more often than "false" ones. But you're unlikely to increase your fifty-fifty odds with true-false questions that you don't know; avoid second-guessing or spending too much time on them.

Multiple-choice Questions. Budget your time carefully. Because multiple-choice items may contain information that will help you answer other questions, always read the whole test once before you mark any answers. If a multiple-choice question seems long or complex, skip it the first time; go back to it only after you've answered the easier questions.

Read all the parts of a multiple-choice item carefully. Misreading can cause you to make the wrong choice even if you knew the correct answer. Notice too whether the instructions call for the *best* answer. This type of multiple-choice question is particularly challenging because you may find two choices attractive. Look for the best one, but don't waste too much time agonizing over the differences: You won't increase your chances beyond fifty percent, and you'll probably need all the time you're allowed to complete the test.

If you have to guess, try to improve your odds by eliminating at least one obvious wrong choice. If you have no clue about the correct answer (and there's no penalty for guessing), research has shown that the longest choice is most likely to be correct.

Sometimes you'll find complex choices in multiple-choice questions: "all of the above," "none of the above," "A and B," as in these sample questions:

1. If you're trying to eat less refined sugar, which foods should you limit?

    a. Jams and jellies
    b. Cake
    c. Fresh fruits
    d. a and b

The correct answer is d.

2. Which strategies can increase your ability to concentrate?

    a. Get less sleep to allow more time for study.
    b. Tune your radio to your favorite station.
    c. Save your most difficult assignments to do last.
    d. All the above
    e. None of the above

The correct answer is e.

Allow extra time for complicated multiple-choice questions, and think about each choice carefully. If you're allowed to write on the test paper, crossing out incorrect choices can simplify questions, increasing your chances of finding the right answer. Do not, however, spend too much time on any question.

Matching Questions. If possible, mark your answers lightly in pencil, or use scratch paper the first time you work through the list of matches. And cross out any matches you make to save time as you look for the remaining ones. Be cautious; one incorrect match can start a chain reaction, causing you to lose many points. Wait till you're satisfied with all the matches to mark them on the answer sheet.

Sample question: Match each number below with one of the letters that follow. Use each number and letter only once.

1. may be long, complex, and time-consuming
2. watch out for chain reactions
3. fifty-fifty chance of choosing the correct answer
a. true-false item
b. matching question
c. multiple-choice item

Either a, b, or c could be applied to #1: "may be long, complex and time-consuming." But if you look for matches for #2 and #3, you'll see that #1 must be matched with c: "multiple-choice item." Taking a second look at choices in a matching question is always a good strategy.

Fill-in-the-Blank Questions. These questions can be troublesome because more than one answer may fit into the blank. An answer that seems correct to you may not be what your professor had in mind. If you run into that problem, you may be able to ask your professor for clarification during the test. Don't ask, "Is my answer correct?" Instead, ask a question like one of these:

Were you expecting a date here?

Are you looking for a person's name?

Is this question about a chemical process?

After reading the following test item, think of a clarifying question you could ask:

What we now call "Massachusetts" was originally a _____.

Here are two clarifying questions:

Are you looking for a descriptive word? [wilderness]

Would a political term fit here? [colony]

Notice that the words in the test question provide an important clue. "Indian settlement" is obviously the *wrong* answer because "a Indian settlement" is grammatically incorrect and wouldn't fit the statement on the test.

Here are a few more suggestions:

1. Don't be influenced by the length of the blank space. A professor may want a long answer even though the blank space is small.

2. Try asking for clarification if you think two words might fit in a single space, as in this question:

Eli Whitney invented the _____. [cotton gin]

3. Read the question carefully to be sure your answer makes sense.

Use Testing Time Effectively on Objective Tests. Time is often an important factor in test-taking—and one that many students misunderstand. If you rush through a test, or budget your time improperly, you may be disappointed in your score.

Make a habit of taking all the time you need to answer the test questions. Sometimes students are afraid to stay for the whole test period, fearing that others will have a low opinion of them. The truth is just the opposite: Successful students always stay long enough to take a test thoughtfully and check their work.

On the other hand, you may miss questions because you run out of time. To conquer this problem, practice placing test questions into A, B, and C categories. The "A" category includes two types of questions: those with high point value assigned by the professor, and ones that you can answer easily and quickly. Tackle these first, skipping over the rest of the test items. Answer "B" questions next—those with lower point value, and ones requiring more thought. The remaining items are "C" questions: Do these last.

Here's a detailed explanation of how this system works:

1. First read the entire test rapidly. This gives your mind a chance to search for information you might have learned once and forgotten. Have you ever suddenly remembered an answer after you handed in a test? This read-ahead system will help you retrieve "lost" information. You may also find that the test itself has information that will help you score better. Facts stated in a multiple-choice item may help you answer an essay question.

2. If the test is long and divided into sections, see if the professor has labeled the point value of each section; then allot your time accordingly. If an essay is worth 25 percent of your total score, you should spend approximately one-fourth of your time on your answer. A question worth only five percent of the total should receive less of your time.

3. If you're not sure of the answer to a question with high point value, try at least to write some kind of relevant information. A history professor may give you partial credit for a list of events and dates, even if you don't organize them into a complete essay. Math and science professors may give you points if you make a diagram or list the steps needed to solve a problem, even if you don't complete it.

4. After you've answered questions with high point value, take a close look at the remaining questions. Mentally label them "A"—questions you're likely to get right; "B"—questions you're unsure about; "C"—questions requiring guessing.

5. Begin with the A questions, skipping over the ones you labeled B and C. (If you're using an answer sheet, be careful not to lose your place.) At first you may feel uncomfortable skipping questions like this. Remember, though, you want to earn points for anything you know. If you slow down to think about a difficult test item, you may not have time for questions you could have answered easily on the last part of the test.

6. Now answer the questions you labeled "B"—items you're unsure about. Don't spend too long on any one of them. If they're multiple-choice, eliminate any answers you know are wrong, and choose quickly from the remaining choices. Don't spend too long on true-false questions either; at best you have a fifty-fifty chance of guessing correctly.

7. Answer C questions last. If there's a penalty for guessing, and you have no clue to the correct answer, leave a C question blank. If you think you have a chance at getting the question right, or there's no penalty for guessing, make the best choice you can. But don't spend too long on any question.

8. If time remains, check your work; by now your mind may have retrieved some "lost" information from your memory. You may also be able to correct a few careless errors you'd made. Don't outsmart yourself, however. Usually your first answer to a test question is the correct one. Don't change an answer without a very good reason.

After a few tests, you'll develop confidence in this A-B-C system, and time limits will seem less threatening. Strategic use of your time combined with thorough preparation are keys to success on tests—make use of both.

Essay Tests. Many students say they find essay tests more challenging than any other type of college examination. But with careful planning and ample study, you can learn to write superior answers to the essay questions on college tests.

1. Begin your preparation by listing all the important ideas, events, principles, or names that might appear as essay topics on your test. Decide which you already know

Make an informal outline before you answer an essay question, and find out ahead of time if you'll be allowed to use a dictionary.

thoroughly and which need more study. In your study plan, set aside time to learn and review them.

2. Invest a significant part of your study time outlining and creating mind maps of the material you've listed. Your outlines don't have to be elaborate; just write a heading on your paper, and jot down supporting ideas, details, and examples. Remember that professors look for well-developed essays; list as many facts as you can, and commit them to memory.

3. Remind yourself that essay tests often require critical thinking skills. You may be asked to evaluate a government policy or apply a psychological principle, for example. Participation in class discussions is probably the best way to prepare for tasks like these. Study groups are helpful as well because they give you an opportunity to develop critical-thinking skills with other students.

4. When you're taking the test itself, begin by making a quick, informal outline or mind map of the information you plan to include in your answer. Then start your essay with your main idea, based on the test question, and develop it with details, explanations, and examples. Refer to the outline or mind map occasionally to ensure that your essay is well organized and complete. If time is short, or you don't think you can write a passable essay, hand in the mind map or outline you made; it may earn partial credit for you.

5. Be neat. Professors try not to be influenced by handwriting, but it's best not to make a negative impression. Take two good pens with you to the test. If you use your own paper, bring a supply of clean, straight-edged looseleaf paper with you. Avoid messy correction fluid and erasures; cross out errors with a single neat line. Don't scribble or trace over words.

6. Skip lines, and use only one side of the paper.

7. Ask ahead of time if a dictionary or electronic speller is permitted. If the answer is "yes," come to the test prepared.

8. Allow time to reread your essay, make neat corrections, and check your information for accuracy before you hand it in.

9. Don't write a preliminary first draft of your essay during the test; there's almost never enough time for rewriting.

10. Reread your essay and make neat corrections before you hand it in.

11. If you're given a choice between two or more essay topics, make your decision quickly and stick to it. There's almost never enough time to discard a half-written essay and begin a new one.

Informal outline for an essay question:
    Why is reflective listening important to nurses?

Why nurses listen
a) empathize
b) support
c) clarify
d) learn

Notice that the student incorporates the question into her answer:

Reflective listening is important to nurses for four reasons. First, it helps nurses empathize with their patients. In reflective listening, the nurse avoids directing or discounting the patient's thoughts and ideas. As a result the patient feels that the nurse understands his or her thoughts and feelings. Second, reflective listening

Figure 6.2 Answering the Essay Question

How to Relax

If you get nervous before tests, there's good news for you: Those feelings are perfectly normal—and you can do something about them. You can use the following relaxation exercise to convert nervousness into confidence. The six steps below are ideal to practice when you need a break from studying. When you're accustomed to them, you can quietly go through these steps in the testing room to prepare yourself to do your best.

Don't be fooled by the simplicity of this exercise—it really works. By developing your mental powers through exercises like this one, you're preparing yourself to meet the unknown challenges that lie ahead. The positive results—both now and in the future—are well worth the small investment in time and effort.

Step 1. Sit in a comfortable chair in a quiet, pleasant place. Close your eyes and relax; loosen your shoelaces and belt if necessary. Take five slow, deep breaths.

Step 2. Imagine a warm, pleasant feeling in the toes of your left foot. Now imagine that the warmth is traveling up your leg, across your body, and down your other leg to your right foot.

Step 3. Imagine the warmth is going up your back, down your left and right arms, across your shoulders, across your scalp, and into your face.

Step 4. Take five more slow, deep breaths. Then remember a time in your life when you performed in some way that made you proud and happy. Remember those feelings and savor them.

Step 5. Visualize as vividly as you can the place in which you'll meet your new challenge. (If you're already in the testing room, or another stressful situation, omit this visualization.) Picture yourself smiling, performing the task easily, and feeling proud. Transfer the feelings you had about your past accomplishment into the new one.

Step 6. Take five more slow, deep breaths, holding on to the good feelings, and slowly open your eyes.

Raising Test Scores Through Critical Thinking

You can raise your grades by applying critical-thinking skills during study periods and testing sessions. These skills improve your performance in three important ways. First, you'll be better prepared because thinking critically makes you an active learner. Second, you'll understand and answer test questions more effectively. Third, you'll avoid the thoughtless errors that often lower students' test scores. Many students have found these critical-thinking suggestions helpful:

1. Examine your assumptions about the test. Long hours of review won't help you much if you studied the wrong material or prepared for the wrong type of test. One biol-

ogy student memorized many facts about the Krebs cycle, assuming he would be answering multiple-choice questions. But the test required a detailed diagram explaining all the steps in the cycle—and the student barely passed.

Another student failed an important business law test because he assumed he had to answer all eight questions. Two of the questions were difficult for him, and he ran out of time while struggling to answer them. If he'd read the directions ("Answer four of the following eight questions"), he might have earned an A.

2. Look for meaningful connections in the information you're studying. Factual information may not be enough to pass a college test. Professors frequently want you to use critical thinking to establish relationships between various kinds of information, especially on essay tests. When you're studying, ask yourself relationship questions like these:

> Causes: What were the main causes of the War Between the States?
>
> Effects: How does oxygen deprivation affect the muscles of the human body?
>
> Common features (comparison): In what ways is the United States Congress similar to the British Houses of Parliament?
>
> Distinguishing features (contrast): Explain three features of Sigmund Freud's psychological theory that his student Carl Jung rejected.

You'll find that some of these relationships work especially well with certain types of information. In social science courses, you'll find it helpful to make comparisons and contrasts between the theories you're studying. In the physical sciences, causes and effects are extremely important, especially when you're studying processes. And you'll discover many other relationships if you make the effort to look for them. For example, causes and effects are essential to an understanding of historical events; comparisons are useful when you're learning about literary genres.

Common Thinking Errors on Tests. Always make sure you understand a test's requirements. You may need to reread a question, draw a diagram, ask for clarification, or recheck your work.

One student failed an important exam in Italian because she didn't monitor her thinking processes. The test required students to translate a literary passage from Italian to English. She wrote out her translation word by word without bothering to see if it made sense. Her translation was so garbled that she failed the examination.

In another case, poor thinking skills caused many students to miss this simple question on a math test:

> An executive assistant is making dinner reservations for 57 business managers who will be in town for a meeting. Six managers can sit at each table in the restaurant. How many tables should be reserved?

The students correctly divided 57 by 6, coming up with the answer 9 1/2. But that's wrong because the executive assistant couldn't reserve half a table at a restaurant. Ten tables were needed to accommodate the group. Always ask, "Does my answer make sense?" after you complete a test item.

Here are five common test-taking errors:

1. Applying the wrong rule or formula. Make sure ahead of time that you understand the rules or formulas you'll be using. Students of geometry often make the mistake of using the formula for the *circumference* of a circle to calculate the *area* of a circle. English professors say that many students use commas where semicolons are needed.

2. Skipping steps in the thinking process. Before you solve a problem, use scratch paper to list the steps needed—and make sure you complete each one. Mathematical word problems often require three or more steps; so do explanations of scientific processes. Sometimes students are so proud of their ability to solve a problem "in their heads" that they make careless errors. Research has shown that top thinkers in every field place a high value on accuracy. High performers often work more slowly—drawing diagrams, listing facts, and rechecking their work—than less successful people in the same field. And if you write diagrams and steps on your test paper, you may receive partial credit even if your final answer is incorrect.

3. Failing to apply information taught in class. When you're reading a test question, think first about what the professor said in class: Often you'll find the correct answer there. And be sure to use the procedures you've learned in class. Students often score poorly on English usage tests because they look for an answer that sounds right instead of taking the time to apply a punctuation or pronoun rule. In a psychology case study, many students forget to consider behavioral principles discussed in class.

4. Guessing rather than thinking systematically. In college, the process you use to answer a question may be as important as the answer itself. Students in one reading class earned low grades because they read an essay only once and guessed at the answers to questions about it. They could have raised their scores significantly by checking their answers against the reading passage. Science and math tests often require the same patient, systematic thinking.

5. Providing too little support for a conclusion. Supporting evidence is essential to success on essay tests. On one American history test, students were asked to describe two factors that attracted immigrants to this country. One student wrote about economic opportunity and religious freedom, but he did not support his answer with any specific groups: Russian Jews, Irish farmers, European Protestants. To avoid similar problems on essay tests, prepare outlines and mind-maps when you're studying; make sure you know both the most important concepts and enough supporting information to write an effective essay.

Taking Tests

Most of the tests you'll take in college are designed by professors. But you may also take statewide or national tests published by professional organizations. Licensing examinations fall into this category; so do competency tests, the Graduate Record Examination, and many others. To perform well on these "standardized tests," you should be familiar with their special features:

1. Standardized tests contain only objective questions that can be scored electronically (except for writing samples required on some examinations). Most questions are multiple choice; sometimes true-false questions may also be included. If you find objective questions especially difficult, review pages 196 through 200.

2. These tests are scored electronically. Use only the pencil provided; the scoring machine may not be able to read marks made by an ordinary pencil. Avoid messy erasures and stray pencil marks, which the machine may misread.

3. Many standardized tests are long. Arrive rested, wearing comfortable clothing, and bring a snack with you. Since it's easy to lose your place on the answer sheet during a long test, use a piece of paper as a placeholder. Be especially careful to keep track of your place if you skip questions. Read the instructions carefully, and remember that questions may appear on both sides of the page.

4. Standardized tests are designed differently from tests written by an instructor. To earn a grade of 90 on an ordinary college test, you have to answer ninety percent of the questions correctly. But standardized tests report how you compare with other students who have taken the test. You will *not* be graded on the percentage of questions you answer correctly.

If most students had difficulty with a standardized test, and you perform slightly better than 89 percent of them, you will be placed in the ninetieth percentile. It doesn't matter that you missed many questions *if* other students missed even more than you did.

It's important to remember this information if a standardized test seems very difficult. Don't get discouraged; you may still receive a high percentile score.

5. Many standardized tests contain experimental questions that aren't figured in your final score. These questions are there for research purposes, to see if they can be included in future tests. Since it's impossible to tell which questions are experimental, don't spend too long on any test item: It may not count in your final score.

6. Time is an important factor. Most professors try to design tests that students can complete successfully during the test period. But some standardized tests are extremely long, and students may not be expected to finish. Make the best use of your time by following A, B, C method explained on pages 199–200.

7. Many standardized examinations emphasize vocabulary questions. Much current research suggests that the size of your vocabulary is a better predictor of academic ability than a standard I.Q. (intelligence quotient) test. The Johnson O'Connor Foundation, famous for its career testing and counseling service, doesn't even administer I.Q. tests; it relies on vocabulary testing. If you're dissatisfied with the size of your vocabulary, see the suggestions on page 289.

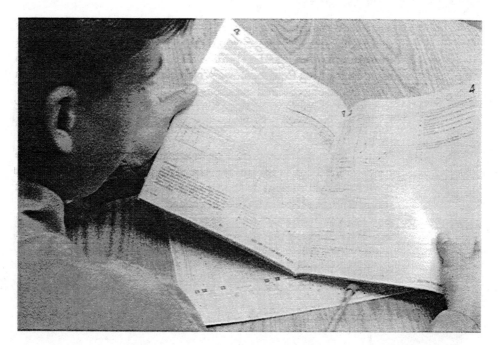

Acquaint yourself with the special features of a standardized test well before the test date.
The testing office on your campus is a good information source.

8. Reading is another important factor in standardized tests. If you can't comprehend the test questions, or your reading rate is extremely slow, you won't score well. The next chapter in this book offers many suggestions for improving your reading skills.

9. Often practice tests and review materials can be purchased or borrowed from a library. Well before you plan to take a standardized test, purchase or borrow a book about it. Familiarize yourself with the test, and work as many of the practice questions as you can.

10. If possible, attend preparatory workshops and review classes. Your campus may offer these several times a year; they may also be sponsored by the public school system in your area, or by a privately owned company specializing in test preparation. Notices about these services often appear on bulletin boards and in campus publications. The testing office on your campus is another good source of information.

 USING WHAT YOU HAVE LEARNED

1. List the important concepts you learned this week in a course you're taking then develop each concept with definitions, examples, and facts. Ask a study partner to prepare a similar list, then compare the results. Would you benefit by studying with

a partner throughout the course? Or do you seem to be able to cover the material thoroughly yourself? Or can you think of other strategies that might be helpful?

2. Prepare a mind-map and an outline for a concept you've been studying. Then try reproducing both from memory. Which experience was more successful for you?

3. Make up ten objective test questions for a subject you're studying. Then ask a study partner to answer the questions you wrote and give you feedback about them. Finally, evaluate this experience. What did you learn that might be helpful when you take your next test?

4. Write a letter to a friend (real or imaginary) who's worried about failing a test. Emphasize that "A" is for attitude, not achievement; use examples and ideas of your own to help your friend develop a more positive attitude. Then save the letter to reread before each test you take in college.

5. Buy a review book about a course you're taking now, or borrow one from the college library. Pretend that the review questions are test items, and apply the test-taking strategies in this chapter as you answer them. Keep practicing as you prepare for upcoming tests in college.

 EVALUATING YOUR PROGRESS

1. As I look back on the past seven days, I've seen an improvement in these areas:

_____   organizing my life

_____   protecting my health

_____   planning my time

_____   concentrating

_____   taking notes

_____   active learning

_____   reading critically

_____   writing effectively

_____   thinking critically

_____   communicating with important people in my life

_____   enjoying my free time

_____   allowing myself to be imperfect

2. In the coming week, I plan to invest five minutes a day working towards this goal:

CHAPTER SEVEN

Active Reading

It is impossible to read properly without using all one's engine power.

ARNOLD BENNETT

PREVIEW

1. Systematic reading practices can help you get maximum benefit from your college reading.

2. Reading critically is vital to your success in college.

3. Comprehending and remembering what you read are more important than speed.

IN-CLASS INTRODUCTORY ACTIVITY: WHY DO YOU READ?

How do you feel about this statement?

I get more information through reading than any other activity.

Strongly disagree	Neutral	Strongly agree
1	5	10

Mark the point on the line that best represents your position; then complete the activities.

ACTIVITIES:

1. *List the information sources you're likely to use in a typical week. (Remember that information comes in many ways—through bus schedules and bulletin boards as well as more obvious ways, like books and radio broadcasts.)*

2. *List as many advantages and disadvantages of reading as you can think of. For example, books are convenient because they're portable, but reading may be less entertaining than getting information from TV.*

COLLABORATIVE ACTIVITY

Meet with a small group of other students to discuss and compare your answers to the previous questions. Then work together to list ways to get the greatest benefit from the reading you do in college. For example, you could suggest taking notes while you read, underlining key ideas, and having a well-lighted place to read. What other ideas come to mind?

◆ THE IMPORTANCE OF READING ◆

In both college life and your career, you will depend heavily on reading for the information you need. You can learn a great deal from lectures, videos, television programming, conversations, and personal experience. But reading is still one of the most inexpensive, convenient, and reliable ways to gain knowledge. Because written matter is compact and portable, it is unlikely to be replaced by other information sources.

If you're not satisfied with your reading skills, resolve to improve them by transforming yourself into an *active* reader. This chapter offers several practical strategies to help you make this transformation. You can preview assignments to schedule your reading time effectively, and you can choose supplementary activities for better comprehension—such as talking to a student or tutor who can help you understand new concepts. This chapter will particularly emphasize your ability to read critically—to evaluate and apply what you're reading.

As you'll see in the reading selection that follows, you can apply these strategies to almost anything you read, including the daily newspaper. The key is to start thinking of reading as an active process—and of yourself as an active, thoughtful reader.

READING THOUGHTFULLY: AN ACTOR BECOMES AN ACTIVE READER

Actor Sidney Poitier, who won an Academy Award for his performance in *Lilies of the Field*, had to overcome many obstacles early in his career. After leaving his home in the Bahamas at the age of sixteen, he came to New York City and worked as a dishwasher. He dreamed of an acting career, but he encountered an obstacle he hadn't expected: his poor reading skills. In his excerpt from his autobiography, *This Life*, he relives that first audition and explains how he improved his reading skills. Before you begin reading, complete the activity below.

BEFORE YOU READ

1. How important do you think reading skills are to an actor?

2. If you wanted to help a friend read more effectively, what steps would you follow?

from **This Life**
by Sidney Poitier

It is the first time I have ever been on a stage—I didn't even know what a stage looked like—but I'm up there now and I open this "script," but I don't know what it is. The director told me to read the part of "John." Everywhere I see "John" I'll read everything under that.

Then I see him sitting in the orchestra staring at me with the most peculiar look. He says, "Get off that stage." I say, "What do you mean?" He says, "Just come on down off that stage and stop wasting my time. You're no actor. You don't even know how to read."

I leave and walk off down 135th Street saying to myself, "You can hardly read. You can't be an actor and not be able to read." I begin to contemplate what he'd said to me. Now I knew I couldn't read too well. Here I am, I'm eighteen years of age, and if I live to be eighty, for the next sixty-two years I'm going to be a dishwasher. I'm not going to be able to impress people.

During the next six months, I spent as much time as possible reading. One of the restaurants I worked in during that period was in Astoria, Long Island.

Sidney Poitier had to improve his reading skills to become a successful actor.

The work was hard and heavy, but we would almost always have most of the dishes cleared away by 11:00 or 11:15 p.m. It was my custom to sit out near the kitchen door and read the newspaper.

At the waiters' table there was an old Jewish man who used to watch me trying to read that paper. I asked him one night what a word meant, and he told me. I thanked him and went back to my paper. He went on watching me for a few seconds and then said, "Do you run across a lot of words you don't understand? I said, "A lot—because I'm just beginning to learn to read well," and he said, "I'll sit with you here and I'll work with you for a while."

So at about eleven every night when he sat down for his meal, I would come out of the kitchen and sit down next to him and read articles from the front page of the paper. When I ran into a word I didn't know (and I didn't know half of the article, because anything past a couple of syllables and I was in trouble) he explained the meaning of the word and gave me the pronunciation. Then he'd send me back to the sentence so I could grasp the word in context.

Then I would take the paper away with me, armed now with the meaning of those words, and reread and reread the article so that the meaning of those words would get locked into my memory. Every evening we did that.

I stayed there at that job for about five or six weeks and I learned a pattern from him, and then I was off to other things. I have never been able to thank him properly because I never knew then what an enormous contribution he was making to my life. He was wonderful, and a little bit of him is in everything I do.

After my relationship with him, I always looked for the meaning of words, and when I ran into words I couldn't pronounce and didn't understand, I would work on them until some sense began to come. I would keep going over and over the sentence they were in, and after a while I would begin to get an idea of what the word meant just by repeating the sentence. That became a habit, as did all the other things he left me with.

AFTER YOU READ

1. Did you encounter any new words in this selection? What strategy will you use to learn them?

2. Do you have any questions about this selection? How will you find the answers?

3. What reading strategies did the waiter teach Poitier?

4. Recall the A-B-C study time strategy you learned in Chapter Five. Was Poitier making use of A, B, or C time?

5. Poitier worked with the waiter for only five or six weeks. Why did the waiter's help have such lasting impact?

6. What motivated Poitier to improve his reading skills? Why do you want to read more effectively?

7. Which of the waiter's strategies do you already use?

8. Which new strategies do you plan to begin using?

GETTING IN TOUCH THROUGH FREEWRITING

1. *Spend four or five minutes writing about your usual reading habits: When, where, what, and how do you generally read? Keep the ideas flowing; don't worry about spelling, punctuation, sentence structure, or organization.*

2. *Freewrite about two past reading experiences—one that you enjoyed and one that you didn't. Recall as many details as you can: What were you reading, and where and why? What made the two experiences different for you?*

3. *Now that you've written about your reading experiences, what insights do you have into your own reading habits and preferences? How can you apply these insights to the reading you'll be doing in college?*

◆ STEPS TO BETTER READING ◆

The waiter taught Sidney Poitier two important skills. First, he showed Poitier how to discover the meanings of words he didn't know by seeing how they were used in the newspaper. Reading experts call this skill "using the context for vocabulary development." Second, the waiter emphasized the importance of review. With his encouragement, Poitier learned to reread a selection until he recognized and understood most of the words there. (Notice that the waiter never pushed speed; he correctly emphasized comprehension first.)

The same principles apply to the reading tasks you encounter in college. Whether you're reading a poem by John Donne or a pharmacology chart, you'll often need to develop your vocabulary and review what you have read. For maximum effectiveness, you should incorporate these two skills into a reading system used successfully by thousands of students: SQ3R—Survey, Question, Read, Recite, Review. (Later you'll focus on another approach—a three-step critical-reading process.) Although you might expect to need longer study periods to work through all five steps, this system (invented by psychologist Francis Robinson during World War II) can actually save you time by making you a more efficient reader. And because you'll be reading actively, you'll find it easier to concentrate and retain new information.

SQ3R: Study, Question, Read, Recite, Review

1. Survey

Begin by establishing your purpose in reading: Facts? Ideas? Pleasure? Be as specific as possible about your expectations. When you know what you're looking for, you're more likely to find it.

If you're learning a new skill, preparing for a test or mastering body of information for a college course, you'll have to read thoroughly and carefully, noting the connections between ideas and the organization of the content.

At other times, you'll be looking only for particular information for a paper or project: statistics for an education course, stories about Native Americans for a humanities paper, or an explanation of Aristotle's political philosophy for a philosophy report. Scan the content rapidly until you find the information you need.

1. Survey	2. Question	3. Read	4. Recite	5. Review

Figure 7.1 SQ3R

When you've decided on your purpose, make a high-speed survey of your reading selection. If you're looking for specific information, this survey will help you find it quickly. If your goal is mastery of the reading selection, the survey will prepare you to absorb what you read and help you devise an effective working strategy. Read the first and last paragraphs, along with any study aids: headings, subheadings, summary, charts, diagrams, and review questions. If there are no study aids, read the first sentence in every paragraph.

Decide also whether the selection has any special features that will help you fulfill your purpose. If you're looking for specific information, will the table of contents or index help you? Sometimes headings and illustrations can help. Does the selection have a glossary—a short dictionary to help you understand what you're reading?

Now you're ready to make a reading plan. Was the content more challenging than you'd expected? Will you refer to the glossary or a dictionary to find the meaning of unfamiliar words and terms? Do you need more background information to understand what you'll be reading? (Additional suggestions for reading about science appear in Chapter Ten; advice for reading mathematics texts appears in Chapter Eleven.)

If necessary, set aside extra "A" time for reading and rereading the selection you're working on. Decide whether you want to use other strategies as well: a talk with your professor? a visit to the library or learning center? a session with a study group?

Finally, consider your learning style. If you're an auditory learner, for example, you may want to read the selection aloud—or take turns reading with a study partner. If you're a pragmatic learner, consider the usefulness of the information you're learning; if you're more conceptual, focusing on abstract ideas may be more helpful. Decide too whether you prefer to read primarily on your own or with a group. (Other supplementary activities are suggested on pages 219 through 221 of this chapter.)

2. Question

Write down any questions that occurred to you during your survey; make up questions from the study aids (headings, charts, summary) and other information as well. You'll be looking for the answers during the next step.

These questions will help you concentrate on, comprehend, and retain what you're reading in the next step. They're especially useful if you're going to be tested later. (All the "Reading Thoughtfully" selections in this book encourage you to ask questions as preparation for reading.)

3. Read

This is the heart of the reading process. In this step you'll read the selection thoroughly, as many times as necessary, for maximum comprehension and retention, and you'll look for answers to the questions you've written.

Your first priority is comprehension. Read thoughtfully, referring to the dictionary when necessary, checking your understanding of the passage. Then decide upon the selection's main point (often subheadings will help you find it, especially if you're reading a magazine article). Look up any unfamiliar terms and references to make sure you comprehend what you've read.

Working with a reading partner can make a difficult text easier to understand.

You'll want to use "one of the best of eyes"—a pencil or marker—to mark up the reading selection and make it your own. (If you've borrowed the selection from the library, make a photocopy to write on.) But read the selection thoroughly at least once to make sure you understand it before you get out your pencil or marker: lines, circles, stars, and question marks in the wrong places can be distracting.

Be cautious about using a highlighter (marking pen used to cover words with a thick, bright, transparent line). Scholar Lawrence Beyer explains, "highlighter use in fact encourages passive reading habits in young adults who very much need to learn to read actively, critically, and analytically." Beyer recommends instead using a pen or pencil for underlining and, more importantly, writing notes in the margins. "The highlighter is virtually useless for this purpose," he notes.

If you have difficulty with the content, set aside time to ask a friend or tutor for help—or talk to your professor. Avoid working on one assignment too long: You'll be most alert if you schedule reading assignments for several "A" and "B" periods during the day.

When you feel that you understand the selection thoroughly, look for answers to the questions you asked in the "question" step. These questions and answers will be helpful later, when you recite and review what you've learned.

Finally, look for connections between the reading selection and your own experience. Is the information related to what you already know? Will it be helpful to you academically, professionally, or personally? If you're a conceptual learner, make sure you haven't missed any practical details; if you're a pragmatic learner, check your understanding of any abstract ideas you've read. These strategies help you comprehend and retain what

If you're a social learner, plan to meet with other students to discuss what you've read.

you've read; they also develop the insightful outlook that is the hallmark of every truly educated person. As you'll see later, they're a vital part of the critical-reading process.

4. Recite

In this step you check your understanding by restating what you learned from the selection. Cover the answers to the questions you wrote in the previous step, and see if you can recall the answers. Another good strategy is asking yourself the meaning of each heading, chart, diagram, and illustration. A third possibility is to write a summary of what you've read; then compare your version with summaries written by other members of your class or study group. Finally, make sure you can answer any review questions that appear at the end of the selection.

5. Review

Don't put your reading selection away after you've read it. Since most forgetting takes place within 24 hours, you'll have to review the reading selection to retain what you've read.

Make sure your review strategies are appropriate to the length and difficulty of the reading selection. A short, easy selection may require only five minutes of review every day or two; a long or difficult selection may require extensive rereading and review. Choose one or more of the following strategies:

Retention Strategies

- reread the entire selection
- answer the questions you've written about the selection
- repeat the survey step, reading only selected parts of the selection
- try explaining what you've read to a friend
- redo the review questions at the end
- write a summary
- without looking, recite your summary from memory
- make a mind map or outline
- without looking, redo your mind map or outline from memory
- make flash cards and study them

EXERCISE 1: TRY THE SQ3R PROCESS

Apply SQ3R to a current reading assignment. If you don't have one right now, invent one for yourself, using a textbook from one of your courses or a book or magazine article that interests you.

Take notes as you go through the SQ3R process. What steps did you follow? How did each step feel? Did you encounter any difficulties—or any breakthroughs?

When you're finished, write a few sentences evaluating your experience. What worked for you? What might you do differently next time?

Getting the Most from Your Reading. In addition to "SQ3R," you can employ a variety of other activities to get maximum benefit from your reading. Perhaps the survey step showed that you need more background information before you tackle your reading assignment. Or you may have found the content so challenging that you want to check your understanding with one or two additional activities—or you may simply want to learn more. Here's a list of supplementary activities that many students have enjoyed using:

1. Preread the jacket, preface, foreword	2. Read the summary	3. Read a children's book on the subject	4. Make an outline or a mind map	5. Read an article in an encyclopedia	6. Discuss what you read	7. Read a condensed version

Figure 7.2 More Active-Reading Strategies

1.   "Preread" a book by reading the entire book jacket, the preface, foreword, introduction, acknowledgments and table of contents.

Like a reconnaissance pilot preparing for a landing, you'll have a useful overview of the new territory you'll be exploring. When you clearly understand the main idea of a reading selection, the reading task itself becomes much easier.

2.   When possible, read a summary before working through an entire scientific article.

Articles in professional journals often include a concise and useful summary. It may be called an "abstract," "summary," or "conclusion," and it can appear at the beginning or the end of the article. Experienced readers look for this summary and read it before they tackle the article itself. If you're doing research, reading just the summary can save you a great deal of time. If you find the information you need quickly, you can skip lengthy explanations about research methods and other details. If you're trying to master the content in the whole article, the summary will increase your understanding of what you're about to read.

3.   Borrow a book on the subject from a children's or young people's library.

Many children's books are well-researched introductions, in simple language, to important subjects. Sometimes the authors of adult books also write for children and young adults. *The Rise and Fall of the Third Reich*, an authoritative book about World War II Germany, was written by William L. Shirer; he also produced a biography of Adolf Hitler for young people. Isaac Asimov has written many excellent scientific works for both young people and adults.

Books for children can't take the place of college texts. But they can introduce you to a subject that's new to you, and their diagrams and illustrations can be especially helpful. When novelist Marilyn Durham was writing *The Man Who Loved Cat Dancing*, a novel about nineteenth-century America, she went to a children's library to learn about weapons from that time.

4.   Make an outline or mind map.

Here you're again using "one of the best of eyes"—a pen or pencil. Outlining and mind-mapping encourage you to read actively, looking for the relationships between ideas. (The previous chapter, "Active Learning," can refresh your memory about these activities.)

5.   Read an article in an encyclopedia.

Encyclopedias are excellent learning aids if you need more background knowledge, or a reading selection stimulated you to learn more, or you feel overwhelmed by the subject you're studying. A good encyclopedia can offer you recent research, helpful illustrations, useful summaries, and reliable information. Start with a general encyclopedia, such as the *Americana* or *Britannica*. If you need more depth, libraries have specialized encyclopedias about a wide variety of subjects.

You can also find recommended reading lists (called *bibliographies*) in encyclopedias and other reference books. The editors of the *Encyclopedia Britannica*, for example, ask noted authorities to contribute articles and compile annotated (expanded) bibliographies.

6. Discuss what you've read.

Talking about what you've read automatically makes you an active learner. Other students are good possibilities for discussions; professors and librarians may also suggest people to contact, and the classified telephone directory may be helpful. A short conversation with a stock broker, architect, biologist, or minister can enliven the ideas you've been reading. You can even telephone an author or another authority in your field if you follow these guidelines: Plan what you're going to say, be willing to call again if you've telephoned at an inconvenient time, keep your call brief, and thank the person who talked to you.

7. Read a condensed (shortened) version of a book that interests you.

A condensation can't replace a complete book, but it can provide valuable information about a subject. If you plan to read the complete book, a condensed version can familiarize you with the author's style and content, making the book easier to read later. Condensations are also useful for increasing your knowledge of a subject that interests you. Many magazines (*The New York Times Magazine, Good Housekeeping, Psychology Today* and others) print excerpts from books. *The Reader's Guide to Periodical Literature* in the reference section of the library is a good place to start looking.

EXERCISE 2: GET MORE FROM YOUR READING

A list of strategies for getting more from your reading appears below. Put a check in front of any you've already tried; circle those you'd like to begin using.

_____ *look for an abstract, summary, or conclusion first*

_____ *reread the selection several times for better understanding*

_____ *make flash cards about the selection*

_____ *practice answering the review questions at the end*

_____ *write your own review questions and answer them*

_____ *read a children's book on a subject you're studying*

_____ *make an outline or mind map*

_____ *read an article in an encyclopedia*

_____ *discuss what you're reading*

_____ *read a condensation*

What about Speed?

Many college students mistakenly define good reading as fast reading. But they do have a point: Slow readers can have difficulty completing the extensive reading requirements in college. Comprehension can also be a problem; if you're plodding through a reading selection, you can completely lose the sense of what the author has written.

To read faster, try to move your eyes across the page more quickly and concentrate harder as you read. Specialized computer programs and reading courses can also increase your speed.

Reading as a Lifelong Project

The love of reading is a common thread in the lives of many influential people. Often the biographies of famous men and women mention a well-loved book that they returned to again and again. David Fairchild reread *The Malay Archipelago*, by naturalist Alfred Russel Wallace, throughout his life; it was particularly special to Fairchild because the author had once visited Fairchild's childhood home. Actor Richard Burton, himself a lifelong reader, discovered during a performance of *Hamlet* that Prime Minister Winston Churchill was an avid student of Shakespeare. Churchill sat in the first row and spoke the lines of the play right along with the actors—from memory.

George Bernard Shaw, also a student of Shakespeare, returned to John Bunyan's *The Pilgrim's Progress* again and again. Thérèse Martin of Lisieux, a spiritual model for many modern Christians, memorized *The Imitation of Christ* by Thomas à Kempis when she was a teenager. Scholar C.S. Lewis said that Virgil's epic *Aeneid*, which he read in the original Latin, helped him make the transition from a boy to a man. The great Belgian novelist Georges Simenon particularly loved the novels of Honoré de Balzac.

These examples suggest that "SQ3R," while valuable, is not the only way to read. If you are gripped by a particular book, make it your own. Buy a copy, keep it with you, mark it up, read and reread it. British writer Harold Nicolson suggests, "mark your books and write a personal index for yourself on the flyleaf." Have a pen or pencil nearby when you're reading so that you can list useful information and ideas, along with their page numbers, inside the front cover. This practice helps make you an active reader, increases the usefulness of your books, and saves time later, when you refer to the book again.

Sometimes magazine and newspaper articles are worth saving and rereading. They may be helpful in a course you take later on, a job, or a research project. Don't underestimate the value of a pair of scissors as a reading tool: Clip interesting articles, note the date and title (if it doesn't appear on the section you cut), and file it for future reference. (If you find the article in a library, make a photocopy.) Most successful people keep—and use—extensive files; now is a good time to develop this habit yourself.

Returning to a fascinating book over and over, finding more in its pages each time, is one of the most valuable and lasting learning experiences you can have. And the thoughts stimulated by your favorite book are likely to be excellent examples of critical thinking. You'll learn more about this important approach to reading beginning on page 224.

But don't sacrifice comprehension and retention in the quest for speed. Reading authority Rudolf Flesch warned, "Reading at double speed may be only half as effective." Thoughtful prereading is a better road to efficiency than rushing through a book or article. Good preparation saves time by making a selection easier to read. Several of the suggestions earlier in the chapter (studying the book jacket and table of contents, looking for a summary, reading a condensation) are excellent preparation strategies.

Ignore anyone who urges you to increase your speed by reading only the important words. Dr. Arthur Whimbey, another reading authority, notes that you can't tell which words are important unless you read them all.

Before you start pushing yourself to read faster, ask yourself whether you really need to feel guilty about your current rate. You can't rush through every college reading assignment at top speed: Different kinds of reading matter demand different levels of speed and concentration. Although efficiency is a worthy goal, you should make *effective reading* your top priority.

Learn to make a realistic evaluation about the time needed for each reading assignment. (You'll make this evaluation during the survey step of SQ3R.) Even if you read quickly, expect your comprehension, speed, and retention to slow down when you tackle unfamiliar concepts and terminology. Sometimes you'll also need extra time to clarify what you're reading; critical thinking is likely to take even more time—and to yield significant benefits. A study partner or study group can also help you solve reading problems. For example, you can ask each group member to study part of an assignment in depth and clarify it for the rest of the group.

The two reading selections that follow will help you experience these shifts in speed, comprehension, and retention yourself. Both excerpts are taken from novelist Nevil Shute's autobiography, *Slide Rule*.[1] In addition to writing *On the Beach* and many other novels, Shute was an aeronautical engineer. During the late 1920s, he helped create a British airship called R.100. In the first excerpt he describes one of the final stages in the stress calculations for the transverse frame:

> When a likely-looking solution had at last been obtained, deflection diagrams were set out for the movements of the various corners of the polygon under the bending moments and loads found in the various portions of the arched rib, and these yielded the extension of the radial wires under load, which was compared with the calculated loads found in the wires. It was usual to find a discrepancy, perhaps due to an arithmetical mistake.

The second excerpt appears on the next page of *Slide Rule*, where Shute describes the team's excitement when the calculations finally balanced perfectly. Notice that this excerpt is much easier to read.

> As I say, it produced a satisfaction almost amounting to a religious experience. After literally months of labour, having filled perhaps fifty sheets with closely penciled figures, after many disappointments and heartaches, the truth stood revealed, real, and perfect, and unquestionable; the very truth. It did one good; one was the better for the experience.

---

[1] A slide rule is a ruler-like device with a sliding center, marked with number scales, and used to calculate various mathematical operations. It was commonly used by math and science students and professionals before the days of pocket calculators.

So when you make a resolution to improve your reading skills, don't overemphasize speed. Adjust your reading rate to the kind of material you're reading.

EXERCISE 3: EXAMINE YOUR READING

Examine the kinds of reading you do regularly to survey the reading speeds required for each. (This is a useful exercise to do twice: once by yourself, and again with two or three other students.)

1. *Select a recent issue of a newspaper and a magazine you read regularly, along with any textbooks you're currently using.*
2. *Spend ten or fifteen minutes browsing through them, noticing the levels of reading difficulties. (Magazine advertisements may be easy to read; news articles may require slower reading; advanced textbooks may be difficult.)*
3. *List the reading materials you surveyed, and write a sentence or two about the level of difficulty of each.*

4. *Evaluate the results. What conclusions can you draw from this exercise? What have you learned about reading rates?*

Reading Critically

You've already seen that effective reading requires more than comprehension and retention: You must also read *critically*—evaluating, applying, and challenging what's written on the page. The habit of reading critically strengthens your intellect and prepares you for the working world. Much of your college coursework is designed to familiarize you with the predominant issues in your major field, and to encourage you to develop your own viewpoint about them. Here are the three steps followed by good critical readers:

Task 1 Forming expectations	**Task 2** Reading with a pencil	**Task 3** Evaluating what I've read
What do I already know?	Mark up the text with:	Did it meet my expectations?
What do I expect?	Questions	Was it covered thoroughly?
What will I gain?	Reactions	Do I need to read more?

Figure 7.3 Reading Critically

Task 1: Forming Expectations. By completing this first task, you get in touch with what you expect from the reading selection. (You can incorporate this activity into the Survey step of SQ3R.) When you're aware of your expectations and assumptions, you can concentrate better and read more thoughtfully. Good readers ask four questions before they start reading:

1. What do I already know about this subject?
2. How do I expect the author to treat this subject?
3. What do I expect to gain from this reading selection?
4. What is the publication date?

1. What do I already know about this subject? You're more likely to understand and retain what you read if you already know something about the subject. If you're going to read about government policies for senior citizens, spend some time thinking about the retired people you know. What is special about this group and their needs? If you haven't had any personal experience with a subject—military service, for example—try to remember what you've heard about it from friends, family, newspapers, books, magazines, and teachers. If the author's views are very different from yours, you can try to find out why—a vital step in critical reading.

2. How do I expect the author to treat this subject? Before you begin reading, decide what you expect from the author (or authors). Book jackets often provide valuable clues. Is the author a journalist, a scholar, or a popular writer? Scholars usually immerse themselves in written information; journalists are more likely to rely on interviews. Popular writers make information accessible to large numbers of people, but they may not have done the exacting research you'd find in a scholarly book.

Authors' backgrounds can shape their writing in other ways too. For example, you can expect the autobiographies of famous people to cast favorable light on their actions and decisions. An ex-president's autobiography will probably give a positive account of his administration. Career information may provide other important clues: Officials from the American Medical Association are likely to defend current medical practices and oppose government health plans; representatives of large corporations will argue for legislation that protects big business.

Information about religious affiliations can sometimes be helpful. Expect an article in the Roman Catholic magazine *America* to oppose abortion; a Unitarian Universalist publication is likely to have a more liberal outlook. When business leader Stephen R. Covey wrote a book about success (*The Seven Habits of Highly Effective People*), some readers wondered why Covey mentioned his wife and children so often. But astute readers knew one possible explanation for that emphasis: Covey's Mormon faith stresses family life.

Many other factors can shape a writer's outlook—just as your life is full of events that have helped make you the person you are. William H. Herndon, Abraham Lincoln's law partner, wrote a famous biography trusted by thousands of readers because Herndon knew Lincoln personally. But scholars later discovered that Herndon had misrepresented some of his information, for a variety of reasons. For example, Herndon disliked Lincoln's wife, Mary Todd Lincoln, and tried to prove that Lincoln had never truly loved her.

Professors and librarians can help you look for background information about an author you're reading. Book reviews can also be helpful. Sources include Infotrac (a computerized index), the *Book Review Digest*, and the *Reader's Guide to Periodical Literature.*

3. What do I expect to gain from this reading selection? Here you focus on your purpose in reading. Do you expect the selection to reinforce what you already know, or do you want to be challenged by an opposing viewpoint? If you've just visited a historical site that intrigues you—the cemetery at Gettysburg, for example—you'll probably be reading for additional information and more depth. But if you're preparing to write a paper about a controversy such as abortion or gun control, you'll need to research both sides of the issue.

Reminding yourself of your purpose in reading helps you find what you want efficiently. It also prepares you for the evaluation step, when you'll decide whether the selection fulfilled your purpose or not, and why. Both questions are central to the task of critical reading.

4. When was the reading selection written? "Recent" does not always mean "reliable," but a book or article may be so out of date that it has little value. Recent information is vital when you're researching timely subjects like careers, scientific trends, and current issues. If you're studying AIDS, communism, or astronomy, for example, older books will lack essential information about recent developments.

But some older writings retain their importance as time passes. Karl Marx (1818–1883) is still widely studied by students of economics, political science, and rhetoric. Students of psychology continue to read the works of Alfred Adler (1870–1937). John Holt (1923–1985) and John Dewey (1859–1952) still influence educators; Charles Darwin (1809–1882) is still an important name in biology. You'll be introduced to many timeless authors like these during your college years. Professors and librarians can help you determine which older books are worth careful study; as time passes, your own experience will also help you decide which reading selections have the most to offer.

Task 2: Reading with a Pencil. Here you read, react to, and mark up the selection you're working on. (This task corresponds to Step Three, "Reading," of SQ3R.) You've already learned that an active pencil is a powerful thinking tool. As you read, imagine you're preparing for a conversation for the author. Mark up your text with questions you'd like to ask and reactions you'd like to share: surprise, puzzlement, agreement, doubt. (Note that this process is similar to the Cornell notetaking suggestions on page 105, which encouraged you to think critically, writing questions and ideas in the margins of your notes.)

Active reading takes you beyond comprehending and memorizing what you've read. You're embarking on an important intellectual task: deciding for yourself the value of what you've read. Your pencil can be also be used to link the reading selection to your own experience and knowledge. Ask yourself whether the selection triggers any memories. Can you compare or connect it to anything else you know?

One history student thought of Eli Whitney while she was reading about mass production in her economics textbook. Whitney (1765–1825) was a pioneer in mass production; his factory-produced weapons were a great aid to Americans in the War of 1812. She noted the connection in her text; later she mentioned Whitney on an essay test in her economics class. Impressed, her instructor awarded extra credit for her essay. As you read, make connections of your own to enrich your reading and your knowledge.

Task 3: Evaluating What You've Read. Critical reading culminates in evaluation—making value judgments about the reading selection. (You can incorporate this task into the "Review" step of SQ3R.) Begin by rereading the notations you made as you read the selection; then plan a strategy for dealing with them. What items need to be clarified?

Reading is an active task, challenging you to "make meaning" by relating the printed page to your own experience.

Would it be helpful to read additional material, talk to your professor, or discuss the selection with another student? If you disagree with some points in the reading selection, how will you resolve the disagreement? What further information do you need?

Other questions can also help you evaluate a reading selection:

1. Did the reading selection meet your expectations?

In the first step of the critical-reading process, you formed expectations about your reading selection. Now is the time to ask yourself whether those expectations were met. If the answer is no, ask yourself why. Perhaps you selected the wrong reading for your purpose, or the ideas were inadequately researched, or the author didn't develop them sufficiently. Uncovering such problems is an important task in critical reading. In other cases a writer may surprise you by taking an unexpected position about an issue. For example, you'd expect a psychologist to defend the value of psychotherapy. But Dr. James Hillman questions its effectiveness in his book *We've Had a Hundred Years of Therapy, and the World's Getting Worse*. If you're interested in psychology, you might find it stimulating to read Dr. Hillman's analysis and decide what you think of it. Conservative columnist William F. Buckley is another writer who's taken an unexpected position in a controversy: He favors eliminating many penalties for drug use. Writers like these can spark your intellectual growth by challenging you to take a fresh look at a controversial issue.

2. Is the subject covered thoroughly?

Be wary of a writer who tackles a complex issue superficially. Poor writers look at a problem from only one standpoint—their own; good writers explore issues in depth from a multitude of viewpoints.

One student prepared a political science project comparing newspaper coverage of a zoning controversy in her town. Developers were angry because they could not get permission to erect commercial buildings on property that had been standing idle for fifteen years. One newspaper had a reputation as a strong supporter of local businesses. Its editorials mentioned only the developers, who complained that the zoning board was promoting waste and opposing progress. Editorials in the other newspaper mentioned three additional groups—environmentalists, civic leaders, and residents who lived near the disputed property. Civic leaders pointed out that the developers had bought their land at extremely low prices because there was always doubt that it could be developed; they also noted that roads in the area could not handle heavy business traffic. Environmentalists warned of danger to the town's water supply if the land was developed; residents said they had moved into the area because the land in question was not zoned for commercial use. In her project, the student concluded that the depth of coverage in the second newspaper was superior to the coverage in the first.

3. Do you need to balance your reading with additional research?

If you want to explore a controversy in depth, don't rely on one or two books—undertake an extensive reading program. Totally objective writers are rare, and a book that claims to be both comprehensive and unbiased may not be able to deliver what it promises.

If you've just read an article arguing against a proposed space exploration project, you've been informed about only one viewpoint. To broaden your understanding, you should read at least one article by an author familiar with the advantages of the project.

READING THOUGHTFULLY: FORMING EXPECTATIONS

Imagine that you're studying the history of the nursing profession. You're about to read an excerpt from "Variety," a chapter in Notes on Nursing (1859) by Florence Nightingale (1820–1910). The questions below will help you explore your expectations, choose activities to enrich your understanding, and think critically about what you've read. (Later you can adapt this exercise to your own reading assignments.)

BEFORE YOU READ

1. What do you know about Florence Nightingale? What resources could you use to learn more about her in a short time? To learn more about how and why she wrote *Notes on Nursing*?
2. Nightingale is often considered the founder of the modern nursing profession. What kinds of information do you expect to find in *Notes on Nursing*? What do you *not* expect to find?
3. What might the word "variety" mean to a nurse? What do you think this chapter will be about?
4. Do you expect *Notes on Nursing* to be worth reading today? Why or why not? Who might be interested in Nightingale's book?

---

from   **Notes on Nursing**
by Florence Nightingale

To any but an old nurse, or an old patient, the degree would be quite inconceivable to which the nerves of the sick suffer from seeing the same walls, the same ceiling, the same surroundings during a long confinement to one or two rooms.

The superior cheerfulness of persons suffering severe paroxysms of pain over that of persons suffering from nervous debility has often been remarked upon, and attributed to the enjoyment of the former in their intervals of respite. I incline to think that the majority of cheerful cases is to be found among those patients who are not confined to one room, whatever their suffering, and that the majority of depressed cases will be seen among those subjected to a long monotony of objects about them.

The nervous frame really suffers as much from this as the digestive organs from long monotony of diet, as e.g. the soldier from his twenty-one years' "boiled beef."

The effect in sickness of beautiful objects, of variety of objects, and especially of brilliancy of colour is hardly at all appreciated.

Such cravings are usually called the "fancies" of patients. And often doubtless patients have "fancies," as, e.g. when they desire two contradictions. But much more often, their (so called) "fancies" are the most valuable indications of what is necessary for their recovery. And it would be well if nurses would watch these (so called) "fancies" closely.

I have seen, in fevers (and felt, when I was a fever patient myself) the most acute suffering produced from the patient (in a hut) not being able to see out of window, and the knots in the wood being the only view. I shall never forget the rapture of fever patients over a bunch of bright-coloured flowers. I remember (in my own case) a nosegay of wild flowers being sent me, and from that moment recovery becoming more rapid.

People say the effect is only on the mind. It is no such thing. The effect is on the body, too. Little as we know about the way in which we are affected by form, by colour, and light, we do know this, that they have an actual physical effect.

AFTER YOU READ

1. List any words that are new to you. How will you learn their meaning?

2. Write any questions you have about this selection. What strategies will you use to find the answers?

3. Review the questions and answers in Step 1. Did the passage meet your expectations? Why or why not? What answers would you change now that you've read the selection?

4. What is your opinion of Nightingale's advice to nurses about providing variety for the sick?

5. What resources might give you greater in-depth information about Nightingale, *Notes on Nursing,* her impact on the nursing profession, and the value of her advice today?

 ## COLLABORATIVE ACTIVITY: CONSIDER READING EXPERIENCES

Meet with a group of three or four other students to read and discuss the five stories below. Which reading experiences are effective, and which are not? Why?

1. A pre-med student has just read a journal article about stress experienced by preschool children in hospitals. She expected the article to discuss the emotional effects of pain, fear, and homesickness. But the article also discusses two other stresses: unfamiliar food and limited opportunities for play.

2. A criminology major has just read a textbook chapter about cell searches in correctional institutions. He expected the chapter to discuss body language—actions, gestures, and posture—that reveal what a person is feeling. During his summer job in the county jail, another officer showed him how inmates' body language sometimes signals that they are hiding forbidden items. But body language is never mentioned in this text.

3. A home-economics major is writing a nutrition paper. She has just collected several articles about nutritional breakfast choices. One article was written by a researcher for a major food company; the other appeared in a magazine distributed free in health-food stores.

4. A psychology student finds long descriptions of Asian spiritual practices in a book about psychotherapy for women. She wonders whether ideas imported from a culture so different can really help American women. The author spent three years as a nun in a Buddhist monastery in Asia, earned a doctorate in psychology from an important American university, and has been a therapist in the United States for eight years.

5. *An elementary education major is reading an article criticizing government child-abuse policies. The author believes that children should remain with their parents unless there is proof of severe physical abuse.*

JOURNAL ACTIVITY: PRACTICE CRITICAL READING

Critical-reading skills, like anything new you're learning, develop gradually. This week spend a few minutes daily focusing on one of the three critical-reading steps in connection with your college reading. (Be sure to alternate the steps, so that you'll develop confidence in all three: forming expectations, reading with a pencil, evaluating what you've read). Use the spaces below for personal notes about your critical-reading experiences this week.

DAY 1

What you read:

The step you chose:

How it worked:

DAY 2

What you read:

The step you chose:

How it worked:

DAY 3

What you read:

The step you chose:

How it worked:

DAY 4

What you read:

The step you chose:

How it worked:

DAY 5

What you read:

The step you chose:

How it worked:

DAY 6

What you read:

The step you chose:

How it worked:

DAY 7

What you read:

The step you chose:

How it worked:

READING THOUGHTFULLY: PRACTICE CRITICAL READING

This is an excerpt from *Do What You Love, The Money Will Follow* by author and psychologist Dr. Marsha Sinetar. Before you begin reading, complete the following activity.

BEFORE YOU READ

1. What do you think the title means? Do you agree or disagree with it?

2. What ideas do you expect Dr. Sinetar to discuss in this selection?

3. Do you believe that if you do what you love, the money will follow?

4. Do you think that principle would work for other people?

---

from **"The Psychology of Right Livelihood" from Do What You Love, The Money Will Follow**
by Marsha Sinetar, Ph.D.

Almost any job has benefits. "At least I don't have to take it home with me," "It's only five minutes away," "It pays the bills," are some of the advantages people identify in their otherwise uninteresting, tedious, or unrewarding work. Moreover, even in situations not particularly suited to them, people are able to develop new abilities. A shy person can learn to be more socially comfortable by selling vacuum cleaners, cars, or Tupperware. An extrovert can learn to work in solitary, focused settings. A technical specialist can become a good manager of people. Clearly we can see that people do grow through "staying the course," through facing difficulty, through self-discipline, through toughening their resolve and perseverance.

Yet, even though we are all fairly adaptable, elastic, and multi-dimensional, we are not born to struggle through life. We are meant to work in ways that suit us, drawing on our natural talents and abilities as a way to express ourselves and contribute to others. This work, when we find it and do it—even if only as a hobby at first—is a key to our true happiness and self-expression.

Most of us think about our jobs or our careers as a means to fulfill responsibilities to families and creditors, to gain more material comforts, and to achieve status and recognition. But we pay a high price for this kind of thinking. A large percentage of America's working population do not enjoy the work they do! This is a profoundly tragic statistic considering that work consumes so much time in our lives. In a few brief decades, our working life adds up to be life itself.

Such a nose-to-the-grindstone attitude is not even a good formula for success. When you study people who are successful, as I have over the years, it is abundantly clear that their achievements are directly related to the enjoyment they derive from their work. They enjoy it in large part because they are good at it. A bright client of mine once told me, "I'm at my best when I'm using my brain. My ideal day is when my boss gives me lots of complex problems to solve." Another client remarked, "I like people, and when I'm involved with them, time just flies by. Since I've been in sales, I find everyone I meet interesting and fun to talk to. I should be paying the company for letting me do this work."

Right Livelihood is an idea about work which is linked to the natural order of things. It is doing our best at what we do best. The rewards that follow are inevitable and manifold. There is no way we can fail. Biology points out the logic of Right Livelihood. Every species in the natural world has a place and function that is specifically suited to its capabilities. This is true for people too. Some of us are uniquely equipped for physical work, athletics, or dance; some of us have special intellectual gifts that make possible abstract or inventive thinking; some of us have aesthetic abilities and eye-hand coordination that enable us to paint, sculpt, or design. Examples are numerous of natures way of directing us to the path that will support us economically and emotionally; this is the path that we were meant to travel.

Any talent that we are born with eventually surfaces as a need. Current research on child prodigies—youngsters who, from an early age, are mathematical wizards, virtuoso musicians, brilliant performers—tells us that they possess a burning desire to express themselves, to use their unique gifts. In a similar fashion, each of us, no matter how ordinary we consider our talents, wants and needs to use them. Yet many of us cannot imagine that what we enjoy doing, what we have talent for, could be a source of income for us or even a catalyst for transforming our relationship to work. But indeed, it can be. Leaders in every walk of life who have the drive, skill and compelling vision to advance their ideas, despite obstacles, need to exert their influence as much as their solutions, energy and enthusiasm are needed by others.

AFTER YOU READ

1. What new words did you encounter in this excerpt? What strategy will you use to learn their meaning?

2. What questions do you have about the selection? How will you find the answers?

3. What is "Right Livelihood"?

4. On page 235 you answered this question: "What ideas do you expect Dr. Sinetar to discuss in this selection?" Did the selection meet your expectations? Why or why not?

5. What main point do you think Dr. Sinetar is trying to make?

6. What is your opinion of Dr. Sinetar's ideas?

7. Which of these ideas, if any, would you like to apply to your own life? If you think they would be helpful, how would you put them to work for you?

8. How do you feel about this statement?

| If I do what I love, the money will follow. |

Strongly disagree	Neutral	Strongly agree
1	5	10

Mark the point on the line that best represents your position; then meet with a small group of other students to compare and discuss your reactions to the statement.

USING WHAT YOU HAVE LEARNED

1. What advice would you give the following students as they search for solutions to their reading problems?

   a. A student is preparing an oral report about American physicist Enrico Fermi (1901–1954) and his work on controlled nuclear chain reactions. The student found seven books about Fermi in the library, but he doesn't know which ones to read. He's also having trouble understanding Fermi's research, which he is supposed to discuss in his report.

   b. A secondary education major is having trouble understanding the textbook for her course in tests and measurements. The mathematical explanations are difficult for her, and she's especially confused by terms like "mean," "median," and "normal curve." She never has time to study a chapter thoroughly enough to master the content.

   c. An English major came across a book by a psychologist that offers fascinating psychological explanations about familiar fairy stories. The student is enjoying the book, but she wonders whether the interpretations are respected by psychologists. Should she continue to read it? Since she's not a psychology major, she wants to find out whether she really understands what she's reading.

2. Survey a chapter you haven't yet read in one of your textbooks and devise a reading plan. Ask a study partner to do the same tasks for the same chapter; then compare and discuss the results. Did you gain any useful ideas from each other?

3. Apply one of the critical-reading tasks on pages 225 through 229 to something you've read before. Does the selection seem different now that you've read it critically? What did you notice that you'd missed before? Did you learn anything that you can apply to future reading tasks?

EVALUATING YOUR PROGRESS

1. As I look back on the past seven days, I've seen an improvement in these areas:

_____ organizing my life

_____ protecting my health

_____ planning my time

_____ concentrating

_____ taking notes

_____ active learning

_____ reading critically

_____ writing effectively

_____ thinking critically

_____ communicating with important people in my life

_____ enjoying my free time

_____ allowing myself to be imperfect

2. In the coming week, I plan to invest five minutes a day working towards this goal:

CHAPTER 8

Critical Thinking

Thinking is like loving and dying. Each of us must do it for himself.

JOSIAH ROYCE

 PREVIEW

1. Critical thinking is "thinking about thinking"—observing and evaluating your mental processes.

2. Lateral thinking helps you broaden and deepen your assumptions; it also puts you in touch with new ideas, information, and possibilities.

3. Vertical thinking helps you make evaluations: It involves judgments about correctness, usefulness, and truth.

4. Critical thinking skills can help you avoid thinking errors.

 IN-CLASS INTRODUCTORY ACTIVITY: THINK ABOUT THINKING

How true is the following statement about thinking? Choose a point on the scale that best represents your opinion. Then complete the activities that follow.

According to the Chinese philosopher Confucius, "Learning without thinking is useless; thinking without learning is dangerous.

Seldom true	Neutral	Always true
1	5	10

ACTIVITIES:

1. *List as many examples of learning that require thinking as you can.*

2. *What do you think Confucius meant when he said that learning without thinking is "useless"? Do you agree with his choice of words? Why or why not?*

3. *What do you think Confucius meant when he said that thinking without learning is "dangerous"? Give as many examples as you can. Do you agree with his choice of words? Why or why not?*

4. *Can you think of any types of learning or thinking that don't fit Confucius's statement?*

COLLABORATIVE ACTIVITY

Meet with a small group of students to discuss and compare your answers.

◆ THE IMPORTANCE OF CRITICAL THINKING ◆

Many students are wary of the word "critical" because it sometimes has a negative meaning. You may have heard statements like this: "I wish my sister would be less critical about my taste in clothing." But in academic and professional situations, "critical" can also mean evaluative. "Critical thinking," therefore, refers to thinking that meets standards for quality: striving to avoid errors in logic and reasoning, and judging the worth of ideas and conclusions.

Critical thinking begins with curiosity about ideas and mental processes. What thoughts are in your head right now, and where did they come from—school, friends, the media, your own experience? The next step is to evaluate the quality of these ideas. Are the sources reliable? Should other sources be checked? Should any ideas be discarded or modified in some way? Critical thinkers make a habit of "thinking about thinking" in this way.

Developing these mental habits is vital to your success in college courses, which often require you to make connections between the ideas and information you're learning. If you're majoring in business, for example, you'll discover that ethics, business law, psychology, and management share a common concern, despite their differences: They all offer approaches to problem solving. Critical thinking offers other benefits as well, such as increasing your creativity. Whatever your major, your compositions, research papers, and oral presentations will be more interesting because you'll find it easier to discover fresh topics. Your grades are likely to improve as you become a more disciplined thinker. As you saw in Chapter Six, "Active Learning," study is most effective when new material is meaningful to you. When you use study time to probe and challenge the information you're learning, retention is much easier.

The benefits of critical thinking extend beyond college life to both citizenship and your career. Because we rely so much on information from outside sources, we must make intelligent responses to information from the media and other sources. Thoughtful feedback can help initiate far-reaching changes in many areas of life. Fast-food companies, for example, have responded to consumer concerns about pollution by cutting back on excessive packaging. In professional life, thinking skills are essential to decision-making, evaluating trends, and identifying problems before they erupt into crises.

Resolve now to make critical thinking an important part of your daily life both now and after college. As you read through the following pages, look for ways to apply what you're learning to your own ideas and the ideas of others.

Lateral and Vertical Thinking

Effective thinking incorporates two types of mental activities, which Edward de Bono, an authority on thinking, calls "lateral thinking" and "vertical thinking." Both are vital to critical thinking.

Lateral thinking aims to broaden your ideas, generating a wide range of new possibilities. Good lateral thinkers are curious about many subjects, always looking for new information, perspectives, and viewpoints. They're eager to get in touch with their assumptions and broaden their thinking—important traits in college. On pages 248 through 251 you'll learn many lateral-thinking strategies.

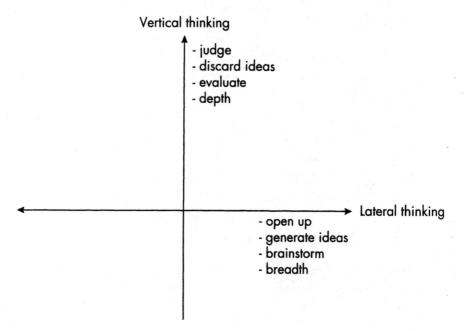

Figure 8.1 Vertical vs. Lateral Thinking

By contrast, "vertical thinking" involves judgments. Good vertical thinkers sort, classify, and evaluate ideas and information—again, important skills in college courses. They ask questions about usefulness, effectiveness, correctness, and truth. You used vertical thinking in Chapter Seven to evaluate the essay about right livelihood by Dr. Marsha Sinetar.

Critical thinkers constantly use both lateral and vertical thinking skills. Often lateral thinking—generating ideas—comes first; vertical thinking—evaluating ideas—follows. You'll probably brainstorm possible solutions to a problem (lateral thinking) before you choose one (vertical thinking). When you're writing a paper, you'll generate ideas through freewriting or research (lateral thinking) before you narrow them (vertical thinking). You'll learn more about this process in Chapter Nine, "Success with Language."

But sometimes vertical thinking will come first. If you evaluate an idea and discover it doesn't work or isn't true, you'll use lateral thinking to discover new possibilities. Suppose, for example, that you decide to begin a jogging program. If it doesn't work for you (a vertical-thinking decision), you might start exploring other fitness possibilities (lateral thinking). Vertical thinking appears again when you make another choice, try it, and evaluate the results. Problem solving often follows this cyclical pattern.

Often, lateral and vertical thinking work together. Imagine that you're listening to a speech about rising crime rates. The speaker says criminals are being set free because jails and prisons are too small. She argues that your state can reduce crime by expanding its correctional facilities. If you think laterally about crime—trying to generate as many causes of crime as you can—you might come up with a list like this one:

Causes of crime:

> alcohol and illegal drugs
> gang activity
> lack of pride in the community
> poverty
> delayed effects of child abuse
> peer pressure
> weak family structure
> inadequate schools
> lack of consequences for minor offenses
> lack of recreation for young people.

The list you generated through lateral thinking can help you make a judgment about the speech (vertical thinking). Building more prisons won't eliminate the causes of crime and probably isn't the best solution. Skilled critical thinkers use both lateral and vertical thinking whenever they examine an issue.

EXERCISE 1: LATERAL VERSUS VERTICAL THINKING

Complete the activities below.

1. *The rest of this chapter will introduce you to many types of lateral and vertical thinking—but they won't always be labeled that way. As you read, circle or underline any examples of lateral thinking (LT) and vertical thinking (VT) that you find. Then meet with another student—or a small group—to compare and discuss your findings.*
2. *Think about the past week. When did you engage in lateral thinking (exploring possibilities) and vertical thinking (evaluating)? List as many examples as you can. Then meet with a small group of other students to discuss your lists.*

◆ THE IMPORTANCE OF ASSUMPTIONS ◆

Getting in touch with your assumptions is one of the keys to skillful critical thinking. Assumptions—the ideas and information we take for granted—shape every aspect of our lives. When you see a green traffic signal, you assume that it's safe to proceed through an intersection. The act of eating is preceded by assumptions about the safety and quality of the meal. Your choices of a college, a major, and a career (vertical thinking) are based on assumptions about the institution where you're enrolled, the lifestyle you want, your aptitudes and ability, and employment opportunities in the future.

Because assumptions are unexamined ideas, they have both negative and positive effects on our lives. If we had to evaluate every daily act, we would have no time left for friendship, learning, or recreation. There's nothing wrong with assuming that your wristwatch is working correctly and the headline in today's paper is accurate.

But assumptions can also be misleading: Life is full of misconceptions and unexpected possibilities. Good drivers, for example, don't assume that a green light guarantees safety; they cover the brake with the right foot while traveling through the intersection—just in case.

Of course, breaking through your assumptions isn't always that easy. Unless you're skilled at lateral thinking—generating new information and ideas—you may not see important possibilities available to you. Aldous Huxley's 1932 novel *Brave New World* has a number of examples of "tethered thinking" (assumptions that limit possibilities). Huxley leaped six hundred years into the future to imagine a world almost free of suffering. Every human is scientifically programmed for happiness; disease, crime, and poverty have been virtually eliminated.

But Huxley's vision of future technology was limited by his own assumptions about what science could accomplish. As a result, his "brave new world" lacks some of the modern technology we take for granted, such as television and contraception. Here, for example, is Huxley's description of a news reporter making a radio transmission six hundred years from now:

> And rapidly, with a series of ritual gestures, he uncoiled two wires connected to the portable battery buckled round his waist; plugged them simultaneously into the sides of his aluminum hat; touched a spring on the crown—and antennae shot up into the air; touched another spring on the peak of the brim—and, like a jack-in-the-box, out jumped a microphone and hung there, quivering, six inches in front of his ears; pressed a switch on the left side of the hat—and from within came a faint waspy buzzing; turned a knob on the right—and the buzzing was interrupted by a stethoscopic wheeze and cackle, by hiccoughs and sudden squeaks.

Huxley did not foresee our widespread use of transistors and other more sophisticated electronic equipment. Although his vision of the future still transcends much of what we are experiencing today, he couldn't break free of his assumptions about radios, which were still bulky, cabinet-sized items in 1932.

Although there are no warranties against mistaken assumptions, you can minimize their dangers. First, be aware of your own assumptions. Second, strive to open yourself up to broad possibilities (lateral thinking). Third, become a lifelong learner and thinker, constantly expanding your knowledge and evaluating your own mental processes.

In everyday life, unexamined assumptions may limit your potential for academic, professional, and personal happiness. The beliefs you formed about yourself in elementary school or your teens may not be accurate. You probably have intelligent friends who mistakenly believe they aren't college material. In the same way, you may have untapped social, artistic, intellectual, or athletic potential.

Finally, mistaken assumptions can lead to errors in judgment: Stereotypes and prejudice grow on unexamined beliefs, as do many of life's errors. Students often mistaken-

Mistaken Assumptions in History

Alexander Graham Bell, inventor of the telephone, assumed it would be used primarily to educate persons who are hearing-impaired. Photocopy machines and cellular telephones took decades to reach the marketplace because their inventors assumed that consumers would not be interested. Composer Scott Joplin (1868–1917) did not foresee the popularity of "mechanical" musical devices—player pianos and phonographs. Because he didn't protect the mechanical rights to his music, Joplin missed a fortune in royalty payments. In 1948, the founder of IBM predicted that someday up to twelve companies would have their own computers.

During World War II, Great Britain and the United States obtained a duplicate of a Nazi machine that sent and decoded secret military messages. The British and Americans worried that the Nazis would eventually realize what had happened and switch to another message system. But the Nazis could not conceive of the possibility that their enemies had obtained the machine. In spite of vast evidence that the Western Allies had discovered their secret, the Nazis continued to rely on their machine.

In World War II, the Western Allies often encouraged incorrect assumptions that confused Nazi leadership. In 1940, a small British fighting force in Egypt needed to convince the enemy that it was actually a large army. The British soldiers obtained hundreds of inflatable rubber tanks and trucks that looked real from a distance. They also hired Arabs to drive huge numbers of camels and horses through the area. When enemy planes flew overhead, they saw great clouds of dust that resembled a large army on the move. The final result was a victory for the outnumbered British soldiers.

Mistaken Assumptions in Everyday Life

Although you may not encounter large-scale deceptions in your everyday life, assumptions can mislead you in many ways. For example, manufacturers of brand-name products want consumers to assume that store brands are always inferior. But all bleach is identical, no matter who manufactured it; so are aspirin, sugar, and a host of other products. Voters can be misled by political assumptions in the same way. For example, a politician who loudly advocates "free enterprise" may also endorse government subsidies for special interests in industry or agriculture. A candidate who favors environmental or consumer concerns may vote quite differently after the election has been won.

ly assume that a difficult assignment can be completed in a short time. They may also harbor mistaken beliefs about tests (assuming that a test will be easy, or will include only multiple-choice questions), purchases (believing that a new product can make life meaningful and fulfilling), and career choices (assuming that jobs in a particular field will be plentiful after graduation).

The following exercise will help you get in touch with some of your own assumptions about college and careers—and to learn more about assumptions and their origins.

EXERCISE 2: EVALUATE YOUR ASSUMPTIONS

1. List the assumptions you held about college before you actually enrolled. (Leave spaces between the items so that you can add notes later.)

2. Put a plus sign in front of every assumption that turned out to be true, and a minus sign in front of each you discovered was false.

3. Reread your list, asking yourself where your assumptions came from. Write informal notes so that you can share your experiences in a group later.

4. List the discoveries about college you've made since you enrolled.

5. Meet with a group of three or four students to compare and discuss the lists you made for this exercise. What has your college experience taught you about assumptions?

6. List the assumptions—positive and negative—you have about a career that interests you. (You do not have to be seriously committed to this career.)

7. *Reread your list, asking where your assumptions came from. Write informal notes to share with your group.*

8. *Meet with a group of three or four students to discuss these career assumptions. Note any insights they offer about the career you selected.*

9. *Evaluate both group activities (5 and 8). What are the benefits of sharing your expectations with others? Did you notice any effects of the group discussion? If so, what were they?*

◆ BROADEN YOUR THINKING THROUGH ◆ NEW EXPERIENCES

You can't think without a store of ideas.

RUDOLF FLESCH

When an athlete breaks a record, other athletes often duplicate that achievement a short time later: The broken record causes them to rethink their assumptions about what an athlete can do.

You may have had a similar breakthrough yourself, in a less dramatic way, when a friend's achievements or a new learning experience inspired you to rethink your assumptions about your own potential. Perhaps a college course showed you that you're better at mathematics, writing, or science than you formerly believed. The seven suggestions that follow will also help you "untether" assumptions that limit your thinking. (Notice that all are aids to lateral thinking.)

Athletes break records when they challenge their old assumptions about what they can and can't do.

1. Read.

Because written words put you directly in touch with another person's thoughts, reading is one of the best ways to broaden your experience. A well-written book or essay can connect you to the mind and heart of great men and women from the past and present. If you have a library card—and you should—you can acquire an extensive education at low cost: The latest and best ideas about technology, ethics, philosophy, psychology, religion, and government are available free of charge.

2. Be curious.

Use the subjects you're studying as a source of new insight into everyday experience. Look for connections between courses in the natural sciences and the physical world around you. Apply sociological and psychological principles as you observe people around you; link education theory to schools you've attended. If you study a foreign language, you may become interested in features of your native tongue that you never noticed before, such as spelling, idioms, verb endings, and word order. You'll find yourself wondering how your language acquired its unique characteristics, and you may be curious about other languages and cultures around the world.

3. Be adventurous.

Every time you venture into the unknown, the familiar begins to look different. Any new experience can open your thinking to new possibilities. In the previous chapter, Dr. Marsha Sinetar suggested that shy persons try activities normally performed by extroverted people—selling Tupperware, for example—and that extroverts try working in solitary settings. If you want to expand your thinking, especially your beliefs about yourself and your abilities, become a risk-taker. Explore new neighborhoods, businesses, holidays, religious outlooks, and ethnic groups. Get to know people whose backgrounds are different from yours. Campus clubs, visiting speakers, and special events can be rich sources for growth.

4. Grab a pen or pencil.

Every chapter in this book includes a journal activity designed to expand your thinking. If you take the advice on these pages—travel, read, meet new people, take risks— you'll learn a great deal. But you'll learn even more if you write about your experiences. The physical movement of the pen or pencil across the page pulls new ideas out of you. If words stifle you, try doodles or cartoons. (The section on drawing and writing later in this chapter offers additional suggestions.)

Become involved in campus activities that will expose you to new ideas and experiences.

5. Make friends.

In-depth conversations with trusted friends can do much to broaden your thinking. Author Eileen Livers has described the profound effect her new college friends had on her thinking:

> Upon leaving the predominantly Jewish community where I was raised, I found myself surrounded by people of all denominations. I soon learned that they were not so different from me. What surprised me was that even though we all had been raised in households with different faiths and traditions, we all had similar values.
>
> All my life I'd thought that Jewish values were different from those values taught by other faiths. But just as I had been taught to be generous and loving, to encourage peace and not war, and to cherish friends and family, so had my friends of other religions.

6. Seek new cultural experiences.

Many college students underestimate their capacity to enjoy and understand great cultural experiences. Seize every opportunity to visit art shows, listen to music, view drama and dance. Keep an open mind: Many cultural experiences can be intensely enjoyable even if you lack formal training in art, music, or dance. You may be astonished and delighted at your ability to be moved by images, color, language, sound, and movement. Such experiences can open your mind and heart to undreamed-of possibilities for enjoyment and self-expression.

7. Take a lively interest in the world around you.

Thomas Alva Edison (1847–1931) is often called a genius by those who have studied his life and accomplishments. An extraordinarily creative thinker, Edison invented the incandescent light bulb, motion picture camera, mimeograph machine, and over a thousand other inventions.

His friend Henry Ford (1863–1947), who developed the gasoline-powered automobile, once told a story that helps explain Edison's "genius." While Ford and Edison were visiting a mutual friend, they were asked to sign the guest book, which had spaces for names, addresses, occupations, and interests. In the last column, Edison wrote just one word: "Everything."

COLLABORATIVE ACTIVITY: LOOK FOR NEW EXPERIENCES

Meet with three or four other students to list opportunities for new experiences on your campus and in the nearby community. Refer to campus publications and community newspapers and magazines for ideas. Look for opportunities to mingle with other cultures, national groups, ethnic groups, age groups, and religions. Also consider gender, business, and government. Finally, list experiences that would expose you to unfamiliar aspects of art, history, philosophy, and science. When you finish your list, put a star in front of any activities that are free.

Seven Common Thinking Errors

1. False choice (mistakenly assuming you must choose between only two possibilities).
2. Oversimplification (failing to see how complex an issue is).
3. Mindreading (guessing, instead of trying to find out, what others are thinking).
4. Ignoring or misreading evidence (evaluating information improperly).
5. Mistaken priorities (failing to determine what is most important).
6. Manipulative language (using words to confuse or mislead).
7. Errors in thinking about time (misunderstanding the effects of time).

Recognizing Thinking Errors

Vertical thinking—the ability to evaluate the quality of ideas—is an important component of critical thinking. Skill in recognizing and correcting thinking errors (often called "fallacies") is vital to your success in college.

Its importance continues after graduation when you're making decisions as a professional, a citizen, and a consumer. Our information-rich age is also, unfortunately, an "error-rich" age. Political and corporate advertising often mixes useful knowledge with misleading claims. Information sources you'll rely on for professional information will also require careful sifting and evaluating.

1. False choice (often called either/or thinking)

Instead of seeing all the possibilities available, unskilled thinkers may limit themselves to two. Perhaps you knew someone in high school who thought that marriage was the only way to escape the restrictions of living at home. Actually the possibilities are almost endless: sharing a home with a friend or relative, living in a "Y," working for room and board, earning enough money to move out, and so on.

Either/or thinking is often seen in family life. For example, parents may believe there are just two ways to rear children: through physical punishment or permissiveness. Only when they meet parents who use other methods do they begin to see broader possibilities.

Either/or thinking is widespread in college as well. Many students mistakenly believe they must choose between college and working, or college and marriage. A young person may abandon the dream of higher education because family finances won't permit it; the possibility of other kinds of financing—or attending a less expensive institution—is never considered.

Either/or thinking can prevent leaders in business, science, and government from exploring all the possible solutions to a problem. Should we prevent crime, or punish it? Protect the environment, or push for prosperity? Experiment on animals, or stop seeking new cures for diseases? All these questions are based on either/or thinking.

2. Oversimplification

People often underestimate the complexity of an issue. For example, some scientists believe that the government should test every citizen's DNA (unique genetic pattern) and keep a DNA file on everyone. They argue that crimes would be much easier to solve, since a criminal's DNA is often found at the crime scene in blood or perspiration stains. But other issues need to be raised. Here are one student's thoughts about required DNA testing:

> In high school I participated in a statewide baseball tournament. That experience taught me a lot about the problems of big projects. The baseball tournament was fun, but many mistakes were made. Names were misspelled, and I heard that one team had a player listed who didn't even attend that school. There was confusion about scheduling the games at each level of competition. Team and player stats weren't always recorded correctly. Drug testing was required for everybody, but the test results sometimes got lost. Some players were tested three times instead of one.
> That experience makes me suspicious about government testing for DNA. How could they be sure the tests were done correctly and recorded correctly? With millions of tests, at least a few mistakes are sure to be made. Suppose an innocent person was accused of a crime because his DNA record was wrong. How could he defend himself? I wonder about people's rights too. Couldn't untrustworthy people get into the DNA files and use DNA to invade their privacy?

3. Mindreading

"Mindreading" happens any time a person assumes he or she knows what another person is thinking. Jan Carlzon, president of Scandinavian Airlines, has described a mind-reading mistake employees at his airline made early in his career, when they organized a series of tours just for senior citizens. Assuming the travelers would be frail and timid, the airline arranged for nurses and slow-paced excursions. Quiet pastimes like bingo and cards were the only forms of entertainment.

Although the airline invested $100,000 in advertising, almost no one signed up. Too late, the organizers discovered that senior travelers are an active group of people who seek adventure and opportunities to mix with young people. The managers should have asked seniors what travel arrangements they preferred—or talked to sales staff and tour conductors who had extensive experience with senior groups.

Mindreading often occurs in business: Top-level managers assume they have all the answers although they have little contact with customers and clients. As a result, some business experts, such as Tom Peters and Karl Albrecht, encourage top management to listen to the employees who are most familiar with people who purchase and use a company's products.

Mindreading also occurs in families. For example, if parents don't seek input from their children, a family outing may be a disaster. Sometimes a surprise gift can turn out to be a mistake: Grown children purchase furniture, a trip, or a dog that their parents can't use and don't want.

In college, mindreading may cause you to miss a friendship you would have enjoyed. One sophomore turned down a date saying, "I know I wouldn't enjoy an evening with a math major—all they think about is numbers." She was dismayed to find out later that he had many of the same interests she did—and was a superb dancer as well.

You can avoid mindreading by testing your assumptions about the ideas, wishes and feelings of others. Ask questions, seek suggestions, and pay close attention to the responses you hear. Attentive listening is a vital skill for critical thinkers.

4.   Ignoring or misinterpreting evidence

In the early 1950s, American schools faced an unforeseen crisis. Thousands of children were ready to enter school—but no classrooms or teachers were ready for them. The "Baby Boom" had begun in 1947, after the end of World War II, when the American birthrate rose dramatically. But local school boards, busy with other tasks, hadn't looked at recent birth statistics. When the children entered kindergarten and first grade, schools had to schedule split sessions, and new schools were hastily built.

Many problems can be traced to evidence that has been ignored or misinterpreted. The Coca-Cola company introduced its "New Coke" when studies showed that customers preferred a sweeter soft drink. But Coca-Cola's market research had underestimated customer loyalty to its original soft drink, which was going to be taken off the market. Although the company had spent vast sums on its marketing and advertising plan, New Coke failed to win customer approval. Coca-Cola returned to its original soft drink, renamed "Classic Coke." After spending huge sums on unsuccessful New Coke promotions, the company was back where it had started.

Daily life is full of similar—if less dramatic—stories. Everyone who buys cigarettes, experiments with illegal drugs, or drives with an unbuckled seat belt is ignoring vast evidence about the risks of such behavior. In family life, many children and parents allow themselves to be influenced by the false statement that "everyone is doing it." In college, students may waste months or years preparing for a career that doesn't suit them or offer sufficient employment opportunities. Thorough and extensive research should always precede an important decision.

5.   Mistaken priorities

In 1912, 1,503 persons drowned when the ocean liner *Titanic* collided with an iceberg and sank in the North Atlantic. Tragically, because the ship had been considered unsinkable, it was not equipped with enough lifeboats to carry all the passengers and crew. But the ultimate cause of the disaster was mistaken priorities. The captain, navigating in fog around many icebergs, should have slowed down the ship's engines. He decided not to cut back the engines, however, because a slower speed would have lengthened the trip and decreased profits for the parent company. His choice of money over safety doomed the ship and many of its passengers and crew.

Critical thinkers know how to choose what's most important and follow through on their decision. But not everyone is a skilled thinker: The results of mistaken priorities appear everywhere. An unsuccessful sales representative may keep calling on the same prospects, despite poor responses, rather than trying to develop new customers. A town that supports itself through hunting or fishing may waste time and money fighting legislation designed to protect a disappearing species. Although the workers know their jobs will be gone in a few years, they may not look for alternative means of livelihood until they're out of work.

Disordered priorities can be seen in families as well. Parents may declare that family life comes first for them, but allow household maintenance or community affairs to consume all their free time. Children can create tension by ignoring values important to their parents—by failing in school, for example, or refusing to join in family activities.

College students too may make poor choices about investing their time and money. The "$25,000 idea" you learned about in Chapter Two is one of the keys to success and happiness. Make thoughtful decisions about what's most important to you, and follow through on them.

6. Manipulative language

According to novelist George Orwell, "If thought corrupts language, language can also corrupt thought." His novel *1984* describes a futuristic world in which the government uses language to confuse and control its followers. The citizens in *1984* are required to practice "reality control"—clearing their memories of past historical events that embarrass the government. Old, shabby apartments are called Victory Mansions, and a Ministry of Love executes criminals.

But you don't have to read fantasy to learn about misuses of language. The famous linguist Noam Chomsky notes the confusing ways in which the political terms "special interest" and "national interest" are often used. The phrase "special interest" is usually applied to mainstream Americans: women, the elderly, labor, and farmers. When we talk about "national interest," however, we often mean only a small sector of American life—corporations and large businesses.

Both consumer and voter behavior can be manipulated by a persuasive device called "glittering generalities." Sometimes a politician will gain popularity by speaking eloquently about a noble concept such as freedom, justice, family values, or equal opportunity. What may be lacking, however, is a specific, workable program to initiate positive changes.

In the same way, advertisers may suggest that a product will bring you fun, popularity, attractiveness, improved health, or a better relationship. In reality, the product may be nothing more than a skin cream, bottled drink, hair preparation, or CD player. No product can be guaranteed to duplicate the eye-catching models and settings you see on TV.

Name-calling is another way to manipulate through words. Critical thinking requires a slow, thoughtful examination of new proposals, programs, and ideas. But name-callers use negative labels to push you into agreeing with their position without taking time to evaluate the evidence. Voters may be urged to vote against a proposal because it is "socialist," "liberal," "reactionary," or "fanatical." Actually it may be none of these. But if the label sticks, voters may not take the trouble to think deeply about the issue and draw their own conclusions.

Personal attacks can also be used to manipulate you into rejecting a person's ideas. To prevent you from listening to a new program or idea, opponents will try to turn you against the person who originated it. You may be told that a public figure is "out of touch," "bigoted," or "close-minded."

People who use personal attack often want you to focus on a person's private life rather than his or her knowledge. A pediatrician who has never been a parent may still have valuable knowledge about rearing a child. A single person may have learned a great deal about marriage from college courses, married friends, and professional study.

Sometimes brilliant thinkers are ignored because they're unknown or have unpleasant personal traits. Scientists, for example, may have difficulty having their ideas published if they're not connected with a famous university or research organization. If you're a critical thinker, you won't allow yourself to be influenced by personal attacks: You'll judge an idea solely on its own merits.

7. Errors in thinking about time

Sometimes a time relationship is confused with a causal one. If you fail a chemistry test after walking under a ladder, you might blame the ladder for your failure. If you do well on the chemistry test, you might credit the "lucky shirt" you were wearing. The truth, however, is that your actions created the test grade.

Many popular—but mistaken—beliefs originate with this mistake. For example, space shots are often said to cause bad weather; a full moon may be blamed for someone's odd behavior; a minor illness might be incorrectly traced to a food eaten earlier in the day; an illness clears up on its own, but the cure is mistakenly attributed to medicine taken the day before.

If you're a sharp critical thinker, you'll discover many more examples. For example, educators have long tried to explain the decline in high-school seniors' SAT scores that begin in the mid-1960's. Television is often blamed, since these students were the first American children to grow up with TV. Some authorities point to Dr. Benjamin Spock, since these children grew up after his book *Baby and Child Care* was published. But far more evidence is needed to prove that TV or Spock's book caused the decline in SAT scores. The truth about the declining scores is probably much more complex than either of these explanations. One possible explanation is put forward by psychologist Stephen Glenn, who has noted that many children from this generation grew up without the love and support of an extended family. As Americans became more mobile, they visited less often with grandparents, aunts, uncles, and cousins. Another explanation is that a different group of students began taking the SAT in 1964, since more low-income families were sending their children to college.

Time errors also occur because people fail to realize when a problem actually started. In *The Seven Habits of Highly Effective People*, author Stephen R. Covey explains how he and his wife, Sandra, successfully traced a problem in their relationship. Covey was puzzled and angry because Sandra insisted on buying only Frigidaire appliances—sometimes at great expense and inconvenience. One day, during a quiet picnic at the beach, Sandra got in touch with some early memories that explained her obsession. Her father, an appliance dealer, had almost lost his business; the Frigidaire company came to his rescue by financing his inventory. Covey wrote, "I came to realize that Sandra wasn't talking about appliances; she was talking about her father, and about loyalty—loyalty to his needs."

EXERCISE 3: LOOK FOR THINKING ERRORS

Fifteen brief stories appear below. Some are examples of effective thinking; in others the thinking is faulty. Evaluate the thinking processes in each one (refer to the list of "Thinking Errors" on page 252). When you're finished, meet with a group of three or four other students to discuss and compare your evaluations.

1. *Several students were planning a class presentation for a political science course. One student, Sue, suggested making a campus political survey and including the results in the presentation. But another student argued that Sue's idea had to be a bad one because she wasn't earning good grades in the course.*

2. *A young Irish woman named Elizabeth Gurley, desperate to leave her unhappy home, married an older man named George Carr Shaw. (Later they became the parents of playwright George Bernard Shaw.) On their honeymoon, Elizabeth Shaw discovered that her husband was an alcoholic. She ran away from her hotel room to the city docks, intending to seek a job on one of the ships. But the dockhands jeered at her, and she ran back to the hotel and her husband.*

3. *In pre-World War II Germany, Adolf Hitler convinced voters that they had to choose between National Socialism (Nazism) and communism. When the Nazi party was voted into office, disastrous consequences followed that eventually plunged Europe and North America into war.*

4. *In 1960, Roman Catholic Senator John F. Kennedy won the Democratic nomination for president of the United States. Some opponents told Americans to vote against Kennedy because of his religion. They claimed that, if elected, Kennedy would be more loyal to his religion than to the people of the United States.*

5. *A first-year college student purchased a new brand of cologne she had seen advertised in a magazine. After she'd worn it for two days, a basketball player she'd been interested in asked her for a date. Five of her friends immediately bought a bottle of the cologne.*

6. *During the Crimean War (1853–1856), many British soldiers died of starvation. At the same time, officials allowed food to rot in military warehouses rather than send it to the front without the proper paperwork.*

7. *A student newspaper carried an advertisement for a diet patch that could be worn on the skin for dramatic weight loss. But when students purchased the diet patch, they discovered it had to be used with a strict diet and a demanding exercise program.*

8. *In his book* Between Parent and Child, *Dr. Haim Ginott urged parents to help their children distinguish between minor and major problems. "Many parents react to a broken egg as to a broken leg, to a shattered window as to a shattered heart. . . . A lost glove need*

not lead to a lost temper; a torn shirt need not serve as a prop for a do-it-yourself Greek tragedy."

9. *When a college student went home for a visit during the holidays, his parents told him that three couples they knew had just been divorced. The student remarked, "Marriage is on its way out. Nobody stays married anymore."*

10. *When television became popular in the 1950's, executives in many film studios worried that Americans would stop going to movie theaters. Walt Disney, however, thought TV could be used to promote his films. He persuaded the ABC network to broadcast* Disneyland *every Wednesday night. This family show offered behind-the-scenes glimpses of old and new Disney feature films. Both the television show and film studio enjoyed enormous success.*

11. *Jan Carlzon, president of SAS airlines, talks about passengers rather than airplanes. Since he took charge of SAS, he's made it a "service-oriented business" rather than an "asset-oriented business." According to Carlzon, businesses need to make distinctions between secondary concerns—buildings and equipment—and primary concerns—satisfied customers who plan to return in the future.*

12. *The director of student activities on a college campus received a brochure advertising a dance festival in a nearby town. He decided not to post the brochure because the students on his campus wouldn't be interested.*

13. *A number of people deny that 6 million Jews died in the Nazi Holocaust of World War II. As proof, they note even before the Holocaust began, Germany's Jewish population was much smaller than 6 million people. Members of this anti-Holocaust group usually don't realize that Jews from other countries, including France, Italy, the Netherlands, Hungary, Poland, Russia, Czechoslovakia, and Yugoslavia died in Nazi concentration camps.*

14. *After baseball star Jackie Robinson left professional sports, he devoted himself to helping other African-Americans. Once a friend remarked, during a conversation about minority problems, "Good schooling comes first." Robinson disagreed. "Housing is the first thing," he said. "Unless he's got a home he wants to come back to, it doesn't matter what kind of school he goes to."*

15. *A pet cat belonging to a monastery was disturbing the evening meditation period by meowing and running among the monks. To solve the problem, a monk was assigned to tie up the cat every evening. Years passed, and the cat eventually died. The monks adopted another cat so they could tie it up every evening just before meditation time.*

READING THOUGHTFULLY: THINKING ABOUT MOTORCYCLES

Good thinkers are skilled at identifying errors in reasoning. But critical thinking includes much more, as you'll see in the description of motorcycle maintenance written by Robert

M. Pirsig. Like Pirsig, good critical thinkers often discover connections between everyday experiences and universal ideas and concepts. His friend John, by contrast, looks only for surface meanings in the world around him. Before you begin reading, complete the following activity.

BEFORE YOU READ

1. Zen Buddhism is a religion that encourages its followers to seek enlightenment through thoughtful observation and meditation. What would you expect to learn by watching a mechanic tune up a motorcycle?

2. What are the advantages and disadvantages of using a motorcycle for transportation?

---

from **Zen and the Art of Motorcycle Maintenance**
by Robert M. Pirsig

Not everyone understands what a completely rational process this is, this maintenance of a motorcycle. They think it's some kind of a "knack" or some kind of "affinity for machines" in operation. They are right, but this knack is almost purely a process of reason, and most of the troubles are caused by what old time radio men called a "short between the earphones," failures to use the head properly. A motorcycle functions entirely in accordance with the laws of reason, and a study of the art of motorcycle maintenance is really a miniature study of the art of rationality itself.

The porcelain inside this first plug is very dark. The carbon molecules in the gasoline aren't finding enough oxygen to combine with and they're just sitting here loading up the plug. Coming into town yesterday the idle was loping a little, which is a symptom of the same thing.

Just to see if it's just the one cylinder that's rich, I check the other one. They're both the same. I get out a pocket knife, grab a stick lying in the gutter and whittle down the end to clean out the plugs, wondering what could be the cause of the richness. The first tappet is right on, no adjustment required, so I move on to the next. Still plenty of time before the sun gets past those trees. . . . I always feel like I'm in church when I do this. . . . The gage is some kind of religious icon and I'm performing a holy rite with it. It is a member of a set called "precision measuring instruments" which in a classic sense has a profound meaning.

In a motorcycle this precision isn't maintained for any romantic or perfectionist reasons. It's simply that the enormous forces of heat and explosive pressure inside this engine can only be controlled through the kind of precision these instruments give. When each explosion takes place, it drives a connecting rod onto the crankshaft with a surface pressure of many tons per square inch. If the fit of the rod to the crankshaft is precise, the explosion force will be transferred smoothly and the metal will be able to stand it. But if the fit is loose by a distance of only a few thousandths of an inch, the force will be delivered suddenly, like a hammer blow, and the rod, bearing and crankshaft surface will soon be pounded flat, creating a noise which at first sounds a lot like loose tappets. That's the reason I'm checking it now. If it *is* a loose rod and I try to make it to the mountains without an overhaul, it will soon get louder and louder until the rod tears itself free, slams into the spinning crankshaft and destroys the engine. Sometimes broken rods will pile right down through the crankcase and dump all the oil onto the road. All you can do then is start walking.

But all this can be prevented by a few thousandths of an inch fit which precision measuring instruments give, and this is their classical beauty—not what you see, but what they mean—what they are capable of in terms of control of underlying form.

The second tappet's fine. I swing over to the street side of the machine and start on the other cylinder. Precision instruments are designed to achieve an *idea*, dimensional precision, whose perfection is impossible. There is no perfectly shaped part of the motorcycle and never will be, but when you come as close as these instruments take you, remarkable things happen, and you go flying across the countryside under a power that would be called magic if it were not so completely rational in every way. It's the understanding of this rational intellectual *idea* that's fundamental. John looks at the motorcycle and he sees steel in various shapes and has negative feelings about these steel shapes and turns off the whole thing. I look at the shapes of the steel now and I see *ideas*. He thinks I'm working on *parts*. I'm working on *concepts*.

AFTER YOU READ

1. Did you encounter any new words in this selection? How will you find out their meaning?

2. What questions do you have about this reading? How will you find the answers?

3. What ideas does Pirsig think about as he cleans the plugs of his motorcycle engine?

4. What is different about John's way of thinking about the motorcycle engine?

5. Think of an item you own that you can think about in two ways—as *parts* or as *ideas*. Write a sentence describing one or more parts of the item you've chosen; then write another sentence about ideas related to the item you've chosen.

6. Share your answers to question 5 with another student. Do both of you see the item, its parts, and its ideas the same way?

7. Reread your answers to the two questions in "Before You Read." How did the reading selection alter your understanding of motorcycles and their maintenance? Be specific about any new ideas or insights that came to you.

Applying Critical Thinking to Human Diversity

The thinking skills you are learning can significantly improve your ability to relate to others—a vital quality in both college and the professional world. Good thinkers appreciate human diversity and avoid hasty generalizations about people. But poor thinkers often feel threatened and judgmental when they encounter others who are different in some way.

Here are four common mistakes related to human diversity:

1. Oversimplification

   If you believe that all women instinctively enjoy child care, or that Asians always do well in school, you're oversimplifying. People are much too varied to be grouped this way: Even children born to the same family are likely to grow up differently. Strive to treat people as individuals, not stereotypes.

2. False choice

   In one big-city high school, the athletics director always urges African-American athletes to try out for track, football, or basketball. Failure to explore other possibilities (swimming, hockey, soccer) is an example of false choice.

3. Mindreading

   Don't let group labels fool you into thinking you know what others want or expect. (Jan Carlzon, you'll remember, made this error when he made travel plans for senior citizens.) Cultivate good listening habits; ask others what they think instead of assuming you already know.

4. Ignoring or misreading evidence

   When others make errors or act foolishly, it's easy to misjudge them. Don't be too quick in your evaluation of people's intelligence or maturity. (You've probably made foolish mistakes yourself—everyone has.) Drawing conclusions without sufficient evidence contributes to prejudice and can cause you to miss rewarding relationships.

EXERCISE 4: THINK ABOUT THE PEOPLE YOU KNOW

Complete the activities below.

1. *Spend a few minutes thinking about your family (both close and distant relatives). List the generalizations an observer could make about your family. Then note the ways in which you are different. Finally, make a list of other relatives who are "different" from the family norm.*

2. *List any comments you remember hearing about people in your age group. Then note the ways in which you are different from this generalized picture. Finally, make a list of others in your age group who are also "different."*

3. *List any comments you remember hearing about college students. Meet with three or four other students to discuss your lists. In what ways are you similar to other students? How are you different?*

4. *Reread your answers to the preceding three questions. What conclusion can you make about generalizations about people?*

◆ AN INEXPENSIVE THINKING TOOL: YOUR PENCIL ◆

Because our society relies so much on technology, we sometimes overlook simple tools that can enhance learning and develop thinking skills. The ordinary pencil is one. You've already seen that Samuel Scudder used a pencil to study his fish (Chapter One). In the last chapter you saw that you can become a more effective reader by marking up a reading selection with a pencil. Writing (and drawing) can be an important component of learning because you become a more active thinker. On the following pages you'll be introduced to nine ways you can use a pencil to develop your ability to think critically.

GETTING IN TOUCH THROUGH FREEWRITING

Spend five or ten minutes freewriting about informal writing and drawing as learning activities. The following list of suggestions may help you get started:

> *writing in margins*
> *diagrams in notebooks*

sketches in lab reports

sketches of what you see outdoors

doodles

notes

mind maps

journals

Think Creatively with the Help of Your Pencil

1. Imagine something new—and draw it.

Aldous Huxley couldn't conceive of a miniature radio—but other thinkers did. Without them, we would still be using the bulky radio sets of the 1930's and 1940's. Imagination is an important component of scientific thinking, as you'll see in Chapter Nine: Scientists—and other skillful thinkers—often work out ideas with a pencil and paper. The great Renaissance artist and inventor Leonardo da Vinci (1452–1519) anticipated many later inventions in his drawings; Thomas Edison relied on sketches to develop his new ideas.

DaVinci invents a bicycle.

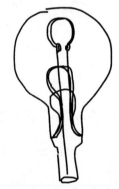

Edison's sketch of a light bulb.
Imagine something new and draw it.

2. Simplify by drawing a sketch.

When you're studying a complex system, such as the workings of the human body, sketch or diagram one component at a time: respiration, reproduction, digestion, or circulation. A simple drawing, diagram, or chart can increase your understanding of history, science, business, economics, psychology, and other subjects.

In Chapter One you read about a ballet student who studied muscle groups in connection with his dance training. He found it helpful to sketch muscles used in various dance movements; he also clipped dance photos from old magazines and labeled the muscle groups at work.

3.   Discover something new by altering a drawing or diagram.

Draw a picture that alters something familiar to you. Often the result will be a new idea or insight. Create a hospital without nurses' stations, a science lab without sinks, or a classroom without desks.

4.   Write about something impossible.

Creative writing is another useful way to discover new possibilities. For example, write a dialogue between Florence Nightingale, the founder of professional nursing, and a modern nurse. You can also use cartoons and drawings to broaden your thinking. Try sketching something familiar in a new way, or making a change in something you know well.

5.   Use words or pictures to sort items or ideas.

Drawing and writing are excellent aids to sorting (classification)—an important process in both the academic and professional world. Sometimes the sorting process will broaden your understanding (lateral thinking). Imagine that you're a criminal-justice major. How would you classify the kinds of forbidden items (contraband) often found in a correctional institution? One student devised three categories: items brought in by outsiders, items stolen by inmates, and items illegally made by the inmates themselves. From there he was able to think of preventive strategies that hadn't occurred to him before.

The sorting process can also help you make judgments (vertical thinking). Fold a piece of paper in half, listing positive factors on one side, and negatives on the other. By comparing both lists, you can evaluate an idea, policy, invention, or event. (For greater insights, thinking expert Edward de Bono suggests adding a third list, "Interesting," to the plus and minus categories.)

6.   Use words or sketches to break a problem into smaller parts.

When you examine inner workings or underlying principles, you are performing an analysis. Both drawing and writing are excellent aids to analysis. Diagraming a scientific process will help you understand the steps more thoroughly; flow charts are helpful when you're studying business and psychology. In English and humanities classes, use informal words and pictures to analyze how a literary work, painting, or symphony was put together.

Drawing and writing are extremely helpful with analytical questions on tests, like this one:

A fox set out traveling west. After an hour it turned right; fifteen minutes later it turned right again. Two hours later it turned left. What direction was it facing then?

Research shows that people who draw sketches and diagrams are the best performers on these tests. With a diagram, it's easy to analyze this question and reach the correct answer.

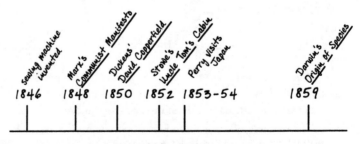

the fox was facing north.

Drawing and writing are extremely
helpful with analytical questions on tests.

7. Make a specialized map or time line.

A time line is an excellent tool for organizing facts about a complex historical event, scientific process, or literary work. You can also use an unlabeled map (available for photocopying in your college library—ask for *Maps on File*) to trace the progress of an exploration or a military invasion, or to understand how a variety of influences can shape a language—English, for example.

You can also use a time line to draw contrasts and similarities between events. The *World Almanac and Book of Facts*, published annually, features time lines comparing American and world history; it's even more helpful to draw your own, especially if you can include events from the history of art, science, literature, and business.

Make a specialized map or time line.

8. Use words or drawings to estimate the answer to a problem.

In mathematics, a quick sketch can help you choose an effective method to solve a problem. Suppose you're solving this arithmetic problem:

A woman who works for a department store has a 25% employee discount. She wants to buy two dresses. The marked price for one is $80; the second is marked $60. How much will the dresses cost her?

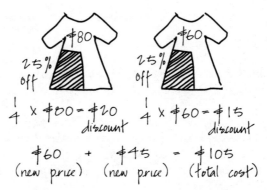

$$\frac{1}{4} \times \$80 = \$20 \text{ discount} \qquad \frac{1}{4} \times \$60 = \$15 \text{ discount}$$

$$\$60 \quad + \quad \$45 \quad = \quad \$105$$
(new price)   (new price)   (total cost)

**Use words or drawings to estimate
the answer to a problem.**

9. Use words and symbols for evaluation.

Use the "plus—minus—interesting" sorting system (Suggestion 5) whenever you're asked to make a value judgment—writing a book report, reviewing a musical performance, evaluating a case study in an ethics or business class.

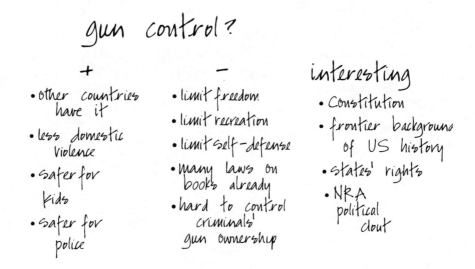

gun control?

+	−	interesting
• other countries have it	• limit freedom	• Constitution
• less domestic violence	• limit recreation	• frontier background of US history
• safer for kids	• limit self-defense	• states' rights
• safer for police	• many laws on books already	• NRA political clout
	• hard to control criminals' gun ownership	

Use words or pictures to sort items or ideas.

EXERCISE 5: USE YOUR PENCIL

PERFORM THREE OF THE ACTIVITIES IN THE FOLLOWING LIST.

1. *Create something new by writing in the two blank spaces:*

   a _____ without _____

(For example, your creation could be "a library without books.") Then draw a sketch or diagram showing what your creation might be like. Add words if you'd like.

2. *Sketch a familiar object; then alter it in some way to create something new.*
3. *Draw a simple sketch to illustrate a concept from a subject that interests you.*
4. *Choose a category that includes several kinds of items. (You could choose "writing instruments," for example.) Use words or pictures to sort them. Put a title on your description or picture.*
5. *Write about something impossible—a dialogue between two people from different centuries, a historical event that didn't happen, an unlikely event in the future.*
6. *In a few words, describe a problem you or another student might have to resolve. Use words or sketches to break the problem into smaller parts.*
7. *Make a list of geographical facts about a subject that interests you. Then arrange the facts on a simple map.*
8. *Make a chronological list of events related to a subject that interests you. Then arrange the events on a simple time line.*
9. *Invent a math problem, or choose one from a math course. Draw one or more pictures that might help in estimating the answer.*
10. *Evaluate a decision, event, invention, or experience using de Bono's "plus—minus— interesting" system.*

Freewrite about your experience with the three activities you choose. How did the activities feel? Did any of the results surprise you? Can you apply any of these activities again to your college studies?

Writing is a critical thinking activity as well as a form of self-expression.

JOURNAL ACTIVITY: DRAW AND WRITE

Each day this week, try one of the "Drawing and Writing" activities in the spaces below. Choose a situation from your daily experience—or an idea you met in a college class—and imagine, simplify, complicate, sort, analyze, make a time line, estimate, evaluate. The examples on pages 264 through 267 will help you get started. Don't limit yourself to the spaces on these pages: feel free to use additional pieces of paper if you'd like.)

DAY 1

DAY 2

DAY 3

DAY 4

DAY 5

DAY 6

DAY 7

USING WHAT YOU HAVE LEARNED

1. Clip five advertisements from magazines or newspapers. List the assumptions implied in each one. Put a check in front of each assumption you think is correct; draw a line through each one you disagree with.

2. Choose two well-written letters to the editors of magazines or newspapers. Write a few sentences explaining why each one impressed you.

3. Choose two poorly reasoned letters to the editors of magazines, newspapers, or both. Underline statements that demonstrate poor critical thinking. Write a few sentences explaining the thinking errors in each letter.

4. List ten actions you perform regularly. List one assumption related to each action. (For example, you assume that brushing your teeth prevents cavities and bad breath.)

5. Briefly describe an encounter with another person in which your assumptions or first impression turned out to be wrong.

6. Apply one of the nine drawing-and-writing activities on pages 264 through 267 to a subject you're studying now.

7. Discover examples of your own for three of the thinking errors on pages 252 through 256. Use your examples to explain the thinking error to another person.

8. Sometime during the next seven days, try an activity to broaden your experience (see pages 248 through 251). Afterward freewrite for five minutes about the experience. Did it match your expectations? Did you learn anything new? Did it cause you to modify any of your assumptions?

EVALUATING YOUR PROGRESS

1. As I look back on the past seven days, I've seen an improvement in these areas:

   _____ organizing my life

   _____ protecting my health

   _____ planning my time

   _____ concentrating

   _____ taking notes

   _____ active learning

   _____ reading critically

   _____ writing effectively

   _____ thinking critically

   _____ communicating with important people in my life

   _____ enjoying my free time

   _____ allowing myself to be imperfect

2. In the coming week, I plan to invest five minutes a day working towards this goal:

CHAPTER 9

Success with Language

Thought is born through words.

LEV VYGOTSKY

PREVIEW

1. Language skills are vital to your success in college and professional life.

2. Thorough preparation is one of the keys to success in public speaking.

3. Effective writers use a three-step writing process: planning, making a rough draft, and revising.

IN-CLASS INTRODUCTORY ACTIVITY: LANGUAGE SKILLS FOR YOUR CAREER

Imagine yourself in a career that sounds interesting to you. List the kinds of writing and speaking tasks you might be performing.

Your career and the writing and speaking tasks that go with it:

COLLABORATIVE ACTIVITY

Meet with a small group of other students to discuss your career choices and your lists of speaking and writing tasks.

GROUP DISCUSSION NOTES

◆ THE IMPORTANCE OF LANGUAGE SKILLS ◆

In almost every professional field, speaking and writing are vital to your success—and their importance increases as you move up to positions of greater responsibility. Anyone who supervises other employees or manages funds must keep records and write reports. Leaders must be able to influence others through spoken and written words. Writing for professional newsletters and journals, and speaking at meetings and conferences provide opportunities to showcase your ideas and abilities.

You can harness the power of language in other areas of your life as well. In your personal life, communication skills can enrich your relationships and help you resolve conflicts. In community life, they can make you a more effective citizen. Almost everyone sometimes feels frustrated about local or national government affairs; not everyone, however, has the skills needed to state a position persuasively and powerfully. By developing these abilities, you'll increase your self-esteem and enjoy the satisfaction that goes with contributing something positive to the world you live in.

How Will Your Language Skills Affect Your Career?

In 1992 a San Francisco software company asked one hundred top business executives how they make hiring and promotion decisions. Sixty-three percent of the executives said they believed poor writing skills were a sign of low intellectual ability. Eighty percent recalled at least one time when they'd decided not to interview an applicant because of a poorly written resume or cover letter. Ninety-nine percent said that poor writing and grammar were an obstacle to promotions.

Think about your own writing skills. Will they help or hurt you in the job market? If you're hired, will they help you earn a promotion? If not, what steps can you take right now to sharpen those skills?

A well-written application letter and resume can help you obtain an interview for a job that interests you.

Finally, language skills offer opportunities for creativity. If you can express yourself effectively, you can envision new ideas and possibilities—and communicate them to others.

READING THOUGHTFULLY: CREATING A PUBLIC SELF

The following selection was written by Richard Rodriguez, who teaches at the University of California at Berkeley. For Rodriguez, the American son of Mexican parents, Spanish was the language of home and family; English was the key to a new identity as an American citizen. Before you begin reading, complete the following activity.

BEFORE YOU READ

1. What do you think the term "public language" might mean?

2. Are there any differences between the way you speak at home and at school?

3. Do you think schools should pressure children to change the speech habits they learned at home?

---

from **"Aria: A Memoir of a Bilingual Childhood"**
by Richard Rodriguez

What I needed to learn in school was that I had the right, and the obligation, to speak the public language. Fortunately, my teachers were unsentimental about their responsibility. What they understood was that I needed to speak public English. So their voices would search me out, asking me questions. Each time I heard them, I'd look up in surprise to see a nun's face frowning at me. I'd mumble, not really meaning to answer. The nun would persist. "Richard, stand up. Don't look at the floor. Speak up. Speak to the entire class, not just to me!" But I couldn't believe English could be my language to use. I continued to mumble. I resisted the teacher's demands. Silent, waiting for the bell to sound, I remained dazed, diffident, afraid.

Sometime afterward it happened: one day in school, I raised my hand to volunteer an answer. I spoke out in a loud voice and I did not think it remarkable when the entire class understood. That day I moved very far from being the disadvantaged child I had been only days earlier. Taken hold at last was the belief, the calming assurance, that *I belonged* in public.

AFTER YOU READ

1. Did you encounter any new words in this selection? How will you learn their meaning?

2. Do you have any questions about this selection? What strategies will you use to answer them?

3. Have you found it easy or difficult to speak up in school and in college? What experiences can you recall about speaking in school?

4. Have you ever had an experience of "belonging in public" similar to the one described by Rodriguez?

5. Now that you've read this excerpt, what do you think a "public language" is? Do you think that you, like Rodriguez, sometimes speak a "public language"? When and where?

Developing Your "Public Language." Sometimes students feel uncomfortable with the sophisticated vocabulary, sentence structure, and style needed for most college writing assignments. Writing for college is a complex process that includes planning activities, a rough draft, and revising and editing for usage, punctuation, and spelling. Your ideas must be consistent, logical, and well developed; your style has to sound sophisticated enough for an academic audience; and your papers must be error-free.

Not surprisingly, college writing skills develop slowly for many students, who feel more comfortable with the spontaneity and flexibility of natural conversation. Sometimes students get frustrated by the requirements of college writing, which seem artificial and unnatural.

A number of strategies can help you feel more comfortable with college writing. First, remember that you're developing a new image: professional, educated, successful. Second, learn to shift gears. Words are flexible tools for self-expression: Many people speak and write more formally in a professional setting than they do with family and friends.

Relax and enjoy this process, and don't get discouraged if your development sometimes seems slow. Think of other challenges you've met—learning to ride a bicycle, drive a stick shift, operate a cash register, fill out a tax form. You probably use many skills today that seemed impossible when you first tried them.

Psychologist James Hillman recalls his struggles with handwriting in the third grade: "I got the lowest marks in the class," he says. "I had to stay after school again and again to practice writing." Today he is the author of an impressive array of essays and books; his language skills were an important factor in his professional development. The same exciting transformation awaits you.

EXERCISE 1: LOOK FOR PUBLIC LANGUAGE

Excerpts from four letters appear below. Which sound spontaneous and natural to you? Which sound like "public language"? Jot down reasons for your answers; then meet with a small group of other students to discuss your responses to these letters.

In 1872, forty-eight years before women were given the right to vote, women's rights leader Susan B. Anthony cast a ballot in a New York election. She was arrested for violating men's rights, found guilty and ordered to pay a fine. Her action inspired many other women to insist on voting. This is a November 5, 1872, letter she wrote to Elizabeth Cady Stanton, another advocate of women's rights:

> Well, I have gone and done it!!—positively voted the Republican ticket—Strait—this A.M. at 7 o'clock—& swore my vote in at that. . . . All my three sisters voted—Rhoda de Garmo too—Amy Post was rejected & she will immediately bring action against the registrars. . . . Not a jeer not a word—not a look disrespectful has met a single woman. . . . I hope the morning's telegrams will tell of many women all over the country trying to vote. . . . I hope you voted too.

In 1963, Dr. Martin Luther King, Jr., was imprisoned because of his protests against Birmingham's racial policies. He wrote his "Letter from Birmingham Jail" to answer criticisms from clergy who disapproved of his actions.

When I was suddenly catapulted into the leadership of the bus protest in Montgomery, Alabama, a few years ago, I felt we would be supported by the white church. I felt that the white ministers, priests and rabbis of the South would be among our strongest allies. Instead, some have been outright opponents, refusing to understand the freedom movement and misrepresenting its leaders; all too many others have been more cautious than courageous and have remained silent behind the anesthetizing security of stained-glass windows.

In 1862, during the Civil War, President Abraham Lincoln thanked General George B. McClellan for sending good news from the battlefront:

A thousand thanks for the relief your two dispatches of 12 & 1 p.m. yesterday give me. Be assured the heroism and skill of yourself, officers, and men, are, and forever will be appreciated. If you can hold your present position, we shall "*hive*" the enemy yet.

In 1945, Aldous Huxley and author Anita Loos planned a filmed version of his novel Brave New World. *In this letter he discusses his ideas for the film:*

In regard to *Brave New World*, I have no very revolutionary ideas, except the notion that it will probably be necessary, for film purposes, to write the scenes of the future in the form of cut-forwards from a contemporary starting point. My feeling is that audiences may be confused and worried, if we plunge straight into the twenty-seventh century a.d. as is done in the book. Also, if we do this, there will have to be a certain amount of retrospective explanation of historical events during the preceding centuries. It is essential, I think, to anchor the brave-new-worldian events very firmly to the present, so as to show that even the most extravagant pieces of satiric fantasy stem inevitably and logically from present-day seeds and are the natural end-product of present-day tendencies.

JOURNAL ACTIVITY: LISTEN FOR PUBLIC AND PRIVATE LANGUAGE

For the next seven days, listen for "private" and "public" language. Examples can include your own experience or your observations of others. Note an example of either "private" or "public" language each day. Add any comments or observations you wish to make. For example, you'll probably notice that "private" language often promotes intimacy, friendship, and fun; "public" language is often a tool for success.

DAY 1

The "private" or "public" language you heard:

Your comments:

DAY 2

The "private" or "public" language you heard:

Your comments:

DAY 3

The "private" or "public" language you heard:

Your comments:

DAY 4

The "private" or "public" language you heard:

Your comments:

DAY 5

The "private" or "public" language you heard:

Your comments:

DAY 6

The "private" or "public" language you heard:

Your comments:

DAY 7

The "private" or "public" language you heard:

Your comments:

Exploding the Myths about Language

Like Richard Rodriguez, most students want to develop the "public language" needed for professional and civic life. But language skills mystify many people. The basic lessons taught in many elementary and high schools do not prepare students for the tougher standards of college and professional life. Although anyone can become an effective writer, some students are afraid to try. Often they are held back by one of the six myths about language described below.

Myth #1: Talent is needed to speak and write effectively. The truth is that instruction and practice rather than talent are the keys to successful speaking and writing.

Whether you have a knack for words or not, you need feedback and practice to develop your language potential.

Hank Ketcham, the cartoonist who created *Dennis the Menace*, describes talent as "the result of intense fascination with a particular art or profession. Perhaps a genetic aptitude is present, but this 'talent' usually doesn't become visible until after a certain amount of despair and perspiration and the celebration of a few small triumphs. Persistence, patience and motivation remain dominant factors in any measure of success."

Myth #2: Inspiration is essential. Actually, inspiration is a rare experience, even for people who are famous. William Faulkner said, "I don't know anything about inspiration because I don't know what inspiration is; I've heard about it, but I never saw it." Oscar Hammerstein II, who wrote some of the most beautiful songs in the American theater, believed that hard work is the secret of good writing. He explained, "A sudden beam of moonlight, or a thrush you have just heard, or a girl you have just kissed, or a beautiful view through your study window is seldom the source of an urge to put words on paper. Such pleasant experiences are likely to obstruct and delay a writer's work."

Myth #3: If your language skills are good, words and ideas will flow naturally. Wrong. Before Lincoln delivered his Gettysburg Address, he worked hard to get the words exactly as he wanted them; so did countless other writers and speakers. Ernest Hemingway revised the conclusion to his novel *A Farewell to Arms* thirty-nine times; he said his greatest problem in writing was "getting the words right."

Libraries and museums are full of messy rough drafts produced by famous men and women. There are two lessons here for students: Don't get discouraged if writing and speaking tasks seem difficult, and allow plenty of time to polish your work.

Myth #4: Writing and speechmaking are solitary tasks. Sometimes social learners have difficulty with writing because they try to force themselves to work alone—and dislike it. The truth is that all writers and speakers—including people who enjoy working independently—need feedback from others, for two reasons.

First, ideas that seem clear when you write or say them may be confusing to others. Feedback helps pinpoint the ideas that need more clarity. Professionals routinely work with editors who suggest improvements and corrections.

Second, creative people don't always know their own strengths. Having others look at your work can help you discover positive features to build on. Walt Disney, passionately interested in quality, was always eager to see how work was progressing on the animated features in his film studio. Because he was an artist himself, Disney understood that his animators didn't want to be disturbed while they were working. So he used to prowl the studios at night, glancing at drawing boards and sketches pinned up on the walls. Sometimes in the morning artists would find that crumpled sketches had been rescued from their wastepaper baskets. On their drawing boards would be a note from Disney: "Quit throwing the good stuff away." Are you throwing *your* "good stuff" away? Seek feedback and affirmation from others.

Out of Gas

There are several reasons why I'll never buy a used car. again. ~~The used car I bought~~
(repititious)
~~a few years ago was a mistake.~~

Two years ago ^when^ I bought a Hyundai ~~thru~~ ^through^ a classified ad, ^I was thrilled.^ ~~At first~~ It seemed like a convenient and economical car, ^But^ ^then I started having problems.

Figure 9.1 Student's Rough Draft

Myth #5: It's hard to find interesting topics for speeches and college papers.
This myth is based on the assumption that you're a dull person with no experiences worth sharing. It's much more likely, however, that you're an interesting, thoughtful person with worthwhile ideas and experiences to write and speak about. On pages 296 to 299 you'll learn how to use thinking skills to discover interesting topics for college assignments.

Myth #6: If you're gifted, you don't have to work at writing or public speaking.
Neither a flair for words nor a dynamic personality guarantees success. Even John Kennedy, one of the most charismatic of modern politicians, had to work hard on his speeches. In 1946, as a young Navy veteran hoping to become a Congressman, he gave a speech to the Polish American Citizens Club in Massachusetts. Several other local officials were on the program; all spoke warmly about distinguished Polish Americans and their contributions to American life. But Kennedy was the only speaker who correctly pronounced all the Polish names in his speech: Pulaski, Kosciusko, Paderewski, and others. Later Kennedy won the election, carrying ninety-five percent of that Polish-American district. Although he did not speak Polish, he had taken the time to learn how to pronounce Polish names. Attention to such details helped him become a successful speechmaker—and President of the United States.

EXERCISE 2: WRITE ABOUT LANGUAGE MYTHS

Imagine that a friend lacks confidence in speaking or writing. Choose one of the six language myths and write a letter to your friend about it. Use experiences you've had—or observations you've made about others—to convince your friend that the myth is invalid. When you're finished, exchange letters with two or three other students in this course; compare, discuss, and evaluate one another's ideas.

◆ TIPS FOR SUCCESS IN WRITING COURSES ◆

1. Sign up for as many writing and public speaking courses as you can.

    College classes offer you opportunities for feedback from both students and professionals. You will receive guidance, encouragement, and up-to-date information about writing and speaking. Consider taking electives in both areas.

2. Get maximum benefit from the classes you attend.

    Prepare for, participate in, and master every concept that's taught. Ask for clarification of anything you don't understand; complete assignments on time, and record your progress in a learning log.

English Learning Log

4/11 Prof. Wiley wrote several positive comments on my essay— interesting intro, good vocabulary choices, strong examples. I need more sentence variety and a stronger conclusion. There are usage problems with commas and apostrophes. See handbook.

4/12 I worked on the usage problems by looking them up in my handbook. Will ask Prof. Wiley about non-restrictive clauses in tomorrow's conference.

Figure 9.2 Student's Learning Log

3. Use the writing services on your campus.

Visit the learning center early in the semester to introduce yourself to the staff and find out what services are available. Often, computers and computer instruction are available to increase your knowledge of usage and grammar. Other instructional resources may include workbooks, learning kits, videotapes, cassettes, and tutoring.

4. Note your professor's office hours and location; make use of them when you're working on a paper or a speech.

Sometimes just a five-minute conversation with your professor can save hours of confusion and frustration when you try to organize a paper at home. To get the most from your visit, arrive prepared: Write your questions beforehand and bring an outline or rough draft with you.

5. Find out which writing handbook your college recommends, and purchase a copy early in the semester.

Keep your handbook in a convenient spot, and refer to it when you have questions about usage, grammar, writing, and research. Writing handbooks offer a wealth of information about planning, writing, and revising papers, as well as grammar, usage, and research skills. Many handbooks also have suggestions about writing papers for science, history, literature, and business courses.

6. Buy an up-to-date dictionary and thesaurus.

Use the dictionary to make sure you've spelled words correctly and that you understand their meaning. Check the copyright date before you make your purchase. Because English changes constantly, and new words are always entering the language, you need a recent edition. An older dictionary might not have definitions for AIDS, anorexia, creationism, modem, or nacho.

A thesaurus is a dictionary of synonyms. When you look up a familiar word, the thesaurus will list others with approximately the same meaning. It's useful for vocabulary building, and it can also add interest to your writing. Instead of writing "happy," for example, you can select a more precise word: cheerful, ebullient, elated, euphoric, exhilarated, glad, joyful, merry.

7. If you can't find the information you need in a handbook or dictionary, visit or phone the library.

Although librarians aren't tutors, they can check reference books to answer questions about spelling, usage, and research. One frustrated writer—an editor of *Saturday Review* magazine—couldn't find the word "miniscule" in his dictionary. A librarian showed him that the dictionary was right, after all: He had been misspelling the word and should have looked for *minuscule*.

8. Make friends with a word-processing program.

Many word-processing programs have a built-in dictionary and thesaurus. Some also include a grammar-check feature—or you can purchase a separate program to use with your word-processor. You can use the computer for a usage check even without this special feature, however. Use the "find" or "search" command to look for the following words, which often confuse students. Every time the computer stops, read the sentence to make sure you've chosen exactly the word you want.

Words Often Confused

its	it's		
your	you're		
affect	effect		
than	then		
to	too	two	
who's	whose		
real	really		
where	wear	were	we're
there	they're	their	

9. Hand in neat, professional-looking papers.

College papers should be typed, unless your instructor accepts handwritten papers. Always double-space, and follow the format instructions you've been given. When you're writing your final draft, neatness is essential. Most professors will permit one or two corrections per page if they're crossed out with a single line. Correction fluid should be used so carefully that it's almost invisible. Write on only one side of each page.

10. Build a network of friends who can give you feedback about your work.

Early in the semester, start seeking other students to help evaluate your papers and speeches. As you learned earlier, professional authors seek feedback about their work; you should follow their example.

Consider forming a weekly study group to read one another's written work and offer suggestions. In both college and the professional world, people who can use language effectively are rare; still rarer are those who can help others polish papers, reports, letters, and speeches. A well-organized study group will help you develop both abilities. As a result, you'll be prepared not only for college assignments, but also for the collaboration and teamwork required in almost every workplace.

11. Utilize your learning style to improve your language skills.

If you're a visual learner, you probably enjoy reading. If this is the case, look for and learn from examples of effective writing when reading. Social learners can read aloud to one another and work together to plan papers and speeches. Remember also to use the *opposite* style to sharpen your skills. If you're a conceptual learner, make sure your speeches and essays include enough examples; if you're a pragmatic learner, unify papers and speeches around a central idea. Auditory learners can benefit from extra reading practice, and visual learners often need practice in public speaking. Remember that successful people, both in college and in professional life, are versatile.

12. Increase your vocabulary.

Having a large vocabulary enhances your ability to express yourself powerfully and precisely. Effective word choices can help you communicate significant distinctions, shades of meaning, and intense feelings.

Introducing the Writing Process

In recent years, writing instruction has changed dramatically. Formerly, students were required to write compositions in one step. Teachers used to walk up and down the aisles as students wrote, pointing out spelling and punctuation errors. Ideas had to be stated perfectly the first time: Crossing out and rewriting were discouraged.

Eventually, research was done into the working methods of successful authors. These studies showed that most professionals write in stages and do a great deal of revising. Preparation (gathering information and planning the paper), drafting (producing one or more rough drafts), and revising (polishing, editing, and refining) are familiar tasks to successful writers.

As a result of this research, students today are taught to follow the same process. Preparation and planning are done at the beginning; punctuation and spelling belong in the last stage, not the first; and messy rough drafts are encouraged.

The research also shows that it's all right to mix up the stages. Professionals often jump back and forth from one stage to another, and you may benefit by following their example: for example, you may want to interrupt your first draft to do some revising. The most important principle is to allow yourself to write imperfectly until you feel satisfied with what you've done. You can keep changing—and improving—a piece of writing as many times as you wish.

The following suggestions will help you make the writing process work for you. More detailed information can be found in a writing textbook or handbook.

Stage 1: Preparation. Begin by generating as many ideas as possible. Use your lateral-thinking skills (see page 242), and allow time for ideas to develop. Your mind is so complex and powerful that it can think about several subjects at the same time. While your attention seems to be focused on errands and routine chores, your mind may be secretly working out the ideas for an assignment.

How to Improve Your Vocabulary

The size of your vocabulary is an important factor in your college success. Students with large vocabularies tend to read and write more effectively, and they often score higher on tests. Here are several suggestions for improving your vocabulary:

1. Keep an up-to-date dictionary in your study area, and refer to it often.
2. Buy a vocabulary-building calendar that features a new word every day (or hint that you'd like one as a gift!).
3. Carry a small notebook with you for writing down and learning new words.
4. When you come across a new word in a book, copy and define it inside the cover.
5. Buy or borrow a book that explains Latin and Greek roots, and study it diligently.
6. Talk about words. Get friends and family members interested; even small children often enjoy experimenting with new words.
7. Practice using new words in conversation and college assignments.
8. Expose yourself to new words. Public radio and television are excellent vocabulary builders; so are many newspapers and magazines.
9. Browse through your dictionary during free moments. Malcolm X, you'll remember, learned a great deal by studying his dictionary. Many people have read dictionaries from start to finish—and acquired impressive vocabularies.
10. Expect irregular progress. Mistakes are inevitable when you're working on vocabulary building. You may mispronounce words or use them incorrectly. A sense of humor is a great help; so are friends who encourage you to continue increasing your vocabulary.
11. Play with words. Crossword puzzles appear in many newspapers and magazines; you can also buy books full of word puzzles—wonderful entertainment on a long trip. Scrabble can be a great vocabulary builder, and you can even buy a computer version to play by yourself.
12. Read. You'll discover words in books that you're unlikely to encounter anywhere else.
13. Seek new experiences. Careers, religions, hobbies, sports, and holidays often have specialized vocabularies. Attend a Kwanzaa celebration, visit a synagogue, shop in an exotic grocery, tour a government office. Accept invitations that expose you to new ideas and customs; be interested and enthusiastic. In addition to increasing your vocabulary, you'll win new friends.

In this planning stage, let your ideas flow freely without censoring them. Then choose your topic and decide what you want to say about it (vertical thinking). The main idea of a paragraph is called a *topic sentence*; the main idea of a longer paper is called a *thesis statement*.

Often, your professor will give you specific instructions about organizing (also called *outlining*) and developing your ideas; ask for guidelines if they haven't been provided. It's also wise to check a writing handbook or visit your learning center for help in planning your paper.

Stage 2: Drafting. Here you write a rough draft by expanding your ideas into complete sentences. Double-space as you write so that you have room for corrections later. Everything in your rough draft should help develop your main idea (topic sentence or thesis statement). Ask your instructor for suggestions about an effective opening and closing; your handbook can also offer good advice.

While you're writing your rough draft, don't stop to check facts or use the dictionary. Keep pushing yourself along, skipping over rough spots and usage corrections until the next stage. Your primary goal is to finish your rough draft, even if you're dissatisfied with it. There's a powerful psychological boost in having written your entire paper once: Revising is less overwhelming when you have a rough draft in front of you.

Stage 3: Revising. In this last stage, polish your rough draft so that it looks professional. Is there any awkward wording to be smoothed out? Are your ideas logical and consistent? Is your paper interesting? Do any facts need to be checked? Did you provide enough support? Refer to your dictionary and handbook for help with editing (making spelling and usage corrections).

If possible, have friends or family members read your paper and offer suggestions. Adopt a professional attitude towards criticism of your work; published authors learn to welcome suggestions for improvements, and you will benefit by following their example.

Gather information in the first step of the writing process–preparation. After you've written your rough draft, check your information and add any new facts you need to make your point convincingly.

Even if you're an independent learner, you'll benefit from feedback about your writing.

Columnist Ellen Goodman says, "What makes me happy is rewriting. . . . It's like cleaning house, getting rid of all the junk, getting things in the right order, tightening things up."

If you know someone who has published a book, ask what the revision process was like; you'll learn a great deal. Carl Barks, a cartoonist whose stories for Walt Disney comics have been reprinted as expensive collector's items, once explained his philosophy about revising: "I think writers should be their own editors and really polish stuff and not fall completely in love with their first draft."

When you're satisfied that your paper is the best work you can produce, make a neat final copy and submit it to your professor. If it's not your best work, continue to revise it. Allow enough time before the due date to do each writing task correctly, getting help if necessary. The good habits you develop will pay off now—in better college grades—and later—with superior performance in your career.

GETTING IN TOUCH THROUGH FREEWRITING

Freewrite about your past writing experiences. Discuss any of the following topics—or any other ideas you want to explore:

> *writing experiences in school*
> *writing experiences outside school*
> *creative writing*

academic writing

private writing

enjoyable and unpleasant writing experiences

successes and disappointments as a writer

publication

feedback

When English Is a Second Language

The following suggestions apply primarily to students whose native language is other than English. But this information can also be helpful to anyone making a transition from "private language" (family and community versions of English) to "public language" (the standard English used in professional circles).

1. Expose yourself to as much English as possible.

Live with an American family if you can. Join a church or club where English is spoken; shop in English-speaking stores; tune to radio and television programming in English; read American newspapers, magazines, and books. Although you may be lonely at first, you'll quickly begin to feel more comfortable. Remember that you can return to your native language later, when your English skills are stronger.

2. Find out what resources are available, and use them.

Many colleges have special, free services for students who are studying English. Learn about tutoring, computer programs, and language laboratories. Ask if there's a campus club for international students: You'll find support there, along with many opportunities to practice your English with students from other countries.

If you're an international student, meet frequently with other students to practice speaking and writing in English.

3. Be patient with yourself.

It takes time to hear the unique sounds of English and learn to reproduce them. Irregular verbs, spelling problems, and idioms can be frustrating until you're used to them. Be persistent, and keep your courage up.

4. Maintain your sense of humor.

Everyone makes mistakes learning a new language; try to take them in stride. If you're feeling very discouraged about your progress in English, try teaching some American friends a few phrases in your native language. Their difficulties will give you a healthy perspective about your struggles with English.

◆ THE IMPORTANCE OF PUBLIC SPEAKING ◆

Perhaps you, like many people, don't enjoy public speaking. You may have decided to leave speechmaking to others and concentrate on developing other skills. If this description fits you, think again! Public speaking offers many opportunities to influence others with your ideas and convictions. In both your professional and community life, the words you speak can influence the people who make decisions and write policies; they can also help you become a decision-maker and policy-writer yourself.

Now is the best time to sharpen your communication skills. Speech consultant Dorothy Sarnoff recalls traveling to the White House to work with a famous student—President Jimmy Carter. Although she saw some improvement in Carter's speechmaking skills after they worked together, he did not have time for extensive training and practice. Later he lost a bid for re-election to a highly skilled speechmaker—Ronald Reagan.

Motivation and preparation will help you become an effective speaker. As you saw in Chapter Three, class participation is an excellent first step. Classes in public speaking can help you tremendously; you can also join campus and community organizations that offer opportunities to speak. Above all, have faith in yourself. Countless other students have successfully transformed themselves into effective speakers. (You read about one of them, George Bernard Shaw, in Chapter Three.) Make friends with others who share your interest in speaking, encourage one another as much as possible, and enjoy the experience.

Most important, get excited about what lies ahead as you develop your speaking ability. Student organizations offer many opportunities to speak out on current issues. Remember too that you don't have to wait for graduation to become involved in local, state, and national organizations: All will welcome your speaking ability. Think also about your future. What professional, political, and personal concerns would you like to address? What forums will be available to you? Imagine yourself speaking in various settings, educating and influencing others. Dare to dream—and use those dreams as motivation to keep improving your speaking abilities.

Speechmaking Tips

Effective public speaking begins with preparation. If your talk is well written and thoroughly rehearsed, you can look forward to making a positive impression on your audience. You'll experience less nervousness when you feel fully prepared for your speech.

Begin by thinking about your audience. What do you know about them? Can you tailor your speech to their interests, experiences, or special concerns? After you've chosen your subject, decide what point you wish to make about it. Then treat your speech like a writing assignment. Get help from your handbook, professor, learning center, or study group to ensure that your ideas are interesting, well developed, and organized logically. Your speech should have three parts:

1. Introduction

Look for a dramatic, funny, or surprising way to introduce your subject and catch your listeners' attention. (Your writing handbook or public-speaking textbook will have many suggestions, such as asking a question, telling a dramatic story, or stating a surprising fact.) Make sure you clearly state your main point early in your speech, as in this introduction from a student speech:

> If you regularly watch football on TV, chances are you've seen your favorite team penalized unfairly at least once by a bad call from a referee. Instant replays make it easy to see when a team is off-sides, and when it isn't. Passes and interceptions can be viewed in slow motion to see where the ball really landed. Fans already appreciate instant replays, and football officials should too. Instant replays should be restored to football officiating.

2. Body

Here you develop your main point with supporting ideas and examples. Make sure you stick to your subject, and look for examples that your audience will understand and find interesting. Use transition words and phrases to help listeners follow your reasoning: *first*, *second*, and *most of all*; *but*, *however*, and *on the other hand*; *for example*, *to illustrate*, *as evidence*. (Your handbook will suggest others.)

3. Conclusion

Restate your main point and thank listeners for their attention. Make a strong final impression with a challenge, prediction for the future, or powerful story. (Again, your writing handbook and public-speaking textbook are good resources.)

After you've written your speech, transfer your main ideas to a set of three-by-five index cards. *Don't* copy each sentence: Get used to speaking from a simple outline. Number the cards so you can put them in order quickly if they're dropped. (You can also write your outline in large, readable letters on sheets of paper. Be sure to write on the front only; otherwise you may forget to turn over a page and lose part of your speech.)

Rehearsing a Speech

It's normal to feel nervous before a speech. But nerves don't have to weaken your performance. You can increase your confidence by staging a successful run-through ahead of time for a friendly audience. Ask friends and family members to listen to your delivery; then ask for both positive and negative feedback. Make notes on their comments and keep improving your performance.

Taping your speech on an audio cassette, and listening to yourself afterward, can be helpful. If possible, practice in front of a video camera and analyze your performance afterwards as you watch your video. (Ask if your college has video facilities for students; many do.)

Here are a few more tips from experienced speakers:

1. Smile.

The muscles that form your smile will also make your words sound more pleasant to your listeners. Radio announcers are taught to smile in front of the microphone even when no one can see them; you'll benefit by following their example.

2. Tighten your diaphragm.

You can control nervousness by tightening the diaphragm (the large muscular structure beneath your lungs). If you tend to giggle or talk too fast during a speech, you'll find this tip especially helpful.

3. Check your posture.

Lean forward, and put your weight equally on the balls of both feet. Be careful not to shift your weight; small body movements may distract your listeners from your message.

4. Practice in the room where you'll be speaking.

You'll feel more comfortable if the room is familiar to you, and you can practice making yourself heard. While you're rehearsing, ask a friend to sit in back of the room and signal you to speak more softly or more loudly. (If possible, have a friend in the back signal in the same way when you're presenting your speech to the audience.)

5. Make eye contact with your audience.

Look for listeners with friendly facial expressions, and direct your speech to them.

6. Think positively.

Try making an imaginary "movie" of yourself giving the speech successfully. Visualize the audience; picture yourself talking confidently to them; "listen" to yourself making the speech; get in touch with the good feelings you'll have as the audience responds warmly to your words. When you're actually making your speech, pretend that a beloved friend or family member is sitting in the first row.

7. Get excited about your speech.

As the day of your speech approaches, remind yourself often that you have a worthwhile message for your listeners. Think about the impact your ideas will be making. Recall speeches you've heard that affected your powerfully, and resolve to have the same effect on your audience.

COLLABORATIVE ACTIVITY: PREPARE A GROUP SPEECH

Work with a group of two or three other students to write, rehearse, and deliver a three-minute speech. Following the suggestions you've already read, choose a topic (only one for the group) and prepare your group speech. After it is written, take turns practicing delivering it to group members. Finally, randomly choose one group member to deliver the speech to the rest of your class.

◆ Using Critical Thinking in ◆
Writing Assignments

Chapter Eight introduced you to nine activities you can do with a pencil to broaden your thinking. Many of them appear again below, with a more specific purpose: helping you discover and develop topics for speaking and writing. For example, both "sort" and "analyze" can be used to write about ecology, as you'll see below.

1. Imagine.

Creative writing assignments are ideal opportunities to put your imagination to work in a story or poem. You can invent situations that allow you to explore endless new ideas and possibilities. Many writers have used language to invent new worlds and new societies; examples include, Shakespeare's *The Tempest*, Butler's *Erewhon*, More's *Utopia*, Huxley's *Brave New World*, and Orwell's *1984*.

Sometimes writers will bring characters together in unusual ways to create interesting problems. In Nevil Shute's novel *No Highway*, a crisis brings together a glamorous movie star and a timid, eccentric engineer; the result is a unique love story and a surprising ending.

Your imagination can also help you discover an interesting angle for a research paper, composition, or speech. One possibility is to pretend you're a literary, scientific, or historical figure. What are your thoughts and emotions? How does your environment look, sound, smell, and feel to you? One student whose grandfather had been a prisoner of war during World War II tried to imagine how that experience must have felt. The result was a psychology paper about the men who had been imprisoned during the Vietnam War and their readjustment to American life.

Finally, your imagination can help you "dream things that never were," as Shaw put it, to explore possible solutions to political, social, health, or ethical problems. You might even discover a problem that others haven't noticed yet—the mark of a true leader, according to business authority Warren Bennis.

2. Simplify.

When you're writing, "simplify" does not always mean "make easier." Often it calls for a strong, single focus. If you're asked to write a descriptive paper, you'll need to simplify your subject by concentrating on a single idea or effect. A descriptive paper about the place where you work might focus on one of these ideas: friendly atmosphere, valuable learning experience, haphazard management, or exhausting workload. Everything in your descriptions of the physical setting, employees, and customers should have a single purpose: helping your readers see your job the way you do.

3. Complicate.

Here you add something to your subject, as in compare-and-contrast papers. To show the advantages of word processing, for example, you might contrast word processing with typing on a traditional typewriter. The *contrasts*, or differences, demonstrate the advantages of word processing. Revisions are faster with a computer than a typewriter; word processing gives you a choice of printing styles; it's easier to store computer disks than typed pages.

A comparison paper develops an idea by emphasizing similarities rather than differences. For example, you could use a comparison to argue that women should not drink during a pregnancy. Alcohol travels through the placenta and umbilical cord directly to the unborn baby; the effect is the same as giving a newborn an alcoholic beverage.

4. Sort.

Sorting skills can help you take notes and organize them, tasks particularly useful in scientific and technical writing. The ability to sort ideas can also help you write classification papers, which are often assigned in college. Besides creating a system of ideas and information, a well-planned classification paper can make a strong case for a position.

One student, for example, wrote a biology paper classifying three types of environmental attitudes she had noticed among her friends. One group was not interested in ecology at all; they saw no problem with littering and thought recycling was a waste of time. The second group was moderately concerned about ecology and occasionally recycled glass, plastic, and aluminum. The third group had a strong commitment to ecology, recycling whenever possible: They looked for non-polluting packaging and products, and ate vegetarian foods that had been raised without violating rain forests and other delicate ecosystems.

5. Analyze.

Here you systematically look for basic parts, causes, processes, and underlying principles. Analysis papers are especially effective when you're arguing for change. For example, you could write a paper arguing that the landslides that occur more frequently in third-world countries could be prevented. Their underlying cause is a deforestation cycle that begins with overpopulation. Forests are cut down to provide homesites and grazing land; as the trees disappear, rain falls with increasing force on the bare land, eventually causing deadly mudslides. As you saw in Chapter Eight, a sketch or diagram can help you organize your ideas before you start writing.

6. Make a time line.

A time line can help you narrow a large subject into a workable idea for an oral report or research paper. For example, a time line about the history of American music might lead to a paper on African-American contributions to our musical heritage. Perhaps you could trace the development of an idea in history, education, humanities, or the sciences. What have psychologists learned about hypnosis over the last century? How did coeducation develop in the United States?

7. Estimate.

Technical writing and business assignments often require estimates about the cost or potential earnings of a new proposal. Estimates—also called speculation—can be useful in other kinds of writing as well. In an American history paper about the Confederacy, you might try to estimate the importance of Jefferson Davis's leadership; in a literary paper you might speculate about the ways in which Ernest Hemingway and F. Scott Fitzgerald influenced each other.

8. Evaluate.

Critiques (often assigned in humanities courses) and book reports are evaluative papers, as are research papers that present evidence to support a position about an issue. Any time you make a judgment about quality, effectiveness, truthfulness, or correctness, you are evaluating. A good planning strategy is Edward de Bono's plus–minus technique, which was described in Chapter Eight. Fold a piece of paper in half and list positive points on one side, negatives on the other. Use your lists to write a thesis and organize your supporting evidence.

USING WHAT YOU HAVE LEARNED

1. Make a list of resources on your campus that can help you improve your writing and speaking skills. Introduce yourself to at least three college employees to learn more about services you might like to use.
2. Write three or four sentences—or more—describing your public-speaking experiences. They may include formal speeches, informal class participation, performances that involved speaking, or similar experiences. How satisfied are you with your speaking skills? Are there any specific changes you plan to make? How do you plan to achieve your goals as a speaker?
3. Meet with two or three other students to discuss dictionary skills. Your group should have at least two different dictionaries to compare and discuss. What are the special features of each one? How are they organized? How recent are they? Where are the pronunciation keys and other useful sections found?
4. Find out which handbook your college recommends and obtain a copy. How is it organized? What topics would help you successfully complete the writing assignments you've been given this semester? What topics might you use in the future? What special features (index, glossary, appendix) does the handbook include? Meet with a small group of other students to compare and discuss your answers.

EVALUATING YOUR PROGRESS

1. As I look back on the past seven days, I've seen an improvement in these areas:

    _____ organizing my life

    _____ protecting my health

    _____ planning my time

    _____ concentrating

    _____ taking notes

    _____ active learning

    _____ reading critically

_____ writing effectively

_____ thinking critically

_____ communicating with important people in my life

_____ enjoying my free time

_____ allowing myself to be imperfect

2. In the coming week, I plan to invest five minutes a day working towards this goal:

CHAPTER 10

Studying
Science

For years, science has been regarded as dull and nerdy. It's almost been a way of identifying yourself as an American—to know nothing.

ALAN ALDA

PREVIEW

1. Science is both a body of knowledge and a method for solving problems.

2. Familiarity with science is important to your professional and community life.

3. You can increase your chances of success by choosing study techniques that work especially well in science courses.

IN-CLASS INTRODUCTORY ACTIVITY: SCIENCE IN YOUR LIFE

How often does science affect your everyday life? List as many examples as you can. (Your list might begin with weather forecasts, nutritional labeling, and electronics.) Then meet with three or four other students to discuss your lists and compile a group list. Finally, complete the group activities that follow.

Your list:

Your group's list:

COLLABORATIVE ACTIVITY: DISCUSS SCIENCE IN YOUR LIFE

1. *As a group, discuss the ways in which science affects your consumer behavior. Are you ever influenced by advertisements that cite results of scientific tests? How interested are you in technological advances in manufactured goods?*

2. *Discuss the ways in which science affects the lifestyles of group members. Have any members changed sleep patterns, nutritional choices, or physical activities as a result of scientific studies? How many members are interested in research about disease prevention and medication?*

3. *Discuss the ways in which science affects citizenship. Are group members concerned about the effects of new technology on your community (pollution, for example)? How concerned are you about the ways in which your taxes fund scientific research? What about weapons and warfare?*

◆ WHY STUDY SCIENCE? ◆

If you're majoring in science, it's easy to see the relevance of science in your life. But if you're planning a career in another field, you may wonder whether studying science has any relevance to your future life. Be assured that it has.

First, science courses sharpen your ability to observe, analyze, and solve problems: Critical thinking is much more important than rote memorization. Although reading and lecture notes are important, you must also observe, collect, and analyze data in laboratory experiments.

Second, scientific knowledge is vital to responsible citizenship. Government officials use feedback from citizens to formulate policies about environmental, medical, and technological issues. You will have opportunities to express your opinion about scientific programs that could affect millions of people, including your friends and family members. If you have a high level of "scientific literacy," you can have a positive impact on the future of our planet.

To find out how "scientifically literate" you are, try the Test of Scientific Literacy on pages 304 and 305. Microwaves, earthquakes, atoms, and acid rain are familiar to most people. Studies have shown, however, that many college graduates cannot choose the correct answers to basic questions about them.

Your participation in science classes is an important step toward "scientific literacy." You can also read magazine articles and books, discuss current issues with students and professors, and watch public television broadcasts about science. When you understand the specialized vocabulary and thought processes of science, you'll have a better understanding of newspaper stories and television reports, which often deal with scientific discoveries. You'll be able to vote more intelligently on a host of issues, from environmental programs to public health policies. And you'll be better prepared to make lifestyle choices about nutrition, exercise, medical care, and other personal issues.

Your college program is likely to include at least one course in the physical sciences (such as biology, chemistry, geology, or physics) and the social sciences (such as psychology, education, sociology, or anthropology). These courses offer both information and rigorous training in critical thinking. As you get to know your instructors and teaching assistants, you'll see that the scientific method is an extension of the critical-thinking skills introduced earlier in this course.

EXERCISE 1: SCIENCE AND CITIZENSHIP

To increase your awareness of the connection between science and citizenship, look for science-related items in a daily newspaper.

1. *How many stories focus on a scientific issue—medical research, the space program, technology?*

Test of Scientific Literacy from *Science Matters*

1. Summer is hotter than winter because:
   a. Light from the sun travels in a straighter line in summer.
   b. The earth is closer to the sun in summer.
   c. The earth is tilted on its axis.
   d. The moon reflects more sunlight in summer.

2. An atom differs from a molecule because:
   a. Molecules are made of atoms.
   b. Atoms are made of molecules.
   c. Gas is made of molecules, but solids are made of atoms.
   d. Atoms and molecules are two words for the same thing.

3. Earthquakes occur in California because:
   a. Earthquakes always accompany volcanoes.
   b. California is sinking into the Pacific Ocean.
   c. Giant underground explosions occur every few years.
   d. Two blocks of the earth's crust are grinding past each other.

4. Genetic engineers can create new life forms because:
   a. Scientists can build living things atom by atom.
   b. All genes are written in the same genetic code.
   c. Japanese and American scientists have collaborated.
   d. All life is made from the same kind of cell.

5. Galaxies, like our Milky Way, are made of:
   a. Hundreds and hundreds of stars.
   b. Thousands and thousands of stars.
   c. Millions and millions of stars.
   d. Billions and billions of stars.

6. The most abundant gas in our atmosphere is:
   a. Oxygen.
   b. Carbon dioxide.
   c. Nitrogen.
   d. Smog.

7. Acid rain is caused by:
   a. The decay of dead trees near lakes and streams.
   b. Poorly run chemical plants that manufacture acids.
   c. Agent Orange.
   d. Nitrogen and sulfur compounds released into the air from burning coal.

8. Why is the ozone layer of the earth's atmosphere important?
a. It blocks harmful ultraviolet radiation.
b. It reduces the greenhouse effect.
c. It keeps the planet smelling fresh and clean.
d. It prevents oxygen from leaking into space.

9. Which of the following does not travel at 186,000 miles per second (the speed of light)?
a. Microwaves in your microwave oven.
b. Radio waves from your local radio station.
c. The solar wind, streaming from the sun.
d. Light from a fluorescent light bulb.

10. The blueprint for every form of life is contained in:
a. The National Institutes of Health near Washington, D.C.
b. DNA molecules.
c. Proteins and carbohydrates.
d. Viruses.

ANSWERS

1. c. The earth travels in an almost circular path around the sun. Summer in the United States occurs when the Northern Hemisphere is tilted toward the sun.
2. a. Molecules are clusters of two or more atoms.
3. d. Earthquakes and volcanoes usually occur at places where thin, brittle pieces of the earth's crust—called plates—collide, split apart, or scrape against each other.
4. b. Every gene is recorded in the same genetic language, so genes can be interchanged between organisms. This process is the basis of genetic engineering.
5. d. There are billions of galaxies, each with billions of stars.
6. c. Nitrogen makes up about four-fifths of the atmosphere, and oxygen most of the rest.
7. d. Impurities in coal, oil, and gasoline release sulfur and nitrogen compounds into the air, where they are converted into sulfuric and nitric acid. Rain carrying these acids damages forest and lake ecosystems.
8. d. The debate about the future extent of global warming due to the greenhouse effect goes on. Nevertheless, all scientists agree that carbon dioxide and other gases, produced in ever-increasing amounts by natural and human processes (especially by the consumption of fossil fuels), contribute to the effect.
9. c. All kinds of electromagnetic radiation, including radio waves, microwaves, infrared radiation, visible light, ultraviolet, and X-rays, travel at the speed of light. The solar wind is made of matter, which (according to Einstein) can never travel at that speed.
10. b. DNA, a chainlike molecule, contains life's genetic code.

2. *How many stories mention science-related items such as hurricane charts, telescopes, satellites, and medical equipment?*

3. *What connections did you make about the relationship between science and citizenship?*

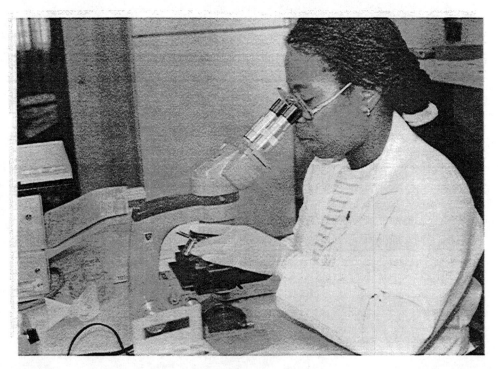

Advances in scientific knowledge may shape government policies that affect millions of people.

◆ HOW TO STUDY SCIENCE ◆

Many of the suggestions made earlier in this text about active learning, listening, note-taking, and preparing for tests can help you achieve success in science courses. Study groups are particularly helpful: The more you talk about scientific facts, ideas, and methods, the more thoroughly you'll understand them. The following suggestions, which deal specifically with science, may be helpful as well:

1. Learn the special terminology of the subject you're studying.

   When used in science, terms like "theory," "food," and "work" have specialized meanings that can be different from their everyday usage. A "theory," according to scientist Hans Selye, is a partially proven law; plants manufacture rather than consume "food," and "work" is force multiplied by distance. If your textbook has a "glossary"—a specialized, miniature dictionary—refer to it often. If it doesn't, make your own by listing unfamiliar words and their definitions. To aid memorization, put the definitions on flash cards and post them on signs in your room.

2. Learn how to read a science textbook.

   Successful students use their textbook as a thinking tool: Their goal is mastery of the mental processes explained in the textbook rather than rote memorization. As you read, look for examples of critical thinking.
   Read actively: Work all the sample problems, learn the definitions of unfamiliar words, and seek help with difficult concepts.
   If you haven't had much experience with scientific reading, be patient with yourself when you start studying your science book; drops in reading speed and comprehension are normal. Schedule enough time to study the text thoughtfully and understand all the information you're reading. Check your understanding by explaining important concepts to a friend or family member.

$$work = force \times distance$$

Figure 10.1 Learn Science Terminology

3. Keep up with homework and reading assignments.

Sometimes students skip assignments early in the semester, thinking they can raise their test average later on with a few high scores. This strategy sometimes works in other disciplines: If you didn't understand *The Great Gatsby* in a literature course, you may do better with *Lord of the Flies*. But science courses are different because later units are based on earlier ones. If you don't study early in the semester, you may not be able to handle more difficult material later on. It's always risky to fall behind in a college course; in science, however, disaster is almost guaranteed.

4. Get maximum benefit from laboratory experiences and case studies.

In the physical sciences, laboratory work is often a significant part of the final grade. Be sure you know the purpose of each experiment, and look for connections between your lab experiences, reading assignments, and lecture material. Check your comprehension of the procedures you're following. If a control is present, make sure you understand why. Ask your professor or a lab assistant to explain any points that aren't clear to you.

Follow laboratory instructions precisely, record your findings accurately, make as many diagrams and drawings as you need, and submit professional-looking lab reports.

In the social sciences, case studies (intensive examinations of a particular group or an individual) are often assigned. Your writing handbook may have useful suggestions for you—other resources include your professor and the library staff. (Chapter Twelve, "Introduction to Research," also has helpful ideas.)

5. Look for opportunities to talk about what you're learning.

Science is a communal undertaking: Scientists constantly question, challenge, affirm, and extend one another's work. Follow their example by talking to other students about your science assignments and laboratory experiences. Many professors encourage scientific dialogue by having students perform experiments in pairs. You can increase this dialogue by sharing ideas with other class members, your study group, and friends and family members outside of college. Even small children may enjoy listening to explanations of simple scientific ideas— and you'll benefit from learning how to express concepts in your own words.

6. Look for opportunities to write about what you're learning.

Keeping a learning log is especially valuable in science classes, for two reasons. First, writing is an important scientific skill. Proficiency with language is necessary for recording observations, formulating hypotheses, and interpreting the results of scientific study. Second, writing about science sharpens your critical-thinking skills. Every time you seek a connection between science and your everyday life, or probe a concept that seems difficult or confusing, you're thinking critically. A learning log in which you can safely record your own learning experiences is an invaluable tool.

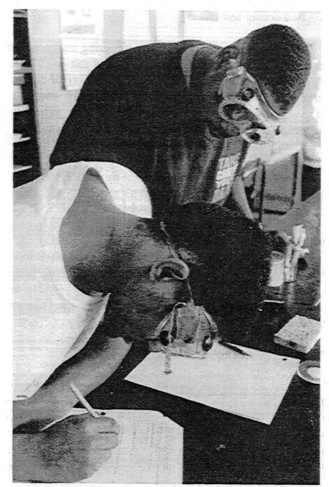

Science is a communal undertaking; look for opportunities to discuss your learning experiences with others.

7. Seek solutions when you encounter a problem.

Earlier you read about Dr. Joyce Brothers, who was unprepared for the sophisticated mathematics required for her advanced psychology courses. Instead of resigning herself to failure, she hired a math tutor. Be a creative and persistent problem solver. If mathematical computations are difficult for you, find out if calculators are allowed. If your writing skills are below par, use a word-processing program for lab reports and science papers.

Visit your professor during office hours to clarify difficult points from lectures and reading assignments. Besides benefiting from one-on-one explanations, you'll be improving your ability to carry on a scientific dialogue with an expert in your field.

8. Be a skillful test-taker.

Begin your test preparation by emphasizing understanding rather than rote memorization. Ask your professor about the type of test you'll be taking: There's a big difference between answering multiple-choice questions about the Krebs cycle and actually reproducing the cycle from memory. Work every sample question in your text until you're sure you understand the procedure. Review difficult points with your professor, an assistant, or a study partner well before the test date. Use a variety of methods to prepare: Flash cards, charts, signs, tape recordings, and self-made tests can help you earn a high score.

When you take the actual test, begin by reading both the directions and all the questions. Make sure you understand what's required, and ask for clarification if necessary. Answer the easiest questions first, saving time for difficult questions later. On long, difficult problems, ensure yourself of at least partial credit by providing formulas, diagrams, and procedures.

When a test is returned, look closely at the questions you missed, and try to discover why you missed them. Since science courses build upon previous knowledge, you need to fill in any gaps before the next test. Reviewing your notes and textbook, working with a study partner, or talking with your professor can help you master the content you missed.

9. Practice thinking scientifically.

Because science classes are usually structured around reading assignments, lectures, and standard experiments, it's easy to forget that science is a *method of problem solving* as well as a body of knowledge. In general, a scientist uses two steps to solve a problem. First the scientist devises a hypothesis (potential solution to the problem); second, the hypothesis is tested through such techniques as observation, measurement, and experimentation. You'll gain more from science lectures, experiments, reading assignments, and study periods if you look for connections between the scientific method of problem solving and the content you're learning.

Be aware of your learning style while you're studying. If you're a pragmatic learner, you may need help with abstract scientific ideas. If you're a conceptual learner, you may have to work harder to memorize facts and details.

GETTING IN TOUCH THROUGH FREEWRITING

In the space below, freewrite about your past experiences in science courses—and your plans for success in future classes. The following questions may be helpful: What did you enjoy most? Least? What study skills did you use? Did you enjoy your laboratory experiences?

Writing down your scientific observations increases your understanding and retention of new material.

Why or why not? What were your most important learning experiences? What changes in your study habits do you plan to make?

SCIENCE STUDY SELF-CHECK

This variation of Chapter Five's checklist emphasizes study techniques for science courses. A daily or weekly self-check can help you uncover trouble spots in your study habits.

_____ *I attend every class and take thorough notes.*

_____ *I get help if my notes are incomplete or confusing.*

_____ *I ask as many questions as necessary to understand the content.*

_____ *I keep up with reading assignments and homework.*

_____ *I schedule at least two hours of study for every hour in class.*

_____ *I work all the sample problems in my text.*

_____ *I seek help if I have trouble understanding a step in the sample problems.*

_____ *I can handle the math that's required in my science class—or I've arranged for tutoring.*

_____ *If there's a laboratory period, I make sure I understand the purpose of the experiment and the procedures I'm following.*

_____ *If I have a laboratory partner, we work well together.*

_____ *My laboratory reports are neatly written (or typed), complete, and accurate.*

_____ *I've learned all the special terms and definitions required in my course.*

_____ *I've discussed what I'm learning with friends or family members.*

_____ *I've invented memory devices (such as mnemonics) for content that must be learned by rote.*

_____ *I've been using study aids (such as flash cards, mind maps, sample test questions, and index card outlines).*

_____ *I have a study partner or meet regularly with a study group.*

_____ *I know the best times of the day for intense study and use them wisely.*

_____ *When possible, I seek connections between what I'm learning and everyday life.*

_____ *I practice thinking critically in my science class, laboratory periods, and study sessions.*

_____ *Before I hand in a test, I check every problem to make sure I solved it correctly.*

_____ *I review returned tests carefully to discover weak areas that need further attention.*

_____ *I regularly write entries in my science learning log.*

_____ *I'm aware of scientific problem-solving methods when I study, perform experiments, and read my textbook.*

Me—A Scientist?

Many people mistakenly assume that scientific problem-solving skills are appropriate only for scientists in white lab coats. The truth is that scientific methods can be applied to many problems in everyday life. Their broad usefulness is one reason science courses are required by most colleges.

Five scientific problem-solving methods are explained below. How many times recently have you practiced these activities?

1. Identifying a particular problem to solve through observation, measurement, logic, or experimentation.

Scientists deal with specifics rather than generalities. When you tackle a problem, define it as clearly as possible. "I want to have fewer arguments with Betty" is better than "I want to improve my relationship with Betty." "I'm doing poorly in school" is not as helpful as "I want to discover study techniques to raise my biology average."

2. Testing a hypothesis to solve the problem.

A "hypothesis" is a guess or hunch about the solution to a problem. Scientists test hypotheses systematically, trying and discarding possibilities until they find the answers they're looking for. This process is equally effective for everyday problems. For example, if your child has sudden bursts of uncontrollable behavior, you might make a list of possible causes and test them one at a time: boisterous playmates, violent TV programs, fatigue, and so on.

3. Observing.

Scientists are attentive observers, for two reasons: Close observation is a powerful learning tool (as you learned from Samuel Scudder in Chapter One), and it is a powerful problem-solving tool. Many pediatricians say that parents who are good observers can provide valuable clues about a child's illness.

Careful observation can teach you a great deal about the physical sciences, as you saw in the Galileo story on page 157; it can also help you understand the behavior and motivation of those around you. A student who was worried about the daily quarrels in his home used observation to solve the problem. He soon discovered that the outbursts began at 5:30 in the evening, when the children were hungry and he and his wife were shifting gears from work and school to family life. When family members understood what was happening, the problem was easily solved: The children were given a nutritious snack at 5:30, and he and his wife agreed to help one another ease back into family life every evening.

4. Measuring.

Careful measurement is a powerful problem-solving tool. One woman, concerned about her family's excessive utility bills, experimented with a variety of energy-saving methods. By checking her electric meter every day, she discovered that most methods had little effect: turning off the TV, cooking one-dish meals and buying low-wattage light bulbs. But the numbers on her meter dropped dramatically when she turned the thermostat on the big hot-water heater down fifteen degrees.

A student used measurement to solve a problem with her fiance, who annoyed her by shouting when he wanted her attention. At a counselor's suggestion, she tried leaving the room when her fiance raised his voice, but the behavior continued and even got worse. The student then began keeping a daily count of the number of shouting occurrences. She found that the behavior increased for three days, but then it began to drop steadily and had almost disappeared a week later. If she hadn't kept a record, she might not have noticed the improvement.

5. Experimenting.

Experimentation happens every time you test a new product or try a lifestyle change. This process acquires a scientific dimension when it's done systematically: observing, measuring, testing. Try keeping a record the next time you purchase a new product or change your eating or exercise habits. What changes did you observe? Are they measurable?

One student, trying to discover the best times of day for intense study, bought a book of word puzzles and tried working on them at various times of the day. He kept a record of his success at solving the puzzles, the amount of time needed for each puzzle, and the way he felt each time. After two weeks he determined that he was most alert and energetic late in the afternoon, after his gym workout. That became his "A" study time, reserved for his toughest academic challenges.

JOURNAL ACTIVITY: PRACTICE SCIENCE ACTIVITIES

During the next seven days, spend a few minutes practicing one or more of the following scientific activities:

Identifying a particular problem to solve
Testing a hypothesis to solve the problem

Observing
Measuring
Experimenting

You may wish to spend the week on just one activity—observing something of interest to you, as Galileo did when he looked out his prison window at the clouds. Or you may want to select a problem and go through all the steps to solve it scientifically: defining the problem, forming a hypothesis to solve it, and testing the solution you devised. Whatever activity you choose, remember that record keeping is an essential part of the process. Record your thoughts and observations in the space below, or on notebook paper if you need more space.

DAY 1

The activity you chose:

Your experience:

DAY 2

The activity you chose:

Your experience:

DAY 3

The activity you chose:

Your experience:

DAY 4

The activity you chose:

Your experience:

DAY 5

The activity you chose:

Your experience:

DAY 6

The activity you chose:

Your experience:

DAY 7

The activity you chose:

Your experience:

Creative Thinking in Science

Scientific thinking involves much more than the problem-solving methods described on the previous pages. Scientists use creativity, hunches, and intuitions to formulate hypotheses and solve problems.

Alexander Graham Bell (1847–1922), fascinated by the possibility of human flight, experimented with aeronautics and invented the aileron (movable flap) still used on airplane wings. Nobel Prize winner Kary Mullis, inventor of the polymerase chain reaction, says, "I was playing. I think really good science doesn't come from hard work. The striking advances come from people on the fringes being playful."

A hypothesis about physics occurred to the Greek scientist Archimedes (287?–212 B.C.) while he was taking a bath; the theory of relativity first appeared to Albert Einstein (1879–1955) as a vision. British scientist Isaac Newton (1642–1727), who formulated the theory of universal gravitation, said, "No great discovery was ever made without a bold guess."

◆ THE HUMAN FACTOR IN SCIENCE ◆

Some students complain that they can't enjoy science because it's too factual and impersonal. But the human factor—individual temperaments, drives, and biases—is always present, even if it's sometimes hidden by the objectivity of scientific writing. Furthermore, scientists themselves are strongly influenced by society's values, biases, and priorities. Awareness of these human factors makes the study of science much more interesting; it also helps you see the vital connection between science and citizenship.

Your elected officials help decide which research projects will be funded by tax dollars; you can offer additional input by working with local and national organizations concerned about scientific issues. You and other consumers influence research decisions in medicine, waste management, and other areas. Scientific issues are debated in books, in newspaper and magazine articles, on television, and in government offices. Biological warfare, animal rights, environmental damage, and overspending are just a few of the issues that have sparked controversy.

As you study science, remember that scientists are people, not data machines. (It can be helpful to read a good biography of a scientist who interests you.) Get to know science professors and other staff members as individuals; search for connections between the information you're learning and your life as a citizen and consumer. The following points will help you make these connections:

1. Scientific advances often raise new legal, economic, and ethical questions that must be decided by society at large.

How much should we rely on nuclear power to solve our energy problems? What guidelines are appropriate for using atomic weapons? Is it ethical to use bio-engineering to improve the human race?

2. Scientists often make use of imagination, intuition, and creativity.

In Chapter Five, David Fairchild observed that science can cause the mind to wander "where perhaps no human imagination has ventured before." Imagination played an important role in the invention of recorded sound. Thomas Edison accidentally made a sound recording on tin foil when he was tinkering with a telephone device. He had never thought of trying to record sound and could not, at first, think of a practical use for his discovery. But his imagination soon envisioned the possibilities: The result was the first phonograph. Today we can hardly imagine life without recorded sound.

The discovery of penicillin, an antibiotic that has been called a "miracle drug," demonstrates why creativity is vital to scientific research. David Fairchild recalled his annoyance when, during his college days, cultures he was growing were destroyed by penicillin spores. For him penicillin was primarily a nuisance. Years later he noted that it took "better brains" than his to see that penicillin's destructive power could be used as a weapon against infections.

3. Scientists are driven by the same motives that drive professionals in other fields.

Some scientists are motivated by ambition; others hope to make discoveries that will aid humanity, and still others view science as a fascinating journey into the unknown. Biographies of scientists are full of human drama: You will encounter stories of greed, generosity, compassion, jealousy, tragedy, and triumph.

4. The values of society at large help determine which research projects will be funded.

The salaries, buildings, and equipment needed for research are too expensive for scientists to provide for themselves. Most support comes from government; other sources are business, industry, educational institutions, and private foundations. Funding decisions are often made by administrators who do not specialize in science. The priorities—and biases—of society help determine how scientists spend their time.

Medical research used to be administered and conducted primarily by men. Researchers included only men in many studies, often overlooking the special needs of women. Heart disease is the top killer of both men and women—but only recently have cardiologists begun to study the prevention and treatment of heart disease in women. On the other hand, our culture considers sexual reproduction a female domain. As a result, most birth-control research has been done on women: So far no pharmaceutical company has attempted to market a birth-control pill for men.

5. Scientists must constantly remind themselves of their human limitations.

Albert Einstein once said, "It is the theory which decides what we can observe." Because scientists are human, they sometimes see what they want to see—not what is actually there.

Psychologist James Hillman notes, "During the seventeenth and eighteenth centuries reasonable scientific men (Dalepatius, Harsoeker, Garden, Bourget, Leeuwenhoek,

Andry), while empirically studying the problems of fertility, conception, and embryology, asserted that they had seen exceedingly minute forms of men, with arms, heads, and legs complete, inside the spermatozoa under the microscope." Because these scientists believed that sperm contained miniature humans, they "saw" what they had expected to see—not what was really there.

At the turn of this century, French physicist Rene Blondlot announced the discovery of N-Rays, which he thought increased the brightness of the electric sparks he measured in his laboratory. The difference in brightness could not be measured, but Blondlot was confident that he was seeing a significant increase in the electric sparks. His mistake was exposed in 1903 when a visiting physicist secretly removed part of Blondlot's apparatus. Not knowing that his apparatus wasn't working, Blondlot performed the experiment for the visitor and confidently pointed out the brighter spark. When the visitor showed him that part of the apparatus was missing, Blondlot realized there could not have been a brighter spark: He had deceived himself, and N-Rays simply did not exist.

6. Scientific knowledge cannot account for much of human experience.

Psychologist Sigmund Freud (1856–1939), son of a physiologist, dreamed of discovering a biological basis for human behavior. But despite his best efforts, Freud felt himself drawn to a larger view of human life. His later books explore such non-biological topics as humor and the problems of civilization. He used a Greek myth—the Oedipus story—to explain how the human personality develops. Ironically, this would-be physiologist was awarded the famous Goethe Prize for Literature.

COLLABORATIVE ACTIVITY: BRAINSTORM THE HUMAN FACTOR IN SCIENCE

You've just read six explanations of the human factor in science. Working with three or four other students, brainstorm as many examples of each one as you can. Here once again are the explanations:

1. *Scientific advances often raise new legal, economic, and ethical questions that must be decided by society at large.*
2. *Scientists often make use of imagination, intuition, and creativity.*
3. *Scientists are driven by the same motives that drive professionals in other fields.*
4. *The values of society at large help determine which research projects will be funded.*
5. *Scientists must constantly remind themselves of their human limitations.*
6. *Scientific knowledge cannot account for much of human experience.*

READING THOUGHTFULLY: SCIENCE AND CITIZENSHIP

You're about to read what one prominent scientist thinks about the connection between science and citizenship. Before you begin reading, complete the following activity.

BEFORE YOU READ

1. What attitudes toward science have you observed in the people you know? In yourself?

2. How much knowledge about science do you think the average person should have? Why?

3. How do people today receive information about science? What sources of science information do you enjoy most? Least?

---

from   **"Public Attitudes Toward Science" from Black Holes and Baby Universes**

by Stephen Hawking

Whether we like it or not, the world we live in has changed a great deal in the last hundred years, and it is likely to change even more in the next hundred. Some people would like to stop these changes and go back to what they see as a purer and simpler age. But as history shows, the past was not that wonderful. It was not so bad for a privileged minority, though even they had to do without modern medicine, and childbirth was highly risky for women. But for the vast majority of the population, life was nasty, brutish, and short.

Anyway, even if one wanted to, one couldn't put the clock back to an earlier age. Knowledge and techniques can't just be forgotten. Nor can one prevent further advances in the future. Even if all the government money for research were cut off, the force of competition would still bring about advances in technology. Moreover, one cannot stop inquiring minds from thinking about basic science, whether or not they are paid for it.

If we accept that we cannot prevent science and technology from changing our world, we can at least try to ensure that the changes they make are in the right directions. In a democratic society, this means that the public needs to have a basic understanding of science, so that it can make informed decisions and not leave them in the hands of experts. At the moment, the public has a rather ambivalent attitude toward science. It has come to expect the steady increase in the standard of living that new developments in science and technology have brought, but it also distrusts science because it doesn't understand it. This distrust is evident in the cartoon figure of the mad scientist working in his laboratory to produce a Frankenstein. But the public also has a great interest in science, particularly astronomy, as is shown by the large audiences for television series such as *Cosmos* and for science fiction.

What can be done to harness this interest and give the public the scientific background it needs to make informed decisions on subjects like acid rain, the greenhouse effect, nuclear weapons, and genetic engineering? Clearly, the basis must lie in what is taught in schools. The science that people learn in school can provide the basic framework. But the rate of scientific progress is now so rapid that there are always new developments that have occurred since one was at school or university. I never learned about molecular biology or transistors at school, but genetic engineering and computers are two of the developments most likely to change the way we live in the future. Popular books and magazine articles about science can help to put across new developments, but even the most successful popular book is read by only a small proportion of the population. Only television can reach a truly mass audience.

There are some very good science programs on TV, but others present scientific wonders simply as magic, without explaining them or showing how they fit into the framework of scientific ideas. Producers of television science programs should realize that they have a responsibility to educate the public, not just entertain it.

AFTER YOU READ

1. What new words and terms did you encounter in this selection? How do you plan to learn their meaning?

2. What questions do you have about this selection? How will you find the answers?

3. How does Stephen Hawking answer questions 2 and 3 in Before You Read on page 320? How are his answers similar to (or different from) yours?

4. Do you agree with Hawking that the public needs to be well informed about science? Why or why not?

5. Have you seen any TV programs that "present scientific wonders simply as magic"? Can you recall any that effectively demonstrated what scientists do and why?

6. Hawking believes that citizens need to make intelligent decisions about "acid rain, the greenhouse effect, nuclear weapons, and genetic engineering." Can you define each item in his list? Do you agree with him?

7. Can you add any scientific issues to Hawking's list in Question 5?

USING WHAT YOU HAVE LEARNED

1. Interview a scientist. Before the interview, meet with a small group of other students to prepare a list of interview questions. Use your own curiosity and interests to generate questions; consider also what you'd especially like to know about a particular area of science. After the interview, prepare a short group presentation for other students in this course.

2. List campus resources that might help you study science successfully. Introduce yourself to at least three college staff members to learn more about services you might use.

3. Meet with a small group of other students to list study techniques that might help you learn about science. Discuss any techniques you've used and found successful.

4. Meet with a small group of students who are taking (or have taken) a science course you have taken or plan to register for. Examine the textbook, noting any helpful features such as a glossary, study questions, or practice tests. Bring a page of notes with you and compare your notetaking techniques. List any new ideas you hear about for success in the course.

5. Reread Samuel Scudder's essay "In the Laboratory" (page 15 of Chapter One). What did you learn about scientific methods from this essay? How many of these methods have you used in your everyday life? Try to give at least one specific example of each method drawn from your own experience.

6. Reread David Fairchild's essay in Chapter Five (page 157). What did you learn about the relationship between science and creativity from this essay? What examples of creative thinking can you remember from your own life? List as many examples as you can.

EVALUATING YOUR PROGRESS

1. As I look back on the past seven days, I've seen an improvement in these areas:

   _____ organizing my life

   _____ protecting my health

   _____ planning my time

   _____ concentrating

   _____ taking notes

   _____ active learning

   _____ reading critically

   _____ writing effectively

_____ thinking critically

_____ communicating with important people in my life

_____ enjoying my free time

_____ allowing myself to be imperfect

2. In the coming week, I plan to invest five minutes a day working towards this goal:

CHAPTER 11

Studying Mathematics

There isn't much teachers can do if so many of us go around saying "Ugh, I hate math" and think we're being funny.

JOHN ALLEN PAULOS

PREVIEW

1. Math skills are important to college life, the professional world, and citizenship.

2. You already know a great deal about mathematics from daily life.

3. "Hands-on," concrete experiences are effective ways to sharpen your math skills.

IN-CLASS INTRODUCTORY ACTIVITY: THINK ABOUT MATH

Mark the point on the line that best represents your feeling about this statement.

I'm looking forward to my math courses in college.

Strongly disagree	Neutral	Strongly agree
1	5	10

Complete the activities below.

ACTIVITIES

1. *Briefly describe your past experiences with mathematics. Were they generally positive or negative? Why?*

2. *If you had the power to change one of your past experiences with math, which one would it be? What change would you make?*

3. *If you would like your mathematical experiences in college to be different from those in high school, what is one change you would make?*

4. *Whether your mathematical background is strong or not, you can probably think of one change you'd like to make in your mathematical study habits. What would it be?*

COLLABORATIVE ACTIVITIES

1. *Meet with a small group of other students to discuss and compare your answers to the previous questions in this activity. What experiences and attitudes, if any, do you have in common? What experiences and attitudes are unique to you?*

2. *The students in your math courses will probably come from a variety of mathematical backgrounds. If you were helping to form a math study group, what plans might you make to help all the members understand one another and enjoy working together?*

GROUP DISCUSSION NOTES:

Adopt a positive and professional attitude toward your math courses.

◆ WHY STUDY MATH? ◆

According to Dr. John Allen Paulos, author of *Innumeracy: Mathematical Illiteracy and Its Consequences*, many people have the unfortunate idea that it's funny to hate or fear math. Some women, believing math is a masculine subject, think it's feminine and appealing to brag that they can't balance their checkbooks. Dr. Paulos accordingly urges all students—both male and female—to recognize the importance of math in both personal and professional life.

The truth is that anti-mathematics attitudes are crippling. Without math skills it's impossible to be sure your paycheck is correct or your bank statement is accurate. The simple act of reading a newspaper or watching a news program becomes difficult: Graphs will be a mystery, and you won't understand any reporting that uses percentage to explain government spending, business trends, or taxes.

Math skills are especially important to leadership positions in any career—not just the sciences—because powerful positions always include financial responsibilities. Women who joke about their weak math skills may find that they're never seriously considered for important promotions. Dr. Paulos explains, "Women who do everything in their power to avoid a chemistry or an economics course with mathematics or statistics prerequisites may end up in lower-paying careers."

Fears and antipathy towards math are so widespread that most campuses offer special math services, including tutoring, computer-assisted instruction, workshops, and study groups. If you're taking a math course right now, your instructor may have office hours when he or she is available for extra help. Every year thousands of students take advantage of these services to succeed in math; the same options are open to you.

If you find math especially challenging, there's really only one obstacle to overcome: your own reluctance to seek help. In the end, you're the person who determines your level of success.

Math in Your Professional Life

A journalism student named Lisa Bintrim mailed the following question to the "Ask Marilyn"* column that appears in many magazines. (Marilyn vos Savant, who writes the column, has the highest I.Q. ever recorded, according to the *Guinness Book of World Records*.)

> Is there any practical use for algebra outside of careers directly related to math and science? I plan on being a journalist. Will I ever need to use algebra in my everyday life on the job?
>
> Lisa Bintrim, New Freedom, Pennsylvania

Here is the reply from Marilyn vos Savant:

> I sympathize, but we all need as many math courses as we can stand, because they teach us how to think logically and to reason through problems in all areas of our lives, not just the more number-related areas. (And, by the way, if a journalist can't cope with algebra, how is she going to cope with things like misleading statistics and economic plans and business trends?)

---

* Reprinted with permission from Parade, Copyright © 1993.

Math in Everyday Life

In 1994 the U.S. government ordered food manufacturers to include more nutritional information on food labels. A group of journalists conducted an informal study to see whether consumers could understand and benefit from the new labels. One of their questions concerned the amount of protein in a popular breakfast cereal. When served with a half cup of milk, the cereal provided 20% of the minimum daily requirement of protein. What percentage, they asked, would a person receive who had two bowls of the cereal with milk? Only 1/4 of the consumers questioned gave the correct answer: 40%.

There are many reasons why large numbers of Americans have difficulty with mathematics. Some people have had such negative experiences that they freeze when they hear words like "percentage" or "algebra." Others have memorized techniques and formulas without understanding the mathematical principles behind them. When they're presented with a problem that's new to them, like the question about breakfast cereal, they don't know where to begin. These are only two causes; math writers Sheila Tobias and John Allen Paulos have discussed many others.

More important than *why* students have difficulty, however, is *what* you can do to get the strong math background you need for professional and personal success. You've already seen the importance of math in professional life: It's just as essential in everyday tasks like shopping, buying and decorating a home, maintaining tax records, reading a newspaper, and budgeting.

EXERCISE 1: MATH IN YOUR EVERYDAY LIFE

Work with a partner to solve the following problems, writing down the steps you used. Check your answers (the answers appear on page 331); then meet with another pair of students to compare the methods you used.

1. *A student needs to earn $150 a week to pay her college expenses. She is offered a part-time job selling shoes at a 20% commission. What dollar amount in shoe sales must she accomplish every week to meet her expenses?*

2. *A couple is going to paint the walls of their living room, which is 18 feet long and 14 feet wide. The walls are 9 feet high. A gallon of paint covers 300 square feet. How many gallons will they need for two coats of paint?*

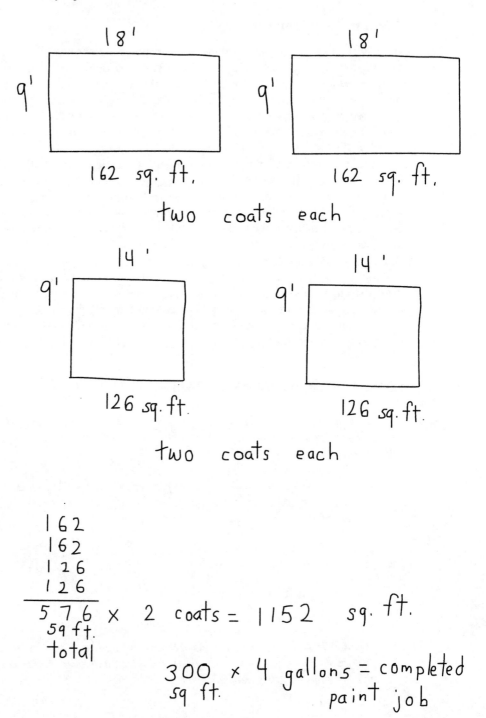

18'

9'

162 sq. ft.

18'

9'

162 sq. ft.

two coats each

14'

9'

126 sq. ft.

14'

9'

126 sq. ft.

two coats each

162
162
126
126
─────
576 × 2 coats = 1152 sq. ft.
sq ft.
total

300 × 4 gallons = completed
sq ft.   paint job

Figure 11.1 Answer: How Much Paint Will They Need?

3. *A student has earned scores of 78%, 91%, 81%, and 77% on his sociology tests this semester. What must he score on the next test to have an average of 85%?*

4. *A newspaper reports that 18% of the employees in a local factory face layoffs in the next six months. Four thousand people work in the factory. How many will be left?*

The answers:

1. 1/5 X = $150; X = $750. (She decided not to take the job.)
2. Two walls are 18 x 9: 162 square feet each. The other two walls are 14 x 9: 126 square feet each. The paint must cover about 1150 square feet (minus a few square feet for the door and windows). At 300 square feet a gallon, they'll need four gallons.
3. 78% + 91% + 81% + 77% + X% = 425%; X = 98%
   (He didn't make it.)
4. 82% of 4,000 employees will remain: .82 x 4,000 = 3,280

READING THOUGHTFULLY: MATHEMATICS SOLVES A MYSTERY

Mathematical skills can be useful in a wide variety of situations. In this condensation of a story by Sir Arthur Conan Doyle (1859–1930), fictional detective Sherlock Holmes used math to solve a mystery. Holmes is telling the story to Dr. John Watson, a close friend who assists the detective in his cases. Before you begin reading, complete the following activity.

BEFORE YOU READ

1. What do you know about Sherlock Holmes? Have you ever read a story about him? If so, what was your response?

2. List all the ways you can think of in which a detective might use mathematics.

3. Give an example of a time when you used math to solve a problem.

---

from **"The Musgrave Ritual"**

[Sherlock Holmes and Watson are relaxing in Holmes's study on Baker Street in London. Holmes has just shown Watson a tin box containing a crumpled piece of paper, an old-fashioned brass key, a peg of wood with a ball of string attached to it, and three rusty old discs of metal. Holmes is reminiscing about a mystery he solved some time ago.]

These are all that I have left to remind me of "The Adventure of the Musgrave Ritual." Reginald Musgrave had been in the same college as myself, and I had some slight acquaintance with him. For four years I had seen nothing of him, until one morning he walked into my room in Montague Street. He had changed little, was dressed like a young man of fashion, and preserved the same quiet, suave manner which had formerly distinguished him.

"I understand, Holmes," said Musgrave, "that you are turning to practical ends those powers with which you used to amaze us?"

"Yes," said I, "I have taken to living by my wits."

"I am delighted to hear it, for your advice would be exceedingly valuable to me. We have had some very strange doings, and the police have been able to throw no light upon the matter."

"Pray let me have the details," I cried.

"I have kept up a considerable staff of servants, for my estate is a rambling old place, and takes a good deal of looking after. Of these servants the one who had been longest in our service was Brunton, the butler. He was quite a well-grown, handsome man, and though he has been with us for twenty years he cannot be more than forty now. With his personal advantages and his extraordinary gifts, for he can speak several languages and play nearly every musical instrument, it is wonderful that he would have been satisfied for so long in such a position, but I suppose that he was comfortable and lacked energy to make any change.

"But this paragon has one fault. He is a bit of a Don Juan.[1] When he was married it was all right, but since he has been a widower we have had no end of

---

[1] A man who obsessively seduces women (after a legendary fourteenth-century nobleman).

trouble with him. A few months ago we were in hopes that he was about to settle down again, for he became engaged to Rachel Howells, our second housemaid. But he has thrown her over since then and taken up with Janet Tregellis, the daughter of the head gamekeeper. She is a very good girl, but she had a sharp touch of brain fever and goes about the house now—or did until yesterday—like a black-eyed shadow of her former self.

"I have said that Brunton was intelligent, and this very intelligence has caused his ruin, for it seems to have led to an insatiable curiosity about things which did not in the least concern him. One night last week I found that I could not sleep. After struggling against it until two in the morning I felt that it was quite hopeless, so I rose and lit the candle with the intention of continuing a novel which I was reading. The book, however, was in the library.

"You can imagine my surprise when as I looked down the corridor I saw a glimmer of light coming from the open door of the library. Brunton, the butler, was there. He was sitting, fully dressed, in an easy chair, with a slip of paper, which looked like a map, upon his knee, and his forehead sunk forward upon his hand in deep thought. I stood, dumb with astonishment, watching him from the darkness.

"Suddenly, as I looked, he rose from his chair, and walking over to a bureau at the side he unlocked it and drew out one of the drawers. From this he took a paper and, returning to his seat, he flattened it out on the edge of table, and began to study it with minute attention. My indignation at this calm examination of our family documents overcame me so far that I took a step forward, and Brunton saw me standing in the doorway. He sprang to his feet, his face turned livid with fear, and he thrust into his breast the chart-like paper which he had been originally studying.

"So!" said I, "this is how you repay the trust which we have reposed in you! You will leave my service tomorrow."

"He bowed with the look of a man who is utterly crushed as I glanced to see what the paper was which Brunton had taken from the bureau. To my surprise it was nothing of any importance, but simply a copy of the questions and answers in the old observance called the Musgrave Ritual. It is a sort of ceremony peculiar to our family, which each Musgrave for centuries past has gone through upon his coming of age—a thing of private interest, and perhaps of some little importance to the archaeologist, but of no practical use whatever."

"We had better come back to the paper afterwards," said I.

"If you think it really necessary," he answered, with some hesitation.

"I relocked the bureau," said Musgrave, "and I had turned to go, when I was surprised to find the butler standing before me.

"Mr. Musgrave, sir," he cried, "I can't bear disgrace, sir. I've always been proud above my station in life and disgrace would kill me. If you cannot keep me after what has passed, then for God's sake let me give you notice and leave in a month, as if of my own free will."

"You don't deserve much consideration, Brunton," I answered. "However, as you have been a long time in the family, I have no wish to bring public disgrace upon you. A month, however, is too long. Take yourself away in a week, and give what reason you like for going."

"He crept away, his face sunk upon his breast, like a broken man, while I put out the light and returned to my room."

[Three days later Rachel Howells, still looking sick, told Musgrave that Brunton had disappeared. She became delirious and was put under a nurse's care.]

"On the third night after Brunton's disappearance, the nurse woke in the early morning to find the bed empty, the window open, and no signs of the invalid. It was not difficult to tell the direction which she had taken, for we could follow her footmarks easily across the lawn to the edge of the lake, where they vanished.

"Of course we had the lake dragged at once, but no trace of the body could we find. On the other hand, we brought to the surface an object of a most unexpected kind. It was a linen bag containing a mass of old rusted and discolored metal and several dull-colored pieces of pebble or glass," said Musgrave.

"I must see that paper, Musgrave," said I, "which this butler of yours thought it worth his while to consult, even at the risk of the loss of his position."

"It is rather an absurd business, this Ritual of ours," he answered, "but it has at least the saving grace of antiquity to excuse it."

He handed me this very paper which I have here, Watson, and this is the strange catechism to which each Musgrave had to submit when he came to man's estate. I will read you the questions and answers as they stand:

"Whose was it? His who is gone. Who shall have it? He who will come. Where was the sun? Over the oak. Where was the shadow? Under the elm. How was it stepped? North by ten and by ten, east by five and by five, south by two and by two, west by one and by one, and so under."

[Sherlock thought he could solve the mystery by counting the steps in this ancient ritual. The oak was no problem—it still stood on the Musgrave estate. But only a stump of the elm remained. How would Sherlock determine the length of the shadow of the original tree? He asked Musgrave how high the old elm had been.]

"I can give you it at once. It was 64 feet."

"How do you come to know it?" I asked in surprise.

"When my old tutor used to give me an exercise in trigonometry it always took the shape of measuring heights. When I was a lad I worked out every tree and building on the estate."

This was an unexpected piece of luck.

"Tell me," I asked, "did your butler ever ask you such a question?"

Reginald Musgrave looked at me in astonishment. "Now that you call it to my mind," he answered, "Brunton *did* ask me about the height of the tree some months ago."

I looked up at the sun. It was low in the heavens, and I calculated that in less than an hour it would lie just above the topmost branches of the old oak. One condition mentioned in the Ritual would then be fulfilled. I had then to find where the far end of the shadow would fall when the sun was just clear of the oak.

[Next, Sherlock put a six-foot-long fishing rod into the ground and measured the shadow it cast—nine feet.]

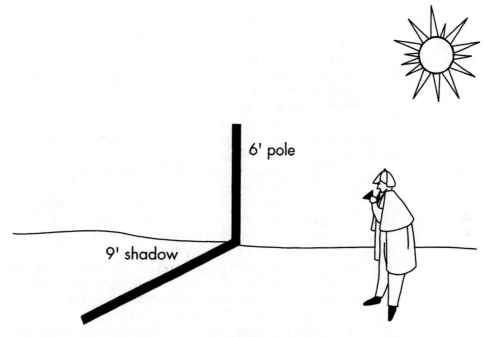

Figure 11.2 Sherlock Holmes Measures the Shadow Cast By a Six-Foot Pole

Figure 11.3 Sherlock Holmes Calculates the Shadow That Would Be Cast By a Ninety-Six–Foot Tree

If a rod of six feet threw a shadow of 9 feet, a tree of 64 feet would throw one of 96 feet. I measured out the distance, which brought me almost to the wall of the house, and I thrust a peg into the spot. You can imagine my exultation, when within two inches of my peg I saw a conical depression in the ground. I knew that it was the mark made by Brunton in his measurements, and that I was still upon his trail.

[Holmes counted off the steps in the Musgrave Ritual and found himself standing on a stone floor in a small room inside the house. The phrase "and under" took him into the basement.]

In the center lay a large and heavy flagstone, with a rusted iron ring in the centre, to which a thick scarf was attached.

"That's Brunton's scarf!" cried my client. "I have seen it on him, and could swear to it. What has the villain been doing here?'

At my suggestion a couple of the county police were summoned, and with the aid of one of the constables I succeeded in raising the stone. A black hole yawned beneath, into which we all peered, while Musgrave, kneeling at the side, pushed down the lantern. Our eyes were riveted upon the figure of a man, clad in a suit of black, who squatted down with his forehead sunk upon the edge of a box. He had been dead some days, but there was no wound or bruise upon him to show how he had met his dreadful end. I sat down upon a keg in the corner and thought the whole matter carefully over.

He knew that something valuable was concealed. He had spotted the place. He found that the stone which covered it was just too heavy for a man to move unaided. But whom could he ask? Rachel Howells had been devoted to him. A man always finds it hard to realize that he may have finally lost a woman's love, however badly he may have treated her.

He tried a few attentions to make his peace with the girl, and then he would engage her as his accomplice. Together they came at night to the cellar, and their united force would raise the stone. But for two of them, and one a woman, it must have been heavy work. What would they do to assist them? Evidently as they had dragged the stone up, they had thrust small chunks of wood under it, until at last, when the opening was large enough to crawl through, they would hold it open by a billet[2] placed lengthwise. Clearly only one person could get into the hole, and that one was Brunton. The girl must have waited above. Brunton then unlocked the box, handed up the contents, presumably—since they are not to be found.

What smouldering fire of vengeance had suddenly sprung into flame in this woman's soul when she saw the man who had wronged her in her power? Was it a chance that the wood had slipped and that the stone had shut Brunton into what became his tomb? Or had some sudden blow from her hand dashed the support away and sent the slab crashing down into its place?

But what had been in the box? Of course, it must have been the old metal and pebbles which my client had dragged from the lake. She had thrown them in there at the first opportunity, to remove the last trace of her crime.

---

[2]A thick stick.

I asked to see the old metal and pebbles. The stones were lusterless and dull. I rubbed one of them on my sleeve, however, and it glowed like a spark in the dark hollow of my hand. The metal was in the form of a double ring, but it had been bent and twisted out of its original shape.

"It is nothing less than the ancient crown of the Kings of England," I said. "Consider what the Ritual says. 'Whose was it? His who is gone.' That was after the execution of King Charles. Then, 'Who shall have it? He who will come.' That was Charles II, whose return was anticipated."

Musgrave asked, "And how was it that Charles II did not get his crown when he returned?"

I explained, "It is likely that the Musgrave who held the secret died, and by oversight left this guide to his descendant without explaining the meaning of it. From that day to this it had been handed down from father to son, until at last it came within reach of a man who tore its secret out and lost his life in the venture."

Of Rachel Howell nothing was ever heard, and the probability is that she got away out of England, and carried herself, and the memory of her crime, to some land beyond the seas.

AFTER YOU READ

1. What new words did you encounter in this story? What strategy will you use to learn them?

2. Briefly describe each major character in the story.

3. What questions came to mind as you read the story? How will you find answers to them?

4. Did you enjoy reading this story? Why or why not?

5. Describe the steps Sherlock Holmes used to solve this mystery.

COLLABORATIVE ACTIVITY: WRITE A MATHEMATICAL MYSTERY

Meet with a group of other students to write a "mathematical mystery." Invent a detective who solves a crime by performing a mathematical calculation. (For example, your detective might calculate how far a getaway car could drive on a tank of gas.) When you're finished, exchange "mathematical mysteries" with another student group. Finally, list the mathematical skills you discussed and used in this exercise.

GETTING IN TOUCH THROUGH FREEWRITING

In the space below, freewrite about your past experiences in math courses—and your plans for success in future classes. The following questions may be helpful: What did you enjoy most? Least? What study skills did you use? What were your most important learning experiences? What changes in your study habits do you plan to make?

◆ HOW TO STUDY MATH ◆

Motivating yourself is the first step in mastering mathematics. The second step is discovering study methods that work for you. In addition to the ideas on class attendance, active learning, and test-taking you met earlier in this textbook, try these suggestions:

1.   Build on what you already know.

If you understand the odometer (mileage instrument) on the dashboard of a car, you know something about how decimals work. Our money system uses decimals too, as well as fractions (quarters and half dollars). You've had additional experience with fractions from using rulers, which measure parts of inches: fourths, halves, eighths, and sixteenths.

You may know more about percentages than you think; most people understand at least the general meaning of signs advertising "10% off" and "25% discount," and restaurant patrons usually know how to calculate a 15% tip.

Negative numbers are another area where you've probably had some experience. You're familiar with temperatures below zero (-10 degrees), and you know that a debt is a negative amount of money.

Everyday life offers many opportunities to understand and practice mathematical skills. Start becoming aware of the math experiences in your everyday life, and make connections between that knowledge and the new concepts you're learning.

2. Use a "hands-on" approach to review basic math concepts.

Many students have difficulty with math because they plunge into abstract concepts and formulas too quickly. Look for ways to make mathematical ideas concrete and real. Browsing through math books in a children's library may clarify concepts you find difficult to understand.

Always draw a picture—even if it's a silly one—before you solve a word problem. Dr. Paulos also suggests writing a dollar sign in front of numbers—especially decimals—to make them seem real.

3.   Study with a group.

As you saw in Chapter Five, "Active Learning," talking about a concept is one of the best ways to learn. Review new concepts and mathematical strategies with your group, and set aside time to study for tests together. For maximum benefit, try the math activities in this chapter with your study group: they'll help you sharpen your understanding of basic concepts.

4.   Practice.

Most math textbooks have model problems, complete with step-by-step explanations and correct solutions. Work the problems on your own, comparing your steps to the ones in your text. Repeat the same model problems (daily if necessary) until you can do them correctly by yourself. If you don't understand a step, seek help from your professor, a tutor, or another student.

5. Check your work.

"Use the opposite process" is the rule for checking math calculations. For example, use division to check multiplication, subtraction to check addition, and so on. (See your math instructor or a tutor for additional explanations.) When you're taking a math test, check every problem before you hand in your paper.

6. Use critical-thinking skills.

"Imagine, estimate, and evaluate" is a useful process for almost any math problem. Imagine—draw a picture—before you tackle a mathematical problem, and estimate the answer before you work out the solution. When you've finished, evaluate—check—your answer against your estimate: they should be close. If they're not, review the steps you used to tackle the problem and check your calculations for errors. Rework the problem—several times if necessary—until you're satisfied with the answer. Seek help if you continue to have difficulty.

7. Learn the language of mathematics.

One successful math instructor teaches her students to connect the word "percent" with "cent"—a practice that makes it easy to visualize math problems. Many students find it helpful to substitute the word "times" when the word "of" appears in a math problem.

Textbooks often have glossaries to help you master mathematical terminology—the difference between integers, "real" numbers, "imaginary" numbers, numerals, and so on. Algebra is easier to understand when you learn to read it as a specialized mathematical language. For example "a number plus 5" becomes "X + 5" in an algebra problem. A restaurant server's 15% tip on a patron's bill, might be expressed like this: 15% x X. Every branch of mathematics has special terminology; begin learning it through flash cards or other memory techniques early in the course.

8. Be precise.

When you're adding and subtracting, write the numbers in neat columns; if decimal points are present, line them up carefully. Write numbers clearly: It's easy to confuse 4 and 9, 7 and 1. When you finish a solution, double-check your calculations and reread the problem to make sure you didn't forget any steps. Many students miss problem 2 on page 329, for example, because they forget that the room needs two coats of paint, not one.

9. Get the most out of class.

Prepare for every class (most students need two hours of preparation for every class hour) and attend every session. Choose a seat front and center: You'll find it easier to con-

Precision and practice are important to your success in math courses.

centrate there. Don't be embarrassed to ask questions: Other students, as well as you, will benefit from your determination to master every problem.

10.   Aim for comprehension.

Successful students strive to understand rather than simply memorize mathematical concepts. Look for connections between lectures, reading assignments, and homework. Never be satisfied with memorization; "cramming" can be disastrous to your math grade because later lessons depend upon thorough understanding of material presented earlier. If tutoring seems necessary, start the process early, before you're dangerously behind. Above all, keep up with homework and lecture material.

11. Be persistent.

Many people mistakenly believe that only gifted students earn A's and B's in math. But the key to good grades is persistence rather than talent. During class, ask questions until you're sure you understand each concept. If class time is limited, save your questions for your instructor's office hours. Make use of tutoring services and computer-assisted learning programs on campus. During study periods, work and rework every problem until you're sure you understand it.

Psychologist Dr. Joyce Brothers says she never mastered the multiplication tables because she skipped grades in elementary school and missed the drills everyone else was doing. In graduate school she had to work harder than most other students to learn the advanced mathematical skills required in her program. Persistence made her a winner—and can do the same for you.

12. Use memory devices.

Many students have benefited from mnemonics like FOIL (*f*ront, *o*utside, *i*nside, *l*ast—a device for remembering the steps to use with binomials). The first letters of "Papa enjoys my dancing and singing" are useful to remind yourself of the order of operations: *p*arentheses, *e*xponents, *m*ultiplication, *d*ivision, *a*dding, *s*ubtracting.

Mnemonics don't take the place of thinking and understanding. But they can help you minimize errors and forgetfulness. Ask professors and tutors to share memory devices they've found helpful—and make up your own as well.

13. Rely on your learning style.

If you're a pragmatic learner, look for practical applications of math theory. Ask learning-center staff what computer programs that suit your learning style are available. Seek connections between everyday math experiences and the principles you're learning in class.

If you're a conceptual learner, abstract principles may come relatively easily to you. Be careful, however, not to overlook important details in math assignments and tests. A misplaced decimal point or an omitted step can cause a wrong answer.

Social and auditory learners are especially likely to benefit from study partnerships and groups. Talk through math problems and new concepts until you're sure you understand them. If you're a visual or an independent learner, set aside "A" concentration time for maximum benefit from individual study and reading.

Overcoming Math Anxiety

Don't allow fears about math to thwart your success in this important subject. Many students who have overcome math anxiety report that the following strategies are especially helpful.

1. Join a math study group—or form one yourself. Talking and working with others builds confidence.

2. Review basic concepts with a tutor or study partner, or work at a computer-learning program. Don't let embarrassment prevent you from building a solid math foundation. It's never too late to start catching up.

3. Practice positive self-talk about math every day (see page 194 in Chapter 5). Replace negative thoughts with positive ones; start telling yourself you *can* succeed.

4. Practice the relaxation exercise on page 203 of Chapter Six, "Taking Tests."

5. If your college offers math-anxiety workshops, sign up for them. If workshops aren't available, ask your college to consider offering them. Your math instructor, a college counselor, or the learning-center staff may be able to get the workshops started.

6. Get to know your math instructor. During office hours, talk about your experiences with math and your hopes for the future. When the instructor is a friend, you may find it easier to ask for help both inside and outside of class.

7. Experiment with a variety of math experiences. Borrow a book of math puzzles from the library; visit the children's library to see if a book there might be helpful. Purchase a math game to play with family members. Invent puzzles and problems of your own to entertain others.

8. If you feel discouraged, review the Five Self-Defeating Beliefs in Chapter Four (pages 132 through 134). Deal firmly with negative feelings; if necessary, ask a friend or family member to help you boost your motivation and courage.

9. Celebrate. Plan a special outing or a treat to reward yourself for sticking to your study schedule, getting help when it's needed, and mastering the new concepts in your classes.

Learning from a Math Learning Log. A learning log can help you reduce math anxiety and develop confidence. Because the log belongs to you alone, it is a safe place to record thoughts, feelings, questions, and problems. If math is difficult for you, the log may help you accept and work with your feelings. If you enjoy math, the log can provide deeper insights into your thinking processes, along with opportunities to probe new ideas and possibilities. The writing process is up to you: You decide the purpose of your log and the kinds of entries you want to write. Here is a list of subjects you may want to explore:

new mathematical concepts
feeling stuck
feeling victorious
feeling confused

what works

what doesn't work

resources

experiments

discoveries

doubts

self-affirmations

math memories

definitions

memory aids

JOURNAL ACTIVITY: KEEP A MATH LEARNING LOG

Keep a math learning log for the next seven days. If you're taking a math course, focus on classwork, assignments, and resources you may be using. If you're not taking a math course, focus on the ways in which you use math in your everyday life. Use the spaces below to explore your experiences, feelings, and ideas about math; experiment with different types of entries.

DAY 1

DAY 2

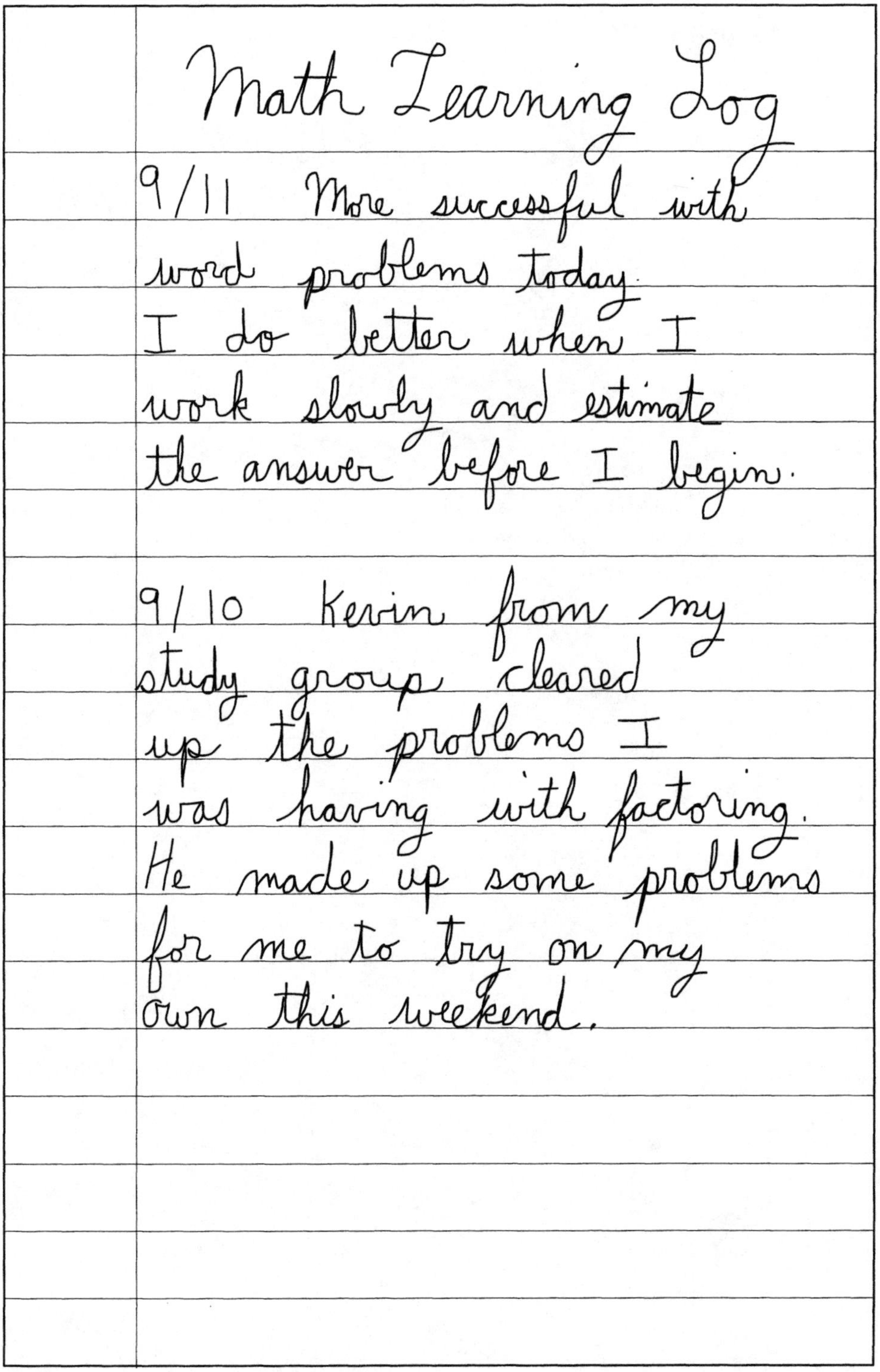

Math Learning Log

9/11 More successful with word problems today. I do better when I work slowly and estimate the answer before I begin.

9/10 Kevin from my study group cleared up the problems I was having with factoring. He made up some problems for me to try on my own this weekend.

Figure 11.4 A Student's Learning Log

DAY 3

DAY 4

DAY 5

DAY 6

DAY 7

EVALUATION

In the space below, freewrite for two or three minutes about this week's journal experience. What did you like about it? What didn't work? What kinds of entries do you plan to try again? Do you intend to continue keeping this journal?

 MATH STUDY SELF-CHECK

This variation on Chapter Five's checklist emphasizes study techniques for math courses. A daily or weekly self-check can help you uncover trouble spots in your study habits.

_____ *I attend every class and take thorough notes.*

_____ *I get help if my notes are incomplete or confusing.*

_____ *I ask as many questions as necessary to understand the lesson.*

_____ *I keep up with reading assignments and homework.*

_____ *I schedule at least two hours of study for every hour in class.*

_____ *I work all the sample problems in my text.*

_____ *I seek help if I have trouble understanding a step in the sample problems.*

_____ *I've arranged for tutoring if it seems necessary.*

_____ *I've learned all the special terms and definitions required in my course.*

_____ *I've discussed what I'm learning with friends or family members.*

_____ *I've invented memory devices (such as mnemonics) for content that must be learned by rote.*

_____ *I've been using study aids (such as flash cards, mind maps, sample test questions, and index-card outlines).*

_____ *I have a study partner or meet regularly with a study group.*

_____ *I know my best times of the day for intense math study and use them wisely.*

_____ *When possible, I seek connections between what I'm learning and everyday life.*

_____ *I practice thinking critically in my math class and study sessions.*

_____ *When I take a math test, I check the answer to every problem before I hand in my paper.*

_____ *I review returned tests carefully to discover weak areas that need further attention.*

_____ *I've embarked on a program to overcome any fears that may slow my progress in math.*

_____ *I regularly make entries into a math learning log.*

Imagine-Estimate-Evaluate

You were introduced to "imagine-estimate-evaluate" on page 340. Many students find that this phrase helps them determine what answer to expect from a problem, what method might be used to solve it, and whether their answer is probably correct. Here's an example of how it works:

If your boss announces a 4% raise, and your current salary is $25,000, here's how to figure your raise:

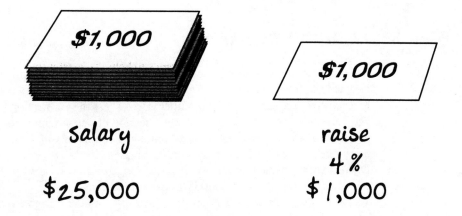

Figure 11.5 Estimate Your Answer

1. Imagine (visualize) the problem.

"Four percent" is "four over a hundred." It's small—like four cents out of a dollar. Don't expect a big raise.

2. Estimate the answer.

A 50% raise—half your salary—would be $12,500. Unfortunately you're getting only a 4% raise. That will be much smaller: less than one-tenth of the 50% raise.

$$4\% \times \$25,000 = ?$$
$$.04 \times \$25,000 = \$1,000$$

3. Evaluate your answer.

If you're earning $25,000, a 4% raise will not be very big: $1,000 sounds right.

COLLABORATIVE ACTIVITY: INVENT AND SOLVE WORD PROBLEMS

Working with two or three other students, invent four math word problems that use basic skills: adding, subtracting, multiplying, and dividing whole numbers or sums of money. When you're finished, exchange problems with another group. Working with your group members, use "imagine-estimate-evaluate" to solve the problems you were given. Take notes on the steps. Then meet with the other group to explain the steps you used, and to listen to their explanations.

USING WHAT YOU HAVE LEARNED

1. List the resources available on your campus to help you master mathematics. Interview at least three college employees to learn more about services you might use.
2. Meet with a small group of other students to discuss the connection between math and current events. Divide the first news section of a newspaper (the pages covering national and international events) among group members. Circle or underline every reference to math. Discuss your findings.
3. Divide another section of the newspaper among group members and look for math references in the advertisements. Discuss your findings.
4. Teach an informal math lesson to someone else—a student, friend, family member, or neighbor. (Don't skip this activity on the grounds that you haven't always been successful with math. Think about the ways in which you use math in your everyday life; be creative as you develop your lesson.)
5. Review this chapter, circling five techniques for learning math that are new to you. Choose two to try before the next class meeting. Take notes on your experiences with these techniques, and evaluate the results.

EVALUATING YOUR PROGRESS

1. As I look back on the past seven days, I've seen an improvement in these areas:

    _____ organizing my life

    _____ protecting my health

    _____ planning my time

    _____ concentrating

    _____ taking notes

    _____ active learning

    _____ reading critically

    _____ writing effectively

    _____ thinking critically

    _____ communicating with important people in my life

    _____ enjoying my free time

    _____ allowing myself to be imperfect

2. In the coming week, I plan to invest five minutes a day working towards this goal:

CHAPTER 12

Introduction to Research

May you be hardworking in the library, as if it were paradise for you.

ERASMUS

PREVIEW

1. Research tasks teach you how to locate, organize, and evaluate information.

2. Research sharpens your critical-reading and critical-thinking skills.

3. You can benefit from practical strategies for conducting research efficiently and effectively.

IN-CLASS INTRODUCTORY ACTIVITY: THINK ABOUT RESEARCH

Mark the point on the line that most closely matches how you feel about this statement.

Curiosity is part of my nature: I always want to know more.

Strongly disagree	Neutral	Strongly agree
1	5	10

Complete the following activities:

ACTIVITIES

1. *What subjects and issues are you curious about? List as many as you can.*

2. *What resources have you used to get information you want? List as many as you can—books, magazines, brochures, television, radio, computer programs, conversations with experts, and so on.*

3. *Have you had any previous experience with research? If so, jot down notes about what you did, how you felt, and the results you obtained.*

COLLABORATIVE ACTIVITY

Meet with a small group of other students to compare and discuss your answers to the first three questions.

◆ GET ACQUAINTED WITH RESEARCH ◆

We live in the Age of Information: Facts and ideas stream into our consciousness via television, radio, newspapers, magazines, signs, posters, billboards, leaflets, and brochures. Even the calendar on your wall may advertise a product or display historical facts. The introductory exercise in this chapter invited you to explore your feelings about our Age of Information. Whether it stimulates or overwhelms you, information is everywhere—and it must be managed.

Organizing and sifting through the avalanche of facts and ideas requires skill. In both college and the professional world, successful people can find and interpret information they need, quickly and effectively. College research assignments can help you acquire those skills. (Sample research projects and term papers are included in many college handbooks. If you're not familiar with college-level research, it's a good idea to read a few sample papers.)

In this chapter you will find practical, proven strategies for discovering, organizing, and interpreting information. You'll learn how to plan research projects that satisfy course requirements and offer personal benefits to you. Most important, you'll discover strategies for overcoming procrastination and fear—the two biggest obstacles to successful research.

The Importance of Research

You can learn a great deal from a well-planned research project; it can also increase your self-confidence, raise your grade in a course, sharpen your critical-reading skills and help you learn how to write like a professional.

A well-written research project can impress a professor and even earn you a nomination for an academic award. Knowledge you uncover in the library this afternoon may be useful on the job three years from now. Your familiarity with research tools may give you a competitive edge in professional report writing and decision making.

Planning is the key to all these benefits. Begin by carefully choosing the topic for your research. Then set up a timetable for the project and visit the library to find out what resources are available. Talk to your professor and a librarian early in the project; their suggestions may save you both time and worry. These preliminary steps, combined with critical-reading and critical-thinking skills, can prepare you for success.

GETTING IN TOUCH THROUGH FREEWRITING

One of the keys to successful research is choosing topics that interest you and will be useful to you. In the space below, freewrite about your favorite subjects. What do you find yourself wondering about? What kinds of stories do you turn to in newspapers and magazines? What do your TV habits reveal about your interests? What specialized knowledge do you expect to need in your professional life? The list of topics below may help you start your freewriting.

> *entertainment*
> *the arts*
> *science*
> *health*
> *relationships*
> *families*

education

religion

nature

geography

languages

social problems

sports

history

technology

business

psychology

children

literature

spirituality

outer space

social groupings

war and peace

philosophy

◆ THE "HOW-TO'S" OF RESEARCH ◆

A successful research project begins with planning. After choosing a suitable topic, you begin learning about it and formulate a *thesis statement* (a one-sentence summary of the central purpose of your research). The next step is gathering information and taking notes so that you can support your thesis. When you have enough information, you can plan, draft, and revise your paper. Finally you submit your paper to your instructor; when it's returned, you carefully read the professor's comments so that you can apply his or her suggestions to your next research project.

On the following pages, you'll take a closer look at each of these steps in the research process.

Five Steps for Effective Research

1.   Select a research project.

Start by looking for a subject that interests you. Past experiences, preliminary reading, and your own curiosity may suggest a suitable topic. "Using Critical Thinking in Writing Assignments" in Chapter Nine can help you select an interesting subject.

One student, fascinated since childhood by the fall migrations of birds, learned that pesticide use in the tropics endangers the breeding and nesting areas of many species. Eventually his findings grew into a term paper for an ecology course.

Consider a research project related to your career goal. Can you investigate a possible career, examine a current issue, or study a specialty that particularly interests you? Look for topics that will acquaint you with important authorities, reference works, and publications in your field.

If you're taking a course outside your field, look for a connection with your career goals. A student majoring in marketing needed a research project for an American history course. She lived near Monticello, Thomas Jefferson's Virginia home, which had recently made news by raising a million dollars to replace the roof. With her professor's approval, she wrote a research paper about the fund-raising project—and discovered several new marketing techniques, along with a wealth of historical information that pleased her professor.

Make sure you can find enough research material to write an effective paper. Check the library first: Are the necessary books and periodicals available? You'll experience delays if the library has to order materials from another library for you (called an "interlibrary loan"). Will you have to wait for replies from government officials or other public figures? If you plan to conduct interviews, will you complete them in time? After consulting a librarian, consider changing your topic if you're finding it difficult to gather the information you need.

The opposite problem should also be avoided: choosing a topic larger than you can manage. If dozens of books and articles have been written about your subject, it needs to be narrowed. Look for a manageable issue within your subject, as in these examples:

abortion	TOO BROAD
government funding of abortions for low-income women	BETTER
illegal drugs	TOO BROAD
illegal drug use in the workplace	BETTER
college sports	TOO BROAD
recruiting practices for college teams	BETTER

2. Gather information.

    a. Get organized. Before you make your first trip to the library, equip yourself with the following:

> change for copy machines
>
> a notebook for research information
>
> a second notebook that will serve as a research log
>
> pens and pencils
>
> a pocket stapler or paper clips
>
> index cards and rubber bands to hold them together
>
> large manila envelopes for storing photocopies

        Write down the library hours, and make sure you take your library card with you. Everything should be labeled with your name, address, and telephone number: Nothing is more frustrating than losing your notes the day before you're ready to start writing your research paper.

        Make sure you have an up-to-date writing handbook or style manual; ask which edition your professor prefers. Many college papers require endnotes, a "works cited" list, or a bibliography. You'll usually be asked to follow either the MLA (Modern Language Association) or the APA (American Psychological Association) system for setting up these references. Detailed instructions appear in most college handbooks and style manuals; ask your instructor for additional guidelines.

    b. Keep a research notebook. Purchase a notebook each time you begin a research project, and use it for reference information about the books and articles you're using. Many students like stenographic notebooks because they're compact and sturdily bound. Be sure to enter call numbers so you can find your references quickly if you need them again. Save the notebook after your paper is completed: The information may be helpful on another project later.

    c. Record useful information. Index cards are useful for short entries; use the photocopier for charts and long quotations. *Always* record bibliographic information (titles, authors, dates, etc.) when you take notes. Some students photocopy the title page—front and back—of every book they use. This practice costs a little extra, but it's worth the savings in last-minute trips to the library for missing information. When you take notes, write only on the front of an index card. Later you'll be spreading your cards onto a table, bed, or floor to organize your paper; information on the back will be lost.

    d. Keep a research log. This is a variation of the "learning log" you read about in Chapter Five, "Active Learning." In a stenographic pad, or a separate section of a notebook, record each day's thoughts, questions, problems, and discoveries. Date each entry, but don't worry about neatness or organization. This log is for your eyes only—a kind of research "diary."

Current Biography Yearbook 1994
ed. Judith Graham   The H.W. Wilson Company
"Angelou, Maya p. 25 - 29   NY, NY
p. 28 Angelou : "All my work is
meant to say, 'You may encounter
many defeats, but you must not
be defeated.' In fact, the encountering
may be the very experience which
creates the vitality and the power
to endure." p. 28

"Maya Angelou: Prime - Time Poet"
Ebony 4/93   Vol 48 #6 pp. 68 - 70

Angelou says composing the poem
"On the Pulse of the Morning" for
Clinton's inaug. was the highlight
of her life. Male and female
forces must work together for
healing of Af. Am. community.

Figure 12.1 Student's Note Cards

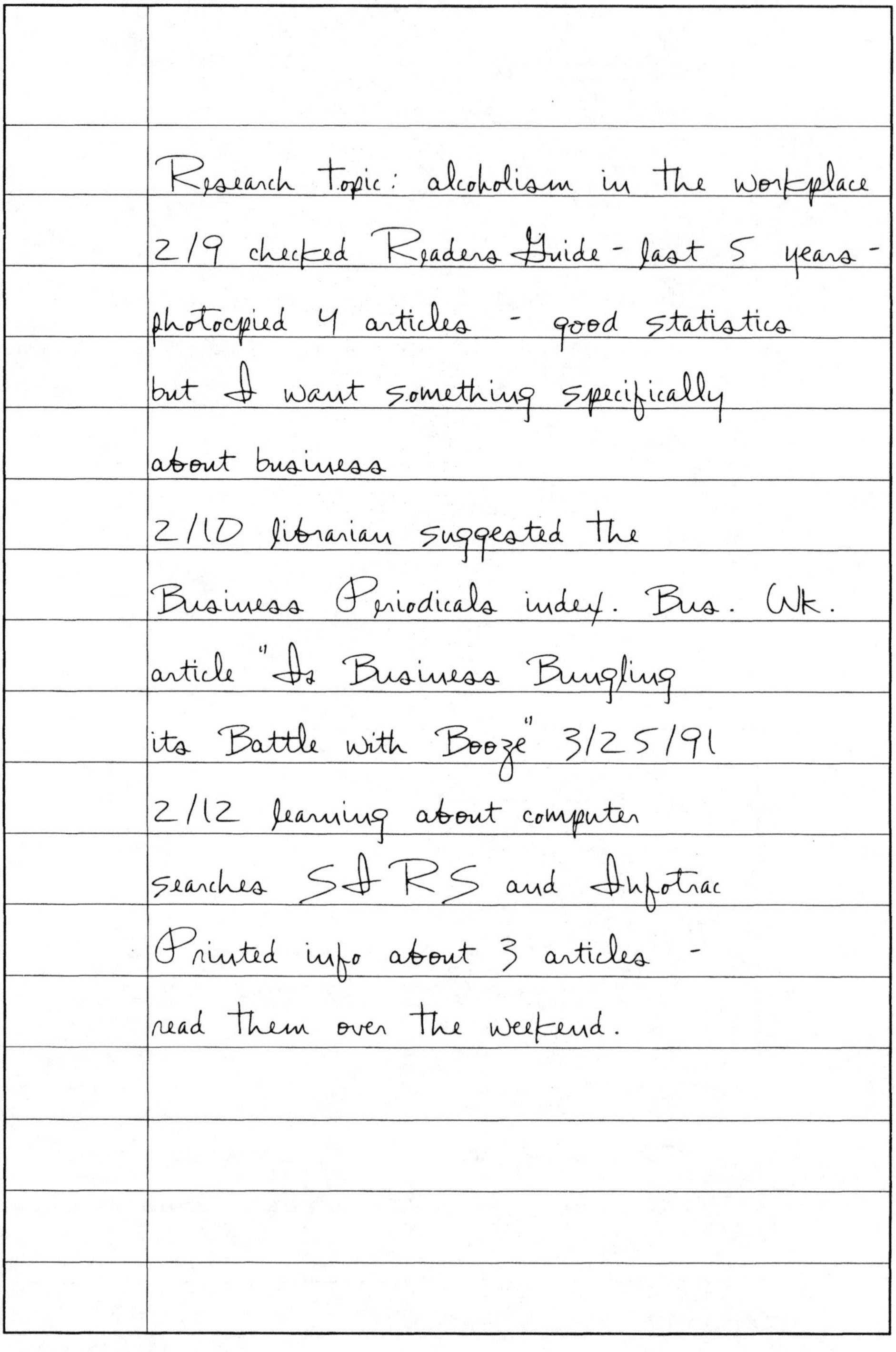

Research topic: alcoholism in the workplace

2/9 checked Readers Guide - last 5 years - photocpied 4 articles - good statistics but I want something specifically about business

2/10 librarian suggested the Business Periodicals index. Bus. Wk. article "Is Business Bungling its Battle with Booze" 3/25/91

2/12 learning about computer searches SIRS and Infotrac Printed info about 3 articles - read them over the weekend.

Figure 12.2 Research Log

The log serves two important purposes. First, writing about your research experiences—ideas, frustrations, and victories—is a great thinking tool. Second, this written record is insurance against forgetting. Most research logs are full of sentences that begin: "I wonder if . . ." "I'm excited because . . ." "I need to ask about . . ." "The librarian suggested . . ." When you return to the library each day, previous entries in your log will help you plan the next steps in your research.

e. Read. In the early stages of research, you may feel overwhelmed by new information. Don't let those feelings discourage you. Even professionals often feel confused in the early stages of research.

With persistence and patience, your project will gradually take shape. Use your research log to record both problems and progress. Sort information into preliminary lists: What are the issues? What points seem most controversial? What kinds of judgments are required? Don't think you have to have all the answers right away; they'll come later.

The following suggestions can save you time and energy during the research process:

• Before you read a journal article, look for a summary, conclusion or abstract. After you've read it, you may not need to read the whole article.

Expect to do a great deal of reading in the early stages of your research project.

- Ask if your library has a computerized database containing summaries of magazine and journal articles. If so, use the summaries to decide whether you want to read the article.

- Pre-reading books can cut down on research time. Scan the jacket, table of contents, index, introduction, and preface. Sometimes you'll quickly decide that

First Steps

"Do-nothingism" often paralyzes student researchers. If you're procrastinating, choose a quick warm-up activity to get you started. One of the best warm-ups is a five-minute visit to the library. If you still have plenty of time before your paper is due, make these visits on three or four consecutive days. Find out where books about your subject are shelved and browse there. Open a drawer in the card catalog, or type a few entries into the computer database to see what's available. You'll soon feel ready to take notes on a book or photocopy an article—and your "do-nothingism" will be gone.

Another good warm-up is talking informally about your research project with a friend. Have a pencil and paper ready for jotting down ideas that come to you during the conversation.

Making a few "get-acquainted" visits to the library is an excellent warm-up for a research project.

the book doesn't have the information you need; at other times your pre-reading will help you find what you want rapidly.

- Most important, seek help when you need it. Expect to learn from each research project; you'll always have problems to solve and victories to celebrate. Pro-

Once your research project starts moving, keep the momentum going. If the process suddenly comes to a halt, seek help. Talk to your professor, a staff member from the learning center, or a student with experience in the kind of research you're doing.

Most important, seek help from librarians, especially in the early stages of research when you're finding out what information is available. Even important scholars rely on their help; you'll often find librarians mentioned on the acknowledgments page of academic books.

Librarians are excellent information managers. Answering your questions is their job.

fessors, librarians, and friends with research experience can light the way and help you sharpen your skills.

3. Select a workable thesis statement.

Your thesis statement—a single sentence that expresses the central idea of your research—is the most important part of a research project. Always ask your professor to approve it before you write your paper. (Refer to your writing handbook for detailed suggestions.)

4. Plan your paper.

Write your paper in stages—planning, drafting, and revising—rather than all at once. (You'll find practical suggestions in "Introducing the Writing Process" in Chapter Nine.) After your professor has approved your thesis statement, start planning your paper. Spread your notecards and photocopies on the floor, a large table, or your bed; then organize your research by grouping related information together. Decide which information should come first, last, and in between; move your cards and photocopies around, imagining how they would fit together in a paper. When you've worked out an organizational pattern you like, write an outline.

5. Write a rough draft of your paper; then revise it.

When you're satisfied with your outline, you're ready to draft your paper. If problems occur at this stage, check your writing handbook or seek help from your professor, a librarian, a friend, or the learning center.

Professors appreciate neatness, accuracy, thoroughness, and error-free writing. Respect your professor's preferences about format, length, references, and other matters: Attention to these details may earn you a higher grade. Call the library if you're missing a date or author's name, but don't expect librarians to provide all your information.

Remember too that plagiarism—copying someone else's work and pretending it's your own—is a serious offense. (Most colleges have an official policy about plagiarism that you can read in your college catalog). To avoid plagiarism, follow these guidelines:

a. Never submit another person's work as your own. Colleges have strict rules against this kind of dishonesty: Offenders may fail a course or even be suspended or expelled from the institution.
b. Use care when copying information from a book, article, or other resource. If you copy a quotation from another source, give credit to the writer. (Refer to your handbook or style manual for specific instructions.) Use endnotes, a works-cited list, or a bibliography to give credit for information you uncovered in your research.
c. Provide sources for any information that might be considered controversial or questionable.

Even if you put information into your own words, you may need to show that you obtained it from a reliable source. The decisive factor is whether the information is easy to verify. No one is going to argue about the date an American president died, the capital of an Asian country, or the composer of a well-known Italian opera, and no sources are required for these kinds of information.

But controversial or questionable information does require documentation (written details about your source): statistics, measurements, quotations, and expert opinions. Expect to spend a great deal of time making decisions about citing sources while you're working on your paper: One purpose of college research projects is to teach you what does and what does not require documentation. You can learn more about documentation from librarians, your writing handbook, and your professor.

6. After you've submitted your paper, take advantage of feedback from your professor.

Your research project doesn't end when you hand in your paper. Many professors offer corrections and suggestions when they grade papers. Respect these comments: They're personal feedback from an expert in the field you're studying. If you're unsure about their meaning, visit your professor during office hours to ask questions.

In general, professors offer three kinds of feedback:

    a.   An explanation of your grade. Use these comments to improve future papers.

    b.   Corrections. Resolve to avoid future errors. If usage mistakes were marked, consult your handbook or discuss them with a tutor. If you made other kinds of errors, ask your professor for advice about avoiding them in the future.

    c.   Suggestions. Sometimes professors offer ideas for future research. These suggestions may prove valuable in later courses.

EXERCISE 1: GET TO KNOW THE LIBRARY

Visit the campus library, introduce yourself to a librarian, and answer the following questions.

1. *Does the library have a card catalog, or is there a computerized database of books?*
2. *Where is the reference area? (It contains encyclopedias and other books of facts that never leave the library.)*
3. *Where are recent issues of magazines displayed?*
4. *Where is the* Readers' Guide to Periodical Literature? *(This reference series lists magazine articles alphabetically, by subject, and by author.)*
5. *Is there a computerized database for magazine and journal articles?*
6. *Where are back issues of magazines and journals kept? Can you get them yourself, or does the library staff get them for you?*
7. *How can you obtain a library card, if you don't already have one?*
8. *How long can you keep a book after you've borrowed it? Can you renew it by telephone? What are the overdue charges?*

9. *Are group study rooms available?*
10. *Can student carrels (semi-private study areas) be reserved?*
11. *If a professor puts a book on reserve for your class, where will it be kept?*

Persuasive or Informative?

Research papers usually have either an informative or a persuasive thesis. The thesis of an informative paper presents a fact or idea without arguing a position or attempting to settle a controversy. But in a persuasive paper, the thesis is usually a controversial idea that the writer wants to prove. (The words *need, should, ought,* or *must* often appear in the thesis.) Here are examples of both informative and persuasive thesis statements:

The availability of DNA testing has created a number of problems for criminal-justice experts.	INFORMATIVE
The results of DNA testing ought to be allowed as evidence when criminal cases are tried in courts.	PERSUASIVE
Automobile manufacturers are thinking about "supercars" that travel hundreds of miles on a gallon of fuel.	INFORMATIVE
By 1998, automobile manufacturers should be required to begin selling "supercars" that can travel hundreds of miles on a gallon of fuel.	PERSUASIVE
Common childhood diseases like chicken pox and measles can have long-term consequences.	INFORMATIVE
Americans need a more aggressive approach to preventing common childhood diseases like chicken pox and measles.	PERSUASIVE

When you're assigned a research project, ask whether your professor prefers an informative or a persuasive paper. If the choice is yours, consider these factors:

1. Often, persuasive papers are easier to organize, since all your information is aimed at proving a central thesis.
2. Persuasive papers may be more enjoyable to read and hence may earn higher grades from professors.
3. Informative papers don't subject you to the risks of taking a position on a controversial subject.
4. An informative paper may allow you to present a variety of viewpoints about the subject you've chosen.

EXERCISE 2: THINK ABOUT THESIS STATEMENTS

Label the following thesis statements either I (informative) or P (persuasive):

_____ 1. Parental consent should be required before a minor can obtain an abortion.

_____ 2. Second marriages involving stepchildren create unique challenges for both adults and children.

_____ 3. Consumer pressure has made fast-food companies more sensitive to environmental and nutritional concerns.

_____ 4. Fast-food employees should not be required to undergo HIV screening.

_____ 5. The writings of American poet Emily Dickinson were strongly influenced by her New England upbringing.

_____ 6. The National Rifle Association exercises too much influence on the American political process.

_____ 7. Although he is most famous for his marches, composer John Philip Sousa did much to broaden the taste and musical knowledge of American concert-goers.

_____ 8. By establishing "magnet schools" in their districts, public-school boards can promote racial integration without forced busing.

_____ 9. Animal testing of consumer products is not cost effective and does little to protect the health and safety of consumers.

_____ 10. Law-enforcement agencies are discovering new solutions to the widespread problem of domestic violence.

_____ 11. Because of his negative attitude toward native peoples, Christopher Columbus should not be honored with a holiday.

Critical Reading and Research

Critical reading is vital to college research. Any subject worth researching will require you to challenge and evaluate written sources. Even if you're relying heavily on interviews, films, television broadcasts, or field studies, you'll begin with critical reading to become familiar with your subject.

Start with the evaluative skills you learned in Chapter Eight, "Critical Thinking." How thoroughly did the author investigate the issue you're researching? Is bias present? What are the author's credentials? Is supporting evidence presented logically?

Research in Your Future

Research doesn't end with college graduation. Businesses use research to test products and evaluate marketing proposals; physicians probe medical literature for new medications and procedures; government-funded organizations of all types (colleges, laboratories, museums, symphony orchestras) perform research to support requests for financial grants.

Consider selecting research projects that will acquaint you with the methods and resources used by professionals in your field. Use a research log to record the process step by step, as it happens; save your note cards and photocopies in case you need them later on.

Acquaint yourself with on-line (computer) aids to research. Ask a librarian to show you how to research a current topic on SIRS or INFOTRAC. You'll discover that computer research programs have special features that save time and put you in touch with a large number of resources. You should also learn about *modems* (devices that allow computer users to communicate with one another through telephone wires). Many professionals use electronic mail to communicate with one another via modems.

Most important, think critically as you work through the research process. If you've chosen a worthwhile topic, you'll learn a great deal about the nature of research, the special issues in your field, and the frustrations and rewards of independent work.

Primary and Secondary Sources. Be aware of the differences between *primary* and *secondary* sources; both have advantages, and both present risks.

Primary sources come from eyewitnesses. They include diaries, letters, official documents, articles, and books written by people close to a person or event. Secondary sources are written by journalists, researchers, and scholars who study, evaluate, and synthesize information they have learned from other writers. Shakespeare's marriage certificate is a primary source; *Shakespeare's Lives*, in which author S. Schoenbaum evaluates all the research on William Shakespeare for the last 400 years, is a secondary source.

Primary sources are important because of their closeness to an event or person. For example, Lincoln scholars are learning a great deal from newly discovered documents connected with his early law career. The new evidence—thousands of legal documents from Lincoln's practice—shows that Lincoln was a serious young attorney who earned substantial fees by handling a huge number of widely varied cases.

But primary sources can also be misleading. As you saw in Chapter Eight, William N. Herndon, Lincoln's law partner, distorted and invented information because he disliked Lincoln's wife. Falsified documents can create additional problems: In the 1930s, a forger named Joseph Cosey circulated many fraudulent "Lincoln letters."

Secondary sources also vary in their usefulness. Carl Sandburg, Lincoln's most famous biographer, is widely respected for his thorough analysis, interpretation, and evaluation of information about Lincoln. But even Sandburg's work has limitations because it covers only the documents that were available during his life. If you were studying Lincoln, you would have to evaluate the research done since Sandburg's death in 1967. A good starting point might be the Lincoln bibliography (reading list) in the *Encyclopedia Americana*. A history professor or research librarian would also be helpful.

Death. Three days later, the President was shot by the actor John Wilkes Booth while attending a performance at Ford's Theater in Washington. He died at 7:22 the following morning, April 15, 1865. After lying in state in the Capitol, his body was taken to Springfield, Ill., where he was buried in Oak Ridge Cemetery. See LINCOLN'S ASSASSINATION.

DAVID HERBERT DONALD, *Harry C. Black Professor of History and Director of the Institute of Southern History, The Johns Hopkins University*

Bibliography

Anderson, Dwight G., *Abraham Lincoln: The Quest for Immortality* (Knopf 1982).

Angle, Paul M., ed., *The Lincoln Reader* (1947; reprint,Greenwood Press 1981).

Barrett, Joseph H., *Life of Abraham Lincoln* (1865; reprint, Darby Bks., 1981).

Bruce, Robert V., *Lincoln and the Tools of War* (1956; reprint, Greenwood Press 1974).

Cox, Lawanda, *Lincoln and Black Freedom* (Univ. of S.C. Press, 1981).

Current, Richard N., *The Lincoln Nobody Knows* (1958; reprint, Greenwood Press, 1980).

De Young, Garry, *Abraham Lincoln: Apostle of Freedom* (De Young Press, 1983).

Donald, David H., *Lincoln's Herndon* (Knopf 1948).

Donald, David H., *Lincoln Reconsidered: Essays on the Civil War Era* (1965; reprint, Greenwood Press 1981).

Foner, Eric and Olivia Mahoney, *A House Divided: America in the Age of Lincoln* (Norton 1990).

Herndon, William H., *Life of Lincoln* (1889; reprint, Da Capo 1983).

McPherson, James M., *Abraham Lincoln and the Second American Revolution* (Oxford 1991).

Neely, Mark E., Jr., *The Fate of Liberty: Abraham Lincoln and Civil Liberties* (Oxford 1991).

Randall, James G., *Lincoln and the South* (1946; reprint, Greenwood Press 1980).

Sandburg, Carl, *Abraham Lincoln: The Prairie Years and the War Years* (1926 & 1939; reprint, Harcourt 1974).

Sloate, Susan, *Abraham Lincoln: The Freedom President* (Fawcett 1989).

Townsend, William H., *Lincoln and the Bluegrass* (Univ. Press of Ky. 1990).

Figure 12.3 Abraham Lincoln Bibliography from the *Encyclopedia Americana*

Evaluating Sources

Skilled researchers ask two basic questions: Who said it? How do they know? Generally speaking, you can trust research that meets these four requirements: The publication date is recent, the author has impressive credentials, the publisher has a reputation for reliability, and the research methods are sound. Always be prepared to consider additional factors, however.

1. Date

Sometimes the newest book on a subject is not as thorough or reliable as an older one. For example, Sir Edward Cook's biography of Florence Nightingale, written in 1913, is still the most respected study of her life. Librarians, professors, and bibliographies can help you decide which authorities are worth reading. Even if an older book has a superb reputation, always look at recent publications to learn about new developments. Remember that articles in periodicals (journals, magazines, newspapers, and newsletters) are especially good sources for current information.

2. Author's credentials

Is the author associated with a well-known college or university? Are any biases present? Where was the research done? Who funded the study that led to the book? What other books has the author written? Does a testimonial from a respected expert appear on the book jacket? Check the *Book Review Digest* if you need to learn more about the author's reputation.

Be careful, however, not to fall into the error of making a personal judgment rather than evaluating information on its own merits. An unknown researcher without important connections may make an important discovery. For example, the nineteenth-century medical community rejected the germ theory of Louis Pasteur (1822–1895) because he was a chemist, not a physician. Scottish surgeon Joseph Lister (1827–1912) met similar resistance because he did not practice medicine in an important medical center.

3. Publisher

In general, you can trust books from established publishers and articles in well-researched professional journals. Many respected journals and publishers remove authors' names from manuscripts being considered for publication. Because the selection board does not know who wrote the article or book they're evaluating, they're likely to be objective. Be aware, however, that even major publications make mistakes. Always use your own knowledge and thinking skills to evaluate what you read.

4. Research methods

Good researchers are methodical and thorough. They know the history of the problem they're studying and the appropriate methods for studying it. They explain exactly where their information came from so that it can be checked for accuracy. In general, they are respectful towards other scholars and previous research that has been done in their area. Be suspicious of any researcher who does not match this description.

In 1974, three years after his death, the research of Sir Cyril Burt, a famous British psychologist, was found to be fraudulent. An American psychologist named Leo Kamin showed that Burt (1882–1971) falsified information to try to prove that intelligence is inborn and unchangeable. (This fallacy about intelligence has since been disproved.) Kamin, who first read Burt's studies in 1972, said, "The immediate conclusion I came to after ten minutes of reading was that Burt was a fraud." Kamin—an experienced researcher—noticed that Burt had failed to explain where, when, and how he had conducted his research. Kamin, amazed that no one had noticed these omissions, started an investigation and eventually exposed Burt's dishonesty.

Similar problems occur in many fields. In 1980 the famous *American Journal of Medicine* published an anorexia study that turned out to be fraudulent. After the article had been published, a reader noticed that no hospital or physicians were named in the study—a violation of research standards. An investigation followed, fraud was discovered, and the journal retracted the article.

In both cases, fraud was exposed by researchers who asked, "How did these experts obtain their information?" An unsatisfactory answer to this question should always trigger doubts. While you may not meet large-scale fraud in your research, you are likely to come across doubtful information. Note such problems in your research log and choose a strategy for further investigation. Often a talk with a professor or librarian will help you decide what to do next.

5. Overall quality

Sometimes your own reading skills will tell you that something is wrong with an article or book. Beware of a researcher who deals superficially with important issues or omits important information. Doubts should also arise when a writer claims to be the first person to discover the answer to a long-standing problem—for example, someone who claims to be the *only* person who can correctly interpret *Hamlet* or explain the disappearance of the dinosaurs.

The following excerpt from Edmund Pearson's *Trial of Lizzie Borden*, a book about the Fall River, Massachusetts ax murders, shows how one writer misled his readers. In 1892 Lizzie Borden was tried for the murders of her stepmother and father, who had been killed by blows from an ax. Lizzie had been home that morning and had gone up the stairs at least once—right past the room where her stepmother lay dead. The prosecution tried to show that Lizzie must have seen her stepmother's dead body on the floor of the guest bedroom. The defense claimed that the body could not be seen unless the person on the stairs knew where to look.

To settle the question, the jury was taken to the house and allowed them to climb the stairs themselves. Here is how Edmund Pearson, who believed Lizzie was guilty, described the jury's staircase experiment:

> The significance of Miss Borden's presence at that precise place at that moment has been investigated with great care; whether anybody descending or ascending the stairs would necessarily see all that was in the guest chamber. Leaving this question, it may be said that one thing is not seriously disputed; anyone on that landing stood within fifteen or twenty feet of Mrs. Borden's dead body as it lay on the floor of the guest chamber.

If you are a sharp reader, you noticed that Pearson omitted the results of the experiment: his phrase "leaving this question" directs the reader's attention elsewhere. But the trial records show that the dead body was *not* visible unless the person on the stairs knew where to look. If you are a particularly skilled thinker, you may have deduced the reason for Pearson's omission: He wanted to make the case against Lizzie as strong as possible. (The jury found Lizzie innocent.)

JOURNAL ACTIVITY: PRACTICE RESEARCH SKILLS

This week spend five minutes a day practicing a few of the research activities from the following list. In the spaces below, note the activity you tried; then write a sentence or two describing and evaluating your experience.

RESEARCH SKILLS

> *browsing through the reference section of the library*
> *browsing through the circulating collection*
> *exploring special library services*
> *using a computer database*
> *exploring the card catalog*
> *reading about research in a handbook*
> *reading critically about a subject that interests you*
> *taking notes from a reading selection*
> *writing an endnote or bibliography entry*
> *reading about plagiarism in your handbook or catalog*
> *reading about documentation in your handbook*

DAY 1

The activity you chose:

Your experience:

DAY 2

The activity you chose:

Your experience:

DAY 3

The activity you chose:

Your experience:

DAY 4

The activity you chose:

Your experience:

DAY 5

The activity you chose:

Your experience:

DAY 6

The activity you chose:

Your experience:

DAY 7

The activity you chose:

Your experience:

READING THOUGHTFULLY: A RESEARCHER AT WORK

The following reading selection about American composer Scott Joplin illustrates why critical thinking is vitally important to a researcher. Joplin, an African American, wrote ragtime compositions that were both elegant and elaborate, but he was never accepted by the American musical establishment. Although Joplin died in 1917, serious research into his life did not begin until the late 1940s. After ragtime music was featured in the Hollywood production of *The Sting*, interest in his life began to grow. In this excerpt, biographer Edward Berlin describes one of the problems he encountered—determining Joplin's birthdate. Before you begin reading, complete the following activity.

BEFORE YOU READ

1. What problems would you expect if you were researching the life of an African American born shortly after the Civil War?

2. What might cause confusion about a famous person's birthdate?

3. If you were researching Joplin's life, what steps might you take to verify his date of birth?

from   **King of Ragtime**
by Edward A. Berlin

T he authenticated facts of Scott Joplin's life are surprisingly scant. Questionable testimony by aged individuals is one problem. Documents may also be seriously flawed. Conflicting and illogical information too often leads to uncertainty. The various problems are illustrated by the difficulty in determining Scott Joplin's date of birth.

November 24, 1868, the date long accepted as Scott Joplin's birth date, is almost certainly incorrect. The date derives from biographical information submitted in 1942 by Lottie Joplin, the composer's widow: Joplin, Scott, composer, pianist; b. Texarkana, Tex., Nov. 24, 1868; d. New York, April 4, 1919.

Lottie demonstrates that her memory in 1942 was faulty. We can overlook her error in placing Joplin's birth in Texarkana. Perhaps Joplin, himself, did not know that there was no Texarkana when he was born, that the town where he spent most of his childhood was founded five years after his birth. But she was present when he died on April 1, 1917, yet remembered the incident as occurring more than two years later.

The information she gave of his birth is also highly questionable. For his death certificate in 1917 she had given his age as 49 and his year of birth as 1868, leaving the month and day blank. If she knew his full birth date in 1942, why did she not know it in 1917? In addition, if he had died at the age of 49, his birthday would have had to be before April 2, 1868.

The U.S. Census of 1870 and of 1880 also indicates that Joplin was born before the middle of 1868. The 1870 census, taken in Davis County, Texas, on July 18, indicates that his age on his last birthday was two. Similarly the 1880 census, taken in Texarkana, Texas, on June 17 and 18, lists his age on his last birthday as twelve.

Later census listings are no help. The 1890 census was destroyed in a fire. The 1900 census taken in Sedalia, Missouri, on June 6, gives his birth date as October 1872—obviously incorrect, for he had already appeared in the 1870 cen-

Until recently, scholars knew little about composer Scott Joplin, who died in 1917. Through persistence and ingenuity, musical scholars have discovered many new facts about his life and work.

sus. His final census entry, that of New York on April 22, 1910, gives his age as 40, also in disagreement with the earlier listings.

Scott Joplin's date of birth is not the important issue. Even if he was not born on November 24, 1868, he was born within a year of that date. The larger issue is that, from the very point of his birth, the facts concerning him are elusive. In studying his life, we are continually faced with conflicting evidence. In view of this general lack of certainty, the approach in this biography is to present all the reasonable information, to discuss the options, and to suggest what seems most plausible.

AFTER YOU READ

1. What new words did you encounter in this reading? How will you learn their meaning?

2. What questions do you have about this reading? What strategies will you use to find the answers?

3. Biographer Edward Berlin disagrees with Joplin's widow about several details. Do you find Mrs. Joplin or Berlin more convincing? Why?

4. Other books about ragtime simply state the November 24, 1868 birthdate for Scott Joplin without challenging it. Did you find Berlin's investigation interesting—or would you have preferred a shorter and simpler explanation? Explain.

5. Reread the last sentence in this reading selection. How does Berlin's biography differ from an encyclopedia article or children's book about Joplin?

6. What are the advantages and disadvantages to Berlin's thoroughness in researching Scott Joplin? Can you think of a situation in which reading an encyclopedia article about Joplin might serve your purpose better than reading Berlin's biography?

Challenging Your Thinking

To thine own self be true.

WILLIAM SHAKESPEARE

One sign of a worthwhile research project is its effect on your biases and blind spots. Even experts are sometimes blinded by their own preference for a particular viewpoint. It's human nature to pay close attention to agreeable evidence and ignore other opinions. You can learn a great deal by weighing and comparing evidence about a controversial issue.

Fortunately there's a simple way to open your thinking to other possibilities. After you've taken a position about an issue, ask yourself what kind of evidence would change your mind. Then find out if that evidence actually exists. For example, many people who don't wear automobile seatbelts claim that they're not yet convinced that seatbelts save lives. But when they're asked what kind of study they're waiting for, they can't answer. They haven't applied rigorous thinking skills to seatbelt use.

What evidence would you need to believe that the Loch Ness Monster really exists? Suppose a Knight Commander of the British Empire, a surgeon, a count, several monks and lawyers, a Nobel-Prize-winning chemist and almost three thousand other people reported sightings of the Monster. Would you accept their evidence? (All of these sightings are on record.) What if a team from the Academy of Applied Science actually photographed one of the Monster's fins? (They have.) What evidence would convince *you*?

When you investigate a controversial issue, decide what evidence you're looking for. It's also helpful to talk with professionals in the field to find out what methods they use.

The ability to evaluate information on its own merits is one of the greatest benefits of a college education. In both everyday life and research, keep asking yourself these vital questions: What factors shape my thinking? What evidence would cause me to change my mind? Does that evidence exist? The following group activity will help you sharpen these thinking skills.

COLLABORATIVE ACTIVITY: LEARNING ABOUT EVIDENCE

On your own, choose five items from the following list. State a position about each one and decide what evidence would cause you to change your mind. Then meet with two or three other students to discuss your ideas.

> *life in outer space*
> *cigarettes*
> *corporal punishment in schools*
> *the 55-mile-per-hour speed limit*
> *the Abominable Snowman*

gun control
extra-sensory perception (ESP)
marijuana
capital punishment
astrology

USING WHAT YOU HAVE LEARNED

1. Work with a group to investigate a topic from the previous activity. Agree on a position, decide what evidence would change your mind, and look for that evidence. When you're finished, present a brief report on your findings to the whole class.
2. Interview a professor, journalist, or local expert in some field to learn about the pitfalls, rewards, and challenges of research. Prepare a brief (two or three minutes) presentation about this experience to deliver to your class.
3. Interview a librarian to find out what research services are available on your campus and how librarians can help.
4. List five experiences you've had or subjects of interest to you that could serve as starting points for college research projects.
5. List three research topics that might help you prepare for a career that interests you.
6. Learn how to use three databases (either print or electronic) in your college library. Use these databases to find two books and two magazine articles about a subject that interests you.

EVALUATING YOUR PROGRESS

1. As I look back on the past seven days, I've seen an improvement in these areas:

   _____   organizing my life

   _____   protecting my health

   _____   planning my time

   _____   concentrating

   _____   taking notes

   _____   active learning

   _____   reading critically

   _____   writing effectively

   _____   thinking critically

_____ communicating with important people in my life

_____ enjoying my free time

_____ allowing myself to be imperfect

2. In the coming week, I plan to invest five minutes a day working towards this goal:

CREDITS

Text Credits: pp. 157-158 Reprinted with the permission of Scribner, an imprint of Simon & Schuster from THE WORLD GROWS ROUND MY DOOR by David Fairchild. Copyright 1947 Charles Scribner's Sons; copyright renewed © 1975 Barbara Muller and Nancy Bell Bates. p. 183 Reprinted with permission from Parade, copyright © 1993. Reprinted by permission of the author and the author's agents, Scovil Chichak Galen Literary Agency, Inc., 381 Park Avenue South, New York, New York 10016. pp. 211–213 From THIS LIFE by Sidney Poitier Copyright © 1980 by Sidney Poitier. Reprinted by permission of Alfred A. Knopf Inc. pp. 235–236 From DO WHAT YOU WILL, THE MONEY WILL FOLLOW, by Marsha Sinetar. Copyright © 1989 by Marsha Sinetar. Reprinted by permission of Dell Books, A division of Bantam Doubleday Dell Publishing Group, Inc. pp. 259–260 Text excerpt as indicated in the request from ZEN AND THE ART OF MOTORCYCLE MAINTENANCE by Robert M. Pirsig. Text Copyright © 1974 by Robert M. Pirsig. By permission of William Morrow and Company, Inc. pp. 304–305 From SCIENCE MAT-TERS: ACHIEVING SCIENTIFIC LITERACY by Robert M. Hazen and James Trefil. Copyright © 1991 by Robert M. Hazen and James Trefil. Used by permission of Doubleday, a division of Bantam Doubleday Dell Publishing Group, Inc. pp. 320–321 From BLACK HOLES AND BABY UNIVERSES AND OTHER ESSAYS by Stephen W. Hawking. Copyright © 1993 by Stephen W. Hawking. Used by permission of Bantam Books, a division of Bantam Doubleday Dell Publishing Group, Inc. p. 328 Reprinted with permission from Parade, copyright © 1993. p. 367 From the *Encyclopedia Americana,* 1992 Edition. Copyright 1992 by Grolier Incorporated. Reprinted by permission.

Photo Credits: p. 8 © Elizabeth Crews/Stock, Boston. p. 10 © Beringer-Dratch/The Image Works. p. 14 Gary Gershoff/Retna. p. 41 © Ex Rouchon/Photo Researchers, Inc. p. 47 © Brian Smith. p. 62 © Patrick James Watson Photography/The Image Works. p. 70 © Spencer Grant/Monkmeyer Press Photo Service. p. 76 © Joseph Schuyler/Stock, Boston. p. 95 © Frank Site-man/Stock, Boston. p. 120 © Topham/The Image Works. p. 129 © Brian Smith. p. 131 © Michael Newman/PhotoEdit. p. 150 Kris Eisenhower/Stock, Boston. p. 162 © Barbara Alper, 1994/Stock, Boston. p. 164 © R. Lord/The Image Works. p. 174 © T. Michael/The Image Works. p. 181 © Brian Smith. p. 187 © Joel Gordon, 1991. p. 190 Joseph Schuyler/Stock, Boston. p. 212 Globe Photos. p. 217 © Brian Smith. p. 218 © Jean-Claude LeJune/Stock, Boston. p. 227 © Brian Smith. p. 249 © Tony Freeman/PhotoEdit. p. 250 © Jeff Greenberg/PhotoEdit. p. 269 © Joel Gordon, 1993. p. 275 © John Coletti. p. 290 © Will Faller. p. 291 © Brian Smith. p. 293 © Jeff Greenberg/Pho-toEdit. p. 306 © Suzanne Arms/The Image Works. p. 309 © Will Faller. p. 311 © Will Faller. p. 327 © Joel Gordon, 1991. p. 341 © Gary A. Conner/PhotoEdit. p. 359 © Joel Gordon, 1994. p. 360 © Spencer Grant/Stock, Boston. p. 361 Laima Druskis Photography/Stock, Boston. p. 374 Music Division, The New York Public Library for the Performing Arts.

INDEX